New Frontiers in Regional Science: Asian Perspectives

Volume 63

This series is a constellation of works by scholars in the field of regional science and in related disciplines specifically focusing on dynamism in Asia.

Asia is the most dynamic part of the world. Japan, Korea, Taiwan, and Singapore experienced rapid and miracle economic growth in the 1970s. Malaysia, Indonesia, and Thailand followed in the 1980s. China, India, and Vietnam are now rising countries in Asia and are even leading the world economy. Due to their rapid economic development and growth, Asian countries continue to face a variety of urgent issues including regional and institutional unbalanced growth, environmental problems, poverty amidst prosperity, an ageing society, the collapse of the bubble economy, and deflation, among others.

Asian countries are diversified as they have their own cultural, historical, and geographical as well as political conditions. Due to this fact, scholars specializing in regional science as an inter- and multi-discipline have taken leading roles in providing mitigating policy proposals based on robust interdisciplinary analysis of multifaceted regional issues and subjects in Asia. This series not only will present unique research results from Asia that are unfamiliar in other parts of the world because of language barriers, but also will publish advanced research results from those regions that have focused on regional and urban issues in Asia from different perspectives.

The series aims to expand the frontiers of regional science through diffusion of intrinsically developed and advanced modern regional science methodologies in Asia and other areas of the world. Readers will be inspired to realize that regional and urban issues in the world are so vast that their established methodologies still have space for development and refinement, and to understand the importance of the interdisciplinary and multidisciplinary approach that is inherent in regional science for analyzing and resolving urgent regional and urban issues in Asia.

Topics under consideration in this series include the theory of social cost and benefit analysis and criteria of public investments, socio-economic vulnerability against disasters, food security and policy, agro-food systems in China, industrial clustering in Asia, comprehensive management of water environment and resources in a river basin, the international trade bloc and food security, migration and labor market in Asia, land policy and local property tax, Information and Communication Technology planning, consumer "shop-around" movements, and regeneration of downtowns, among others.

Researchers who are interested in publishing their books in this Series should obtain a proposal form from Yoshiro Higano (Editor in Chief, higano@jsrsai.jp) and return the completed form to him.

Takahiro Akita • Mitsuhiko Kataoka

Regional Inequality and Development

Measurement and Applications in Indonesia

Springer

Takahiro Akita
IUJ Research Institute
International University of Japan
Niigata, Japan

Mitsuhiko Kataoka
Graduate School of Business
Rikkyo University
Tokyo, Japan

ISSN 2199-5974 ISSN 2199-5982 (electronic)
New Frontiers in Regional Science: Asian Perspectives
ISBN 978-981-19-2970-0 ISBN 978-981-19-2968-7 (eBook)
https://doi.org/10.1007/978-981-19-2968-7

This Springer imprint is published by the registered company Springer Nature Singapore Pte Ltd.
The registered company address is: 152 Beach Road, #21-01/04 Gateway East, Singapore 189721, Singapore

Acknowledgments

A number of people have helped us in gathering the data which made this book possible. We would like to thank all of them. We are especially grateful to Armida Salsiah Alisjahbana, Puji Agus Kurniawan, Rizal Affandi Lukman, Carlos Mendez, and Sachiko Miyata for their supports and stimulating suggestions in writing some of the chapters. We also gratefully acknowledge the financial support of the Japan Society for the Promotion of Science (Grant-in-Aid for Scientific Research 17K03723, 18K01589, and 26380308).

Takahiro Akita, Professor Emeritus, International University of Japan
Mitsuhiko Kataoka, Professor, Rikkyo University

Contents

Chapter 1
Introduction

Abstract Following this introductory chapter, this book consists of six chapters, which are divided into two parts. Part I of this book presents the measurement and analytical methods of regional income inequality, whereas Part II discusses the applications of these analytical methods in Indonesia. Part I consists of two chapters (Chaps. 2 and 3), while Part II consists of four chapters (Chaps. 4, 5, 6, and 7).

Keywords Regional income inequality · National economic development · Williamson's hypothesis

1 Preliminaries

Regions within a country do not usually possess equal capacity and opportunities for economic development. Some regions may be rich in natural resources and have good access to transportation infrastructure; they are likely to grow faster in the early stages of economic development. Some regions may be spatially isolated and lack economic resources; they are likely to lag behind other regions in economic development. Regions with primary cities that are connected to the international economy have strong locational advantages for international investment and trade, while regions that are endowed with abundant tourism resources attract domestic as well as international investment in the tourism industry. These regions could maintain relatively high economic growth for a longer period of time.

If regional barriers to trade and factor flows are high and the growth benefits of some fortunate regions are not easily transmitted to other less fortunate regions, then regional inequality is likely to persist. Williamson (1965) however predicted, in his seminal article on national economic development and regional income inequality, that regional inequality would go through three distinct phases as a country develops. He claimed that in the early stages of economic development, regional

---

This chapter is written by Takahiro Akita.

T. Akita, M. Kataoka, *Regional Inequality and Development*, New Frontiers in Regional Science: Asian Perspectives 63,
https://doi.org/10.1007/978-981-19-2968-7_1

inequality rises, largely because of the dis-equilibrating forces of factor flows, but it is followed by a period of stability, which is characterized by relatively high levels of regional inequality, and finally, as the national economy matures and becomes more integrated, equilibrating forces take effect and regional inequality starts to decline. If regional inequality is plotted against the level of national development, this overall process exhibits a bell-shaped or an inverted U-shaped pattern. Whether this holds true or not is however a subject of empirical investigation.

Alonso (1980) argued that there are some other stylized facts that exhibit a bell-shaped or an inverted U-shaped pattern in the process of economic development. They include geographic concentration, demographic transition, and changing income inequality among individuals. The early stages of economic development are characterized by rapid urbanization, usually concentrated in one or a few major cities. But, as the national economy matures, there is a shift towards population dispersion, though it may be concentrated in secondary cities. A measure of geographic concentration thus follows a bell-shaped pattern. With respect to demographic transition, it is postulated that starting with a situation where both birth and death rates are high, there is a decline in the death rate in the early stages of development, but this is usually followed by a decline in the birth rate. Therefore, the rate of population growth undergoes a bell-shaped pattern with respect to national development.

Regarding the evolution of interpersonal income inequality, Kuznets (1955) advanced the hypothesis that with a population shift from the low-income and low-inequality traditional sector (rural sector) to the high-income and high-inequality modern sector (urban sector), income inequality first rises, but after reaching the peak it starts to decline as more people move to the urban sector. If income inequality is plotted against the share of the urban population, then this overall process follows an inverted U-shaped pattern. Anand and Kanbur (1993) formalized the Kuznets process of income inequality by employing various inequality measures, including the Theil indices (Theil, 1967), the squared coefficient of variation, and the Atkinson indices (Atkinson, 1970).

Williamson's hypothesis of regional income inequality is a spatial version of the Kuznets hypothesis. However, it is quite possible for regional income inequality to rise (or fall) while national interpersonal income inequality exhibits an opposite trend because regional income inequality is based on regional mean incomes relative to the national mean income and fails to explain the dispersion of incomes within regions.

Since all of these bell-shaped processes are concurrent in national development, it may be unlikely that one can gain a deeper understanding of any one of them without considering the other processes at the same time (Alonso, 1980). For example, the concentration of population in and around major cities in the early stages of development is often associated with an increase in regional income inequality due to disequilibrating effects of capital and labor flows. Some researchers have argued that this spatial concentration of population and the concurrent increase in regional inequality do not hinder national economic development, and may stimulate it (Mera, 1973). Nevertheless, many national governments seek to promote balanced regional economic development and reduce regional income inequality, since unbalanced development and higher levels of regional inequality may cause political or ethnic conflicts between different regions of the country.

What is regional income inequality? How is it measured? What is the relationship between national economic development and regional income inequality? In this book, we will address these questions. This book is divided into two parts. Part I presents the measurement and analytical methods of regional income inequality, whereas Part II discusses the applications of these analytical methods in Indonesia. Part I consists of two chapters (Chaps. 2 and 3), while Part II consists of four chapters (Chaps. 4, 5, 6, and 7).

2 Contents of the Book

Chapter 2 starts with the measurement of interpersonal income inequality as a prelude to regional income inequality and introduces four principles that a measure of interpersonal income inequality should satisfy: anonymity, income homogeneity, population homogeneity, and Pigou-Dalton transfer principles. After introducing several inequality measures, including the standard deviation, the coefficient of variation, the Gini coefficient, the generalized entropy class of inequality measures, and the Theil indices, they are summarized according to the aforementioned four principles. The second section also discusses the relationship between the Lorenz curve and the Gini coefficient, where the Lorenz curve is a graphical representation of the distribution of income.

Section 3 of Chap. 2 introduces two types of inequality decomposition methods that are often used to examine the determinants of income inequality. They are decompositions of inequality by population subgroups and by income sources (or factor components). The generalized entropy class of measures (including the Theil indices and the squared coefficient of variation) and the variance of log income are additively decomposable by population subgroups, that is, they can be decomposed into the between-group and within-group inequality components. On the other hand, the Gini coefficient and the coefficient of variation are additively decomposable by income sources or factor components, that is, they can be expressed as the sum of inequality contributions from various income sources. As an application of the first decomposition method (decomposition of inequality by population subgroups), Sect. 4 of Chap. 2 discusses the Kuznets process of income inequality with respect to urbanization (population shift from the rural to the urban sector) using the Theil indices. Under the assumptions that mean income and income inequality are both larger in the urban than in the rural sector and they are kept constant, it is shown that income inequality exhibits an inverted U-shaped curve with respect to urbanization.

Section 5 discusses the measures of regional income inequality by classifying them into three broad types based on how intra-regional income and population distributions are treated. Given an interpersonal distribution of incomes, the first type calculates the contribution of the between-region inequality component to overall interpersonal income inequality using additively decomposable inequality measures, such as the Theil indices and the squared coefficient of variation. This assesses the extent of regional income variation in the interpersonal distribution of incomes. The second type focuses on the between-region inequality component in the decomposition equation of interpersonal inequality by assuming that individuals in each region have their regional mean income and thus there is no income inequality within regions. If the squared coefficient of variation is used as a measure of interpersonal income inequality, the square root of its between-region component is the population-weighted coefficient of variation popularized by Williamson (1965). However, the second type does not measure regional income inequality; in fact, it tries to measure interpersonal income inequality by assuming that individuals in each region have their regional mean income. But, when data on individual incomes are not available, it is reasonable to weigh each region with its population size. Finally, the third type compares regions in terms of their mean incomes, but without taking their population sizes into account. The population-unweighted coefficient of variation is an example of the third type.

Section 6 of Chap. 2 introduces two concepts of regional convergence: β-convergence and σ-convergence. In a cross section of regions, if there is a negative relationship between the initial level of income per capita and the subsequent growth, that is, if poorer regions grow faster than richer regions, then there is β-convergence among them. On the other hand, if the dispersion of income per capita across regions tends to decrease over time, then there is σ-convergence. Regional inequality measures discussed in the previous section are related to the concept of σ-convergence. This section discusses the concept of β-convergence and its relationship with σ-convergence. The section also describes two notions of β-convergence: absolute and conditional. If a negative relationship exists between the initial level of income per capita and the subsequent growth without considering any conditioning factors, then the regions exhibit absolute β-convergence, whereas if a negative relationship exists between these two variables after controlling for some conditioning factors which may affect the steady-state level of income, such as population growth and savings rate, then there is conditional β-convergence.

In the final section of Chap. 2, some useful STATA commands for the measurement and analysis of inequality are introduced, including **`inequal`**, **`ineqerr`**, **`geivars`**, **`lorenz`**, **`sumdist`**, **`ineqdeco`**, **`descogini`**, and **`ineqfac`**. **`inequal`**, **`ineqerr`**, and **`geivars`** estimate various inequality measures, while **`lorenz`** draws the Lorenz curve for the distribution of income or wealth. **`sumdist`** provides distributional summary statistics commonly used by income distribution analysts. **`ineqdeco`** conducts a decomposition analysis by population subgroups, while **`descogini`** and **`ineqfac`** perform a decomposition analysis by income sources (or factor components) using, respectively, the Gini coefficient and the coefficient of variation.

Chapter 3 introduces some analytical methods that could be used to explore the determinants of regional income inequality. The second section of this chapter presents a bidimensional inequality decomposition method. To implement the method, provincial data on population and GDP by industrial sectors are required and all the provinces need to be grouped into mutually exclusive and collectively exhaustive regions. Using the squared coefficient of variation, the method first decomposes overall inequality in GDP per capita across provinces into the within-region and between-region inequality components. Next, it decomposes inter-provincial inequality within each region and inequality between regions by GDP components. Lastly, the method calculates the contribution of each component to overall inter-provincial inequality in a unified framework.

Using provincial data on population and GDP by industrial sectors, the squared coefficient of variation can also be decomposed into variation and covariation components. Section 3 of Chap. 3 introduces this sectoral inequality decomposition method. Unlike the bidimensional inequality decomposition method, covariation components appear in this decomposition method; thus, one can analyze the roles of spatial covariations between industrial sectors in overall inter-provincial inequality in per capita GDP.

Section 4 of Chap. 3 introduces a two-stage nested hierarchical Theil decomposition method. Like the squared coefficient of variation, the Theil indices belong to the generalized entropy class of inequality measures; thus, they can be decomposed into the within-group and between-group inequality components. Using this decomposition property in the three-level hierarchical structure of a country (region-province-district), the method decomposes overall income inequality into three components: the between-region, between-province, and within-province inequality components. The method uses a district as the underlying regional unit to measure income inequality rather than a province and thus can examine the contribution of within-province inequalities as well as between-province and between-region inequalities to overall income inequality in a coherent framework.

The final section of Chap. 3 presents a factor decomposition method for regional income inequality. Unlike the inequality decomposition methods introduced in the previous sections, the method considers labor in addition to GDP and population and expresses GDP per capita as the product of labor productivity and labor participation rate. After linearizing this product using the natural logarithm, it additively decomposes regional inequality in per capita GDP into three components: regional inequality in labor productivity, regional inequality in labor participation rate, and residual component. The first two components in the decomposition equation are regional inequalities measured by the Theil index and take nonnegative values. On the other hand, the residual component represents the interaction between labor productivity and labor participation rate, which can take a negative value.

As the applications of the methods introduced in Chap. 3, Part II of this book presents four independent studies on regional inequality and development in Indonesia. They offer very interesting case studies since as the world's largest archipelagic country with more than 13 thousand islands and 300 ethnic groups, Indonesia is spatially diverse in terms of its ecology, natural resource endowments, economy, ethnicity, and culture.

Over the last four decades, Indonesia has undergone substantial structural changes. While agriculture and mining lowered their GDP shares, the services sector raised its share, particularly after the 1997 financial crisis. Meanwhile, the GDP share of manufacturing exhibited an inverted U-shaped pattern. In the 1980s and 1990s under the Suharto's New Order Regime, it increased gradually; but, after reaching the peak in the early 2000s, it has been declining. Economic tertialization seems to have been associated with output deindustrialization since the financial crisis. Changes in the industrial structure are accompanied by changes in the spatial distribution of economic activities. While Sumatra and Kalimantan regions lowered their GDP shares due to the declining share of oil and gas production, Java-Bali region raised its share. Sulawesi region also increased its GDP share, but Eastern Indonesia did not exhibit a significant change. Against this backdrop, Chap. 4 attempts to explore the determinants of inequality in per capita GDP across provinces in Indonesia over the period 2010–2019 by using the bidimensional inequality decomposition method. In particular, it tries to analyze how economic tertialization and concurrent output deindustrialization affected inequality in per capita GDP.

Over the last two decades, the manufacturing industry has grown at an annual average rate of 4.5% in Indonesia. However, its share in total GDP has fallen gradually. This output deindustrialization appears to be premature in the sense that it started at a much lower development level than in most developed countries. But, if we look at manufacturing subsectors, their growth performances are quite heterogeneous. While labor-intensive industries such as food processing and textile grew relatively rapidly, industries tied to coal, oil, and natural gas were stagnant. Against this background, Chap. 5 attempts to examine how structural changes in the manufacturing industry affected regional income inequality over the period 2010–2019. By using provincial GDP by manufacturing subsectors, the chapter first conducts a shift and share analysis to explore the determinants of provincial growth in the manufacturing industry. It then performs an inequality decomposition analysis to investigate the extent to which each manufacturing subsector contributes to inter-provincial inequality in manufacturing GDP.

During the 1990s, before the 1997 financial crisis, Indonesia achieved an annual average growth rate of more than 7% in real GDP, comparable to the rapid growth period of the 1970s. However, the crisis exerted an enormous impact on the Indonesian economy. It cast a shadow not only on the financial but also on the real sector of the economy; in 1998, the country contracted by 13%. The rapid economic growth before the financial crisis was accompanied by declining regional inequality. However, large disparities persisted in socioeconomic indicators between regions and provinces; in 1997, the per capita GDP of the richest province (Jakarta) was almost ten times that of the poorest (East Nusa Tenggara). How the 1997 financial crisis affected regional economies and income inequality remains one of the important policy questions in Indonesia. Chapter 6 conducts a two-stage nested Theil decomposition analysis to examine the impact of the financial crisis on regional income inequality based on district-level population and GDP data.

Indonesia achieved a substantial reduction in regional inequality in labor productivity (output-labor ratio) over the last three decades. Among its 26 provinces, the ratio of the highest to the lowest labor productivity has declined from 23 to 15. However, as the world's largest archipelagic country with more than 13 thousand islands, large disparities still persist in labor productivity. Based on a balanced panel dataset of 26 provinces, the final chapter of this book examines the sources of inter-provincial inequality in labor productivity in Indonesia over the period 1990–2015. It first conducts a bootstrap as well as conventional data envelopment analysis to obtain efficiency scores for 26 provinces. Using these efficiency scores, it then performs a factor decomposition analysis of inter-provincial inequality in labor productivity measured by the Theil index to explore the sources of the inequality.

References

Alonso, W. (1980). Five bell shapes in development. *Papers of the Regional Science Association, 45*, 5–16.

Anand, S., & Kanbur, S. M. R. (1993). The Kuznets process and the inequality-development relationship. *Journal of Development Economics, 40*(1), 25–52.

Atkinson, A. B. (1970). On the measurement of inequality. *Journal of Economic Theory, 2*, 244–263.

Kuznets, S. S. (1955). Economic growth and income inequality. *American Economic Review, 45*(1), 1–28.

Mera, K. (1973). On the urban agglomeration and economic efficiency. *Economic Development and Cultural Change, 21*(2), 309–324.

Theil, H. (1967). *Economics and information theory*. North Holland.

Williamson, J. G. (1965). Regional inequality and the process of national development: A description of the patterns. *Economic Development and Cultural Change, 13*, 3–45.

Part I
Measurement and Analysis of Regional Inequality

Chapter 2
Measurement of Regional Inequality

Abstract This chapter starts with the measurement of interpersonal income inequality as a prelude to regional income inequality and introduces two types of inequality decomposition methods that are often used to examine the determinants of income inequality. After presenting the Kuznets process of income inequality using the Theil indices, it discusses the measures of regional income inequality by classifying them into three broad types based on how intra-regional income and population distributions are treated. It also introduces two concepts of regional convergence: β-convergence and σ-convergence. In the final section of this chapter, some useful STATA commands for the measurement and analysis of inequality are introduced.

Keywords Interpersonal income inequality · Inequality decomposition methods · Kuznets process of inequality · Regional income inequality · Regional convergence · STATA commands

1 Introduction

Williamson (1965) predicted, in his article on national economic development and regional income inequality, that regional inequality would go through three distinct phases as a country develops. He claimed that in the early stages of economic development, regional inequality rises, largely because of the disequilibrating forces of factor flows, but it is followed by a period of stability, which is characterized by relatively high levels of regional inequality, and finally, as the national economy matures and becomes more integrated, equilibrating forces take effect and regional inequality starts to decline. If regional inequality is plotted against the level of national development, this overall process exhibits a bell-shaped or an inverted U-shaped pattern. Whether this holds true or not is however a subject of empirical investigation. Williamson's hypothesis of regional income inequality is a spatial

This chapter is written by Takahiro Akita.

T. Akita, M. Kataoka, *Regional Inequality and Development*, New Frontiers in Regional Science: Asian Perspectives 63,
https://doi.org/10.1007/978-981-19-2968-7_2

version of the Kuznets hypothesis that describes the relationship between national economic development and interpersonal income inequality (Kuznets, 1955).

Since Williamson's seminal article, regional income inequality has attracted a great deal of attention among economists and regional scientists. What is regional income inequality? How is it measured and analyzed? The main objective of this chapter is to address these questions. One way of examining regional income inequality is to start with interpersonal income inequality and investigate the extent of regional variation in the interpersonal distribution of incomes. This chapter first discusses the measures of interpersonal inequality. The next section introduces four principles that a measure of income inequality should satisfy: anonymity, income homogeneity, population homogeneity, and Pigou-Dalton transfer principles. After introducing several inequality measures, they are summarized according to these four principles. The next section also discusses the relationship between the Lorenz curve and the Gini coefficient.

Section 2.3 introduces two types of inequality decomposition methods that are often used to examine the determinants of income inequality. They are decompositions of inequality by population subgroups and by income sources. The generalized entropy class of measures (including the Theil indices and the squared coefficient of variation) and the variance of log income are additively decomposable by population subgroups, that is, they can be decomposed into the between-group and within-group inequality components. On the other hand, the Gini coefficient and the coefficient of variation are additively decomposable by income sources, that is, they can be expressed as the sum of inequality contributions from various income sources.

As an application of the first decomposition method (decomposition of inequality by population subgroups), Sect. 2.4 discusses the Kuznets process of income inequality with respect to urbanization (population shift from the rural to the urban sector) using the Theil indices. Under the assumption that mean income and income inequality are both larger in the urban than in the rural sector and remain constant, it is shown that income inequality exhibits an inverted U-shaped curve with respect to urbanization.

Section 2.5 discusses the measures of regional income inequality by classifying them into three broad types. Given an interpersonal distribution of incomes, the first type calculates the contribution of the between-region inequality component to overall interpersonal income inequality using additively decomposable inequality measures. This assesses the extent of regional variation in the interpersonal distribution of incomes. The second type focuses on the between-region inequality component in the decomposition equation of interpersonal inequality by assuming that individuals in each region have their regional mean incomes. If the squared coefficient of variation is used as a measure of interpersonal income inequality, the square root of its between-region component is the population-weighted coefficient of variation. However, the second type does not measure regional income inequality; in fact, it tries to measure interpersonal income inequality. But, when data on individual incomes are not available, it is reasonable to weigh each region with its population size. Finally, the third type compares regions in terms of their mean incomes, but without taking their population sizes into account. The population-unweighted coefficient of variation is an example of the third type.

Section 2.6 introduces two concepts of regional convergence: β-convergence and σ-convergence. In a cross section of regions, if there is a negative relationship between the initial level of income per capita and the subsequent growth, that is, if poorer regions grow faster than richer regions, then there is β-convergence among them. On the other hand, if the dispersion of income per capita across regions tends to decrease over time, then there is σ-convergence. Regional inequality measures discussed in the previous section are related to the concept of σ-convergence. On the other hand, Section 2.6 discusses the concept of β-convergence and its relationship with σ-convergence. This section also describes two notions of β-convergence: absolute and conditional β-convergence.

In the final section, some useful STATA commands for the measurement and analysis of inequality are introduced. They include **`inequal`**, **`ineqerr`**, **`geivars`**, **`lorenz`**, **`sumdist`**, **`ineqdeco`**, **`descogini`**, and **`ineqfac`**. **`inequal`**, **`ineqerr`**, and **`geivars`** estimate various inequality measures, while **`lorenz`** draws the Lorenz curve for the distribution of income or wealth. **`sumdist`** provides distributional summary statistics commonly used by income distribution analysts. **`ineqdeco`** conducts a decomposition analysis by population subgroups, while **`descogini`** and **`ineqfac`** perform a decomposition analysis by income sources using, respectively, the Gini coefficient and the coefficient of variation.

2 Measures of Interpersonal Inequality

As a prelude to regional income inequality, we first examine inequality in the interpersonal distribution of incomes. As an example, we consider a small village consisting of 5 individuals. Table 2.1 and Fig. 2.1 present the distribution of incomes for these 5 individuals in US dollars. With an exchange rate of 100 yen per US dollar, Table 2.1 also provides the same distribution of incomes, but in Japanese yen.

2.1 Standard Deviation

How unequal is this distribution or what is the amount of inequality in this distribution? The standard deviation is often used to measure income inequality (Barro and Sala-i-Martin 2004). For a set of incomes for n individuals, $\mathbf{y} = (y_1, y_2, \cdots, y_n)$, with the mean income given by $\mu = \frac{1}{n}\sum_{i=1}^{n} y_i$, it is defined by

Table 2.1 Income distributions in 2010 and 2020: Income homogeneity

	Year 2010 (Distribution 1)				Year 2020	
Individual	Income (dollar)	Share (%)	Income (yen)	Share (%)	Income (dollar)	Share (%)
A	10	20	1000	20	20	20
B	8	16	800	16	16	16
C	12	24	1200	24	24	24
D	4	8	400	8	8	8
E	16	32	1600	32	32	32
Total	50	100	5000	100	100	100
Mean	10		1000		20	
Standard deviation	4.0		400.0		8.0	
Coefficient of variation	0.40		0.40		0.40	

Note: Standard deviation is the population standard deviation, not the sample standard deviation (Sample standard deviation is defined by $\sigma_s = \sqrt{\frac{1}{n-1}\sum_{i=1}^{n}(y_i - \mu)^2}$, while population standard deviation is defined by $\sigma = \sqrt{\frac{1}{n}\sum_{I=1}^{n}(y_i - \mu)^2)}$

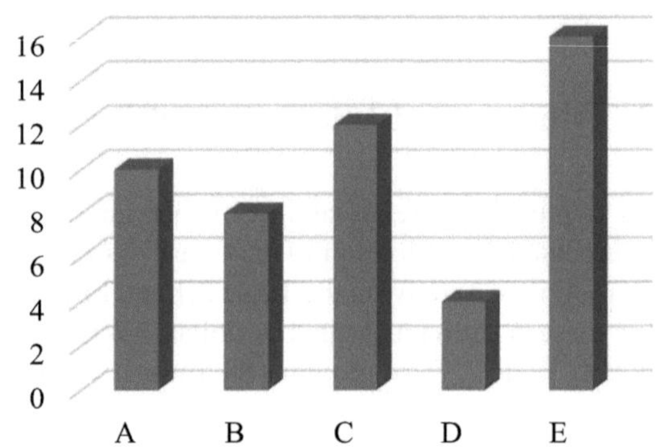

Fig. 2.1 Income distribution in 2010 in US dollar (Distribution 1)

$$\sigma = \sqrt{\frac{1}{n}\sum_{i=1}^{n}(y_i - \mu)^2} \tag{2.1}$$

When all individuals have the same income (perfect equality), we have $y_1 = y_2 = \cdots = y_n = \mu$ and thus $\sigma = 0$. A larger value of the standard deviation indicates that personal incomes are spread out around the mean over a wider range, implying a larger amount of interpersonal income inequality.

We first consider the interpersonal distribution of incomes in US dollars in 2010 (Table 2.1), for which the standard deviation is equal to 4.0.

$$\sigma = \sqrt{\frac{1}{5}\left[(10-10)^2 + (8-10)^2 + (12-10)^2 + (4-10)^2 + (16-10)^2\right]} = 4.0.$$

The problem with using the standard deviation as a measure of income inequality is that it depends not only on the income shares of individuals but also a unit of measurement for incomes. To see this, we calculate the standard deviation for the same distribution but in Japanese yen. Then, the standard deviation will increase to 400. Can we say that the distribution of incomes in Japanese yen is more unequal than the one in US dollars? Obviously no. We measure the same distribution but in different monetary units.

We consider another example. Suppose that due to economic growth, the distribution of incomes changes to the one in 2020 exhibited in Table 2.1, where each individual receives twice as much as the amount received in 2010. Then, the standard deviation will increase to 8.0 from 4.0. However, the income shares of individuals remain constant. Though the absolute income difference between the richest and the poorest doubles (from 12 to 24), the income ratio between them remains unchanged at 4. It is thus reasonable to claim that the income distributions in 2010 and 2020 are equally unequal, that is, they have the same amount of inequality.

2.2 *Coefficient of Variation*

To rectify the problem associated with the standard deviation, the coefficient of variation (*CV*) can be used as a measure of inequality (Anand, 1983: Fields, 2001). It is defined as the ratio between the standard deviation and the mean income as follows.

$$CV = \frac{\sigma}{\mu} \tag{2.2}$$

For all three distributions in Table 2.1, *CV* is 0.4, indicating that these distributions have the same amount of inequality.[1] *CV* satisfies income homogeneity or mean independence principle, described as follows (Anand, 1983; Fields, 2001).

[1] *CV* can be defined by using the sample standard deviation rather than the population standard deviation. But, if the sample size is very large, *CV* using the sample standard deviation is almost the same as the one using the population standard deviation.

Table 2.2 Income distributions in 2010 and 2011: Anonymity and Pigou-Dalton principle of transfers

	Year 2010		Year 2011 (Anonymity)		Year 2011 (Transfer principle)	
Individual	Income (dollar)	Share (%)	Income (dollar)	Share (%)	Income (dollar)	Share (%)
A	10	20	4	8	10	20
B	8	16	16	32	8	16
C	12	24	10	20	11	22
D	4	8	8	16	5	10
E	16	32	12	24	16	32
Total	50	100	50	100	50	100
Mean	10		10		10	
Standard deviation	4.0		4.0		3.6	
Coefficient of variation	0.40		0.40		0.36	

2.2.1 Principle 1: Income Homogeneity or Mean Independence[2]

> When incomes are all multiplied by the same positive scalar, an inequality measure should remain unchanged.

If an inequality measure satisfies income homogeneity or mean independence, then it is called a *relative* inequality measure. If it does not, then it is an *absolute* inequality measure. *CV* is a relative inequality measure, while the standard deviation is an absolute inequality measure.

CV satisfies three other principles, that is, anonymity principle, population homogeneity, and the Pigou-Dalton principle of transfers, which are described below.

2.2.2 Principle 2: Anonymity Principle

> An inequality measure should not depend on who has a higher income or a lower income.

Suppose that in 2011, the distribution of incomes changes to the one shown in Table 2.2. Individuals A, C, and E become poorer, while individuals B and D get richer. But, the 2011 distribution is just a permutation of incomes in the 2010 distribution though the income recipients change. *CV* for the 2011 distribution should be the same as *CV* for the 2010 distribution. It does not matter who earns how much income when we measure income inequality. *CV* satisfies the principle of anonymity because we do not require the names of income recipients when calculating *CV*.

[2] Some researchers use "relative income principle" or "scale independence" to refer to this principle (Ray, 1998; Fields, 2001).

Table 2.3 Income distribution of new village: Population homogeneity

Village in 2010		New Village			
Individual	Income	Individual	Income	Individual	Income
A	10	A	10	F	10
B	8	B	8	G	8
C	12	C	12	H	12
D	4	D	4	I	4
E	16	E	16	J	16
Total	50				100
Mean	10				10
Standard deviation	4				4
Coefficient of variation	0.4				0.4

2.2.3 Principle 3: Population Homogeneity or Population Independence[3]

An inequality measure should remain unchanged if the number of individuals at each income level is changed by the same proportion, that is, an inequality measure should depend only on the relative population frequencies at each income level, not the absolute population frequencies.

To explain population homogeneity, we consider another small village consisting of 5 individuals, which is a replica of the 2010 income distribution shown in Table 2.1. Now, we merge these two villages and create a new village consisting of 10 individuals. The income distribution of the new village is ((10, 8, 12, 4, 16), (10, 8, 12, 4, 16)) (Table 2.3). Do you think that the income distribution of the new village is more unequal than the distribution of the village in 2010? Perhaps, it is not legitimate to judge the former distribution to be more unequal than the latter simply because the new village has more individuals and thus more income differences than the village in 2010. It is reasonable to claim that these two villages have the same amount of inequality. We now calculate *CV* for the income distribution of the new village. Then, we obtain 0.4, which is the same as *CV* for the village in 2010 (Table 2.3). In other words, *CV* satisfies population homogeneity. We should note that the standard deviation also satisfies this principle, though it does not meet the principle of income homogeneity.

[3] Some researchers use "principle of population replication" or "population principle" to refer to this principle (Ray, 1998).

2.2.4 Principle 4: Pigou-Dalton Principle of Transfers or Transfer Principle

Any income transfer from a richer to a poorer person that does not reverse their relative ranks in income should reduce the value of an inequality measure.

Given the income distribution in 2010, consider a transfer of income between individuals C and D. If one dollar is transferred from individual C (richer) to individual D (poorer) in 2011, then the new income distribution is given in Table 2.2. Individual C now has 11 dollars, while individual D has 5 dollars. This income transfer does not reverse their relative ranks in income; individual C is still richer than individual D. In this case, it is reasonable to judge that this income transfer reduces income inequality, that is, the new income distribution is more equal (or less unequal) than the original distribution in 2010. We now calculate *CV* for the new income distribution. Then, we obtain 0.36, which is smaller than *CV* for the original distribution in 2010 (0.40), meaning that *CV* satisfies the Pigou-Dalton principle of transfer.

The main reason why *CV* is used as a measure of inequality in the distribution of incomes is that besides its simplicity, it satisfies the four principles discussed above, that is, anonymity, income homogeneity, population homogeneity, and the Pigou-Dalton principle of transfers.

2.3 Formal Definition of Measures of Inequality

Let us now formally define a measure of inequality. For a given distribution of incomes, $\boldsymbol{y} = (y_1, y_2, \ldots, y_n)$, an inequality measure is defined as a function of the form

$$I = I(y_1, y_2, \ldots, y_n) \geq 0.$$

The function assigns a nonnegative number to a vector of incomes $(y_1, y_2, \cdots, y_n)$. Using this function, income homogeneity, population homogeneity, and the Pigou-Dalton principle of transfers can be described as follows:

Income homogeneity: for any income distribution and any positive number α, we require

$$I(y_1, y_2, \ldots, y_n) = I(\alpha y_1, \alpha y_2, \ldots, \alpha y_n).$$

Population homogeneity: for any income distribution, we require

$$I(y_1, y_2, \ldots, y_n) = I(y_1, y_2, \ldots, y_n; y_1, y_2, \ldots, y_n).$$

The Pigou-Dalton principle of transfers: for any income distribution and any transfer of income $\delta > 0$ between jth individual and kth individual where $y_j < y_k$, we require

$$I(y_1, \ldots, y_j, \ldots, y_k, \ldots, y_n) > I(y_1, \ldots, y_j + \delta, \ldots, y_k - \delta, \ldots, y_n),$$

where $y_j + \delta \leq y_k - \delta$.

2.4 Lorenz Curve

The Lorenz curve is often used to visualize a distribution of incomes (Lorenz 1905). To draw the Lorenz curve of an income distribution, we first order all individuals from the poorest to the richest. On the horizontal axis, we plot the cumulative population shares of individuals. For a village consisting of 5 individuals in 2010 given in Table 2.1, the cumulative population shares are $\left(\frac{1}{5}, \frac{2}{5}, \frac{3}{5}, \frac{4}{5}, \frac{5}{5}\right) = (0.2, 0.4, 0.6, 0.8, 1.0)$. We should note here that each individual has the same population share of $\frac{1}{5} = 0.2$. On the vertical axis, we plot the cumulative income shares of individuals from the poorest to the richest. For the village in 2010, the cumulative income shares of individuals, D (poorest), B, A, C, and E (richest) are $\left(\frac{4}{50}, \frac{12}{50}, \frac{22}{50}, \frac{34}{50}, \frac{50}{50}\right) = (0.08, 0.24, 0.44, 0.68, 1.0)$. Figure 2.2 presents the Lorenz curve for this income distribution (distribution 1), which is the graph of cumulative income shares against cumulative population shares for the village of 5 individuals. It should be noted that to draw the Lorenz curve of an income distribution for individuals, we only need the income shares of the individuals, not their absolute

Fig. 2.2 Lorenz curve

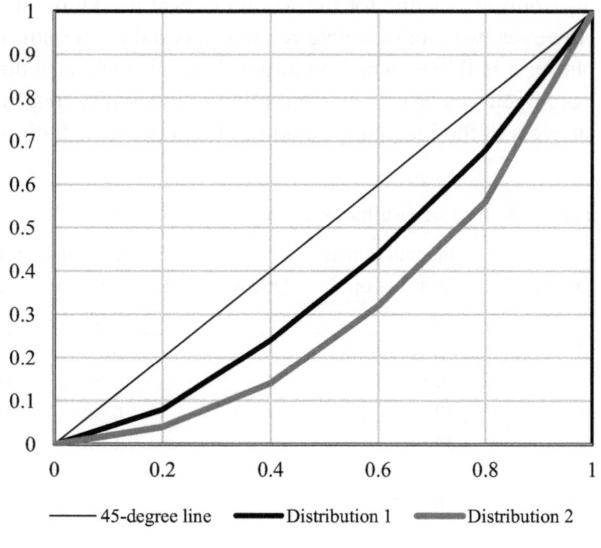

incomes. Therefore, the income distributions presented in Table 2.1 all have the same Lorenz curve, signifying that they have the same amount of inequality, that is, they are equally unequal.

Consider now a distribution of incomes for an infinite number of individuals. If one individual receives all the income and everyone else receive nothing (perfect inequality), then the Lorenz curve lies along the horizontal and right-vertical axes. On the other hand, if all individuals have the same amount of income (perfect equality), the Lorenz curve coincides with the 45° line since each individual's income share is the same as the population share. This suggests that the closer the Lorenz curve to the 45° line, the more equal (or less unequal) is the distribution of incomes.

To see this, consider another village consisting of 5 individuals with its income distribution being (2, 5, 9, 12, 22) (distribution 2). The Lorenz curve of this distribution (distribution 2) is entirely below the Lorenz curve of distribution 1 (Fig. 2.2). Distribution 1 is said to *Lorenz-dominate* distribution 2 (Fields, 2001). It is reasonable to claim that distribution 1 is more equal (less unequal) than distribution 2. This is formally stated as: For two income distributions, $\boldsymbol{x} = (x_1, x_2, \cdots, x_m)$ and $\boldsymbol{y} = (y_1, y_2, \cdots, y_n)$, if distribution $\boldsymbol{x}$ *Lorenz-dominates* distribution $\boldsymbol{y}$, then $\boldsymbol{x}$ is more equal (less unequal) than $\boldsymbol{y}$ by the Lorenz criterion. We should note that *CV* for distribution 1 is 0.40, which is smaller than *CV* for distribution 2 (0.69), indicating that distribution 1 is more equal (less unequal) than distribution 2. In the case of Lorenz-dominance, the inequality ranking of income distributions based on *CV* agrees with the inequality ranking by the Lorenz criterion.

When two Lorenz curves cross, can we compare the inequalities? The answer is that using the Lorenz curve alone, we cannot compare. Table 2.4 and Fig. 2.3 illustrate this situation, where distribution 3 is given by (4, 5, 7, 9, 25). In the table, all individuals are arranged in ascending order of income. For the poorest and second poorest individuals, the Lorenz curve of distribution 3 is above that of distribution 2, while for the second richest individual, the former is below the latter. However, we can calculate relative inequality measures such as *CV*; *CV* for distribution 3 is 0.769, which is larger than *CV* for distribution 2 (0.690). In fact, when Lorenz curves cross, different relative inequality measures would provide different answers in the inequality ranking of income distributions (Fields, 2001). According

Table 2.4 Income distributions: Lorenz curves crossed

	Income (dollar)		Cumulative income share		
Individual	Distribution 2	Distribution 3	45° line	Distribution 2	Distribution 3
1	2	4	0.20	0.04	0.08
2	5	5	0.40	0.14	0.18
3	9	7	0.60	0.32	0.32
4	12	9	0.80	0.56	0.50
5	22	25	1.00	1.00	1.00
Total	50	50			
Mean	10	10			

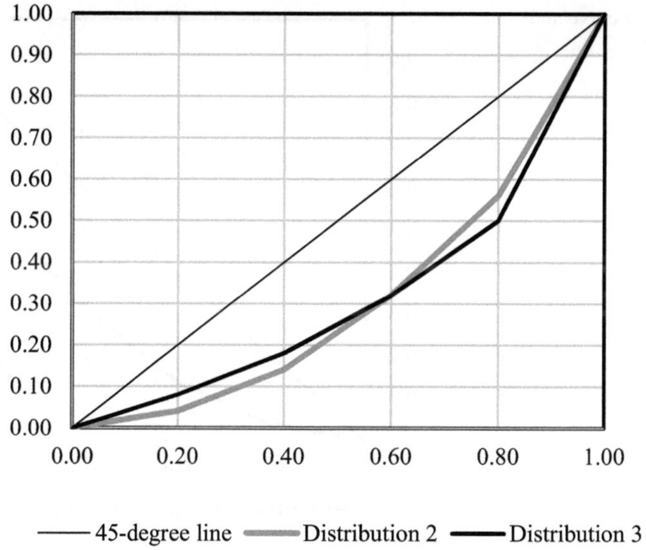

Fig. 2.3 Two Lorenz curves crossed

to *CV*, we could say that distribution 2 is more equal (less unequal) than distribution 3. But, we can find a relative inequality measure which provides the opposite answer.

2.5 *Gini Coefficient*

Many researchers have used the Gini coefficient (or Gini index) as a measure of inequality. The World Bank periodically publishes the Gini coefficient for more than 100 countries in the World Development Indicators (World Bank, 2020). The Gini coefficient can be obtained by using the Lorenz curve. Consider the Lorenz curve of income distribution for *n* individuals (Fig. 2.4). Then, the Gini coefficient is defined as the ratio of the area between the Lorenz curve and the 45° line (*A*) to the area of the triangle below the 45° line and above the horizontal axis (*A* + *B*).

Suppose that F_i and H_i are, respectively, the cumulative population share and cumulative income share of individuals up to individual *i*, where $F_0 = H_0 = 0$ and $F_n = H_n = 1$. Then, the geometric definition of the Gini coefficient is given by:

$$G_1 = 1 - \sum_{i=0}^{n-1} (F_{i+1} - F_i)(H_{i+1} + H_i) = \frac{\mathrm{A}}{\mathrm{A} + \mathrm{B}} \tag{2.3}$$

For the derivation of this formula, please see Appendix 1. The Gini coefficient ranges between 0 (perfect equality) and 1 (perfect inequality). It satisfies all principles discussed before (that is, anonymity, income homogeneity, population

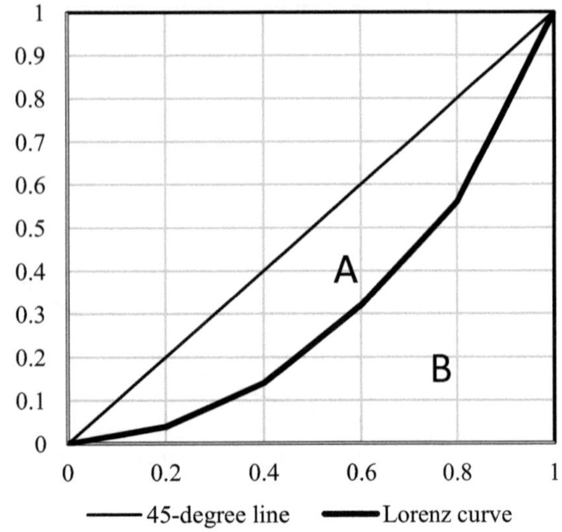

Fig. 2.4 Lorenz curve and Gini coefficient

homogeneity, and the Pigou-Dalton principle of transfers) and is a relative inequality measure. For the income distributions presented in Table 2.1, the Gini coefficient is 0.224 by Eq. (2.3) as follows, where $F_{i+1} - F_i = \frac{i+1}{5} - \frac{i}{5} = \frac{1}{5} = 0.2$ for all i since there are 5 individuals (Table 2.5).

$$G_1 = 1 - [(0.2)(0.08) + (0.2)(0.32) + (0.2)(0.68) + (0.2)(1.12) + (0.2)(1.68)] \\ = 0.224$$

There are some other formulas for the Gini coefficient. Consider an income distribution for n individuals, $\mathbf{y} = (y_1, y_2, \ldots, y_n)$, with the mean income given by μ. The following equation provides another formula for the Gini coefficient.

$$G_2 = \frac{2}{n\mu}\text{cov}(\mathbf{y}, i(\mathbf{y})), \tag{2.4}$$

where $\text{cov}(\mathbf{y}, i(\mathbf{y}))$ is the covariance between incomes $\mathbf{y}$ and the ranking of these incomes, $i(\mathbf{y})$. For the income distributions presented in Table 2.1, the Gini coefficient is 0.224 by Eq. (2.4), which is the same as the one by Eq. (2.3) (Table 2.5).

$$G_2 = \frac{2}{(5)(10)}\text{cov}((4, 8, 10, 12, 16); (1, 2, 3, 4, 5)) = (0.04)(5.6) = 0.224$$

These two formulas (Eqs. 2.3 and 2.4) are equivalent.[4]

[4] Another useful formula for the Gini coefficient considers the differences between all pairs of incomes and sums the absolute differences. It is defined as: $G_3 = \frac{1}{2n^2\mu}\sum_{i=1}^{n}\sum_{j=1}^{n}\lceil y_i - y_j \rceil$. We can show that G_3 is equivalent to G_1 and G_2. For a proof of the equivalence of these three formulas, please see Anand (1983).

Table 2.5 Gini coefficient for distribution in 2010 in US dollars (Distribution 1)

			Cumulative population share		Cumulative income share	
Individual	Income (dollar)	Ranking	F0	0	H0	0
D	4	1	F1	0.20	H1	0.08
B	8	2	F2	0.40	H2	0.24
A	10	3	F3	0.60	H3	0.44
C	12	4	F4	0.80	H4	0.68
E	16	5	F5	1.00	H5	1.00
Total	50					
Mean	10					
G1	0.224					
G2	0.224					

Table 2.6 Income distributions and relative inequality measures

	Income (dollar)			Income share	
Individual	Distribution 2	Distribution 3	Population share	Distribution 2	Distribution 3
1	2	4	0.20	0.04	0.08
2	5	5	0.20	0.10	0.10
3	9	7	0.20	0.18	0.14
4	12	9	0.20	0.24	0.18
5	22	25	0.20	0.44	0.50
Total	50	50			
Mean	10	10			
Standard deviation	6.9	7.7			
Coefficient of variation	0.690	0.769			
Gini	0.376	0.368			
Theil T (E_1)	0.238	0.247			
Theil L (E_0)	0.287	0.231			

We now return to the case where two Lorenz curves cross (Table 2.4 and Fig. 2.3). The Gini coefficient for distribution 2 is 0.376, while that for distribution 3 is 0.368 (Table 2.6). By the Gini coefficient, we could say that distribution 2 is more unequal than distribution 3. This result disagrees with the case based on *CV* where distribution 2 is less unequal than distribution 3 (0.690 vs. 0.769). This implies that when two Lorenz curves cross, we need an additional criterion for the inequality comparison of income distributions.

2.6 Generalized Entropy Class of Measures and Theil Indices

Another commonly used inequality measure is the generalized entropy class of measures, which is defined for the parameter α other than 0 and 1 as:

$$E_\alpha = \frac{1}{\alpha(\alpha-1)}\frac{1}{n}\sum_{i=1}^{n}\left[\left(\frac{y_i}{\mu}\right)^{\alpha}-1\right] \text{ for } \alpha \neq 0,1 \tag{2.5}$$

where the parameter α is an indicator of inequality aversion, that is, a smaller α indicates more averse to inequality (Sen, 1997). E_1 is called the Theil T index (or the Theil measure)[5]

$$E_1 = T = \frac{1}{n}\sum_{i=1}^{n}\frac{y_i}{\mu}\ln\left(\frac{y_i}{\mu}\right), \tag{2.6}$$

while E_0 is called the Theil L index (or the mean logarithmic deviation)

$$E_0 = L = \frac{1}{n}\sum_{i=1}^{n}\ln\left(\frac{\mu}{y_i}\right), \tag{2.7}$$

where $\ln(x)$ is the natural logarithm of x. Some properties of the natural logarithm function are discussed in Appendix 2. The generalized entropy class of measures satisfies all principles discussed before (that is, anonymity, income homogeneity, population homogeneity, and the Pigou-Dalton principle of transfers) and is a relative inequality measure. When all individuals have the same income (perfect equality), the generalized entropy class of measures is 0.

If $Y = \sum_{i=1}^{n} y_i$ is total income, then we have $n\mu = Y$ by definition, and thus we have $\frac{y_i}{\mu} = \frac{y_i/Y}{1/n}$ and $\frac{\mu}{y_i} = \frac{1/n}{y_i/Y}$. Since $\frac{1}{n}$ and $\frac{y_i}{Y}$ are respectively the population and income shares of individual i, the Theil T and L indices are given, respectively, by:

$$E_1 = T = \sum_{i=1}^{n}(\text{income share})_i \times \ln\left(\frac{(\text{income share})_i}{(\text{population share})_i}\right) \tag{2.8}$$

and

$$E_0 = L = \sum_{i=1}^{n}(\text{population share})_i \times \ln\left(\frac{(\text{population share})_i}{(\text{income share})_i}\right). \tag{2.9}$$

The Theil T and L indices for distributions 2 and 3 are given in Table 2.6, where the Lorenz curves of these two distributions cross. For distribution 2, we obtain

[5] E_1 is also called Theil's entropy index (Theil, 1967).

$$
\begin{aligned}
E_1 &= T \\
&= (0.04)\ln\left(\frac{0.04}{0.2}\right) + (0.10)\ln\left(\frac{0.10}{0.2}\right) + (0.18)\ln\left(\frac{0.18}{0.2}\right) + (0.24)\ln\left(\frac{0.24}{0.2}\right) \\
&\quad + (0.44)\ln\left(\frac{0.44}{0.2}\right) \\
&= 0.238
\end{aligned}
$$

$$
\begin{aligned}
E_0 &= L \\
&= (0.2)\ln\left(\frac{0.2}{0.04}\right) + (0.2)\ln\left(\frac{0.2}{0.10}\right) + (0.2)\ln\left(\frac{0.2}{0.18}\right) + (0.2)\ln\left(\frac{0.2}{0.24}\right) \\
&\quad + (0.2)\ln\left(\frac{0.2}{0.44}\right) \\
&= 0.287
\end{aligned}
$$

It is interesting to observe that the inequality ranking of distributions 2 and 3 by the Theil T index disagrees with that by the Theil L index; while distribution 2 is less unequal than distribution 3 by the Theil T index, the former is more unequal than the latter by the Theil L index.

We should note that E_2 is one half of the squared coefficient of variation, that is,

$$E_2 = \frac{1}{2}CV^2. \tag{2.10}$$

Therefore, the squared coefficient of variation belongs to the generalized entropy class of measures. For detail, please see Appendix 3.

2.7 *Other Relative Inequality Measures*

Other commonly used relative inequality measures include the range, the relative mean deviation, the variance of log income, and the Atkinson class of inequality measures. The definitions of these relative inequality measures are given in Appendix 4, while their characteristics are summarized in Table 2.7. When all individuals have the same income (perfect inequality), the values of these inequality measures are 0. We should note that while the Atkinson class of inequality measures satisfies the Pigou-Dalton principle of transfers, the range, the relative mean deviation, and the variance of log income do not (Atkinson 1970).

Table 2.7 Inequality measures and their characteristics

Inequality measures	Anonymity	Population homogeneity	Income homogeneity	Pigou-Dalton principle
Relative inequality measures				
Range (D)	○	○	○	×
Relative mean deviation (M)	○	○	○	×
Variance of log income (V)	○	○	○	×
Coefficient of variation (CV)	○	○	○	○
Gini coefficient (G)	○	○	○	○
Generalized entropy class of measures (E_α)	○	○	○	○
Theil T (E_1)	○	○	○	○
Theil L (E_0)	○	○	○	○
Squared CV ($CV^2 = 2E_2$)	○	○	○	○
Atkinson class of inequality measures (A_ε)	○	○	○	○
Absolute inequality measures				
Standard deviation (σ) and variance (σ^2)	○	○	×	○

Note: ○ shows that an inequality measure satisfies the principle

3 Decomposable Inequality Measures

In empirical researches on income inequality, inequality decomposition methods are often used. This section introduces two types of inequality decomposition methods: decomposition by population subgroups and decomposition by income sources.

3.1 Inequality Decomposition by Population Subgroups

One of the questions that are raised in the analysis of interpersonal income inequality is concerned with the extent to which overall income inequality can be ascribed to income differences between population subgroups such as age groups, education groups, rural and urban areas and regions. To answer this question, the generalized entropy class of measures (including the Theil T and L indices and the squared coefficient of variation) and the variance of log income are commonly used, because they are additively decomposable by population subgroups, that is, they can be decomposed into the within-group and between-group inequality components (Anand, 1983; Bourguignon, 1979; Shorrocks, 1980).

As an example, consider a country consisting of 10 individuals, of which 6 are in rural areas and 4 in urban areas (Fig. 2.5 and Table 2.8). By the Theil L index, interpersonal income inequalities within rural and urban areas (rural and urban inequalities) are, respectively, 0.069 and 0.099 (see Eq. 2.9 for the formula of the

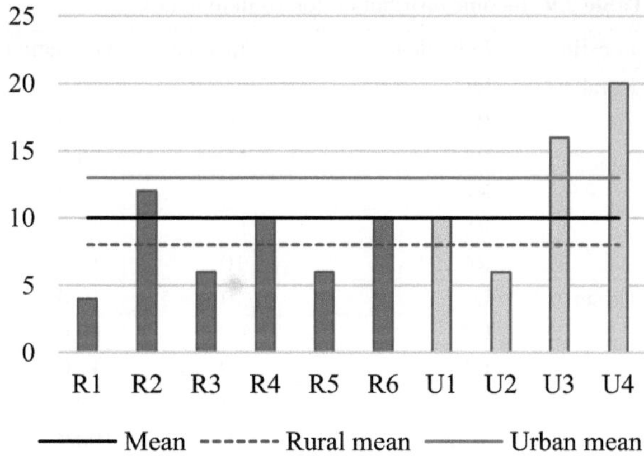

Fig. 2.5 Income distribution for 10 individuals classified into rural and urban areas

Table 2.8 Income distribution for 10 individuals classified into rural and urban areas

Location	Individuals	Income	Population Share (%)	Income Share (%)
Rural	R1	4	16.7	8.3
	R2	12	16.7	25.0
	R3	6	16.7	12.5
	R4	10	16.7	20.8
	R5	6	16.7	12.5
	R6	10	16.7	20.8
	Subtotal	48	100.0	100.0
	Rural mean	8		
	Standard deviation	2.83		
Urban	U1	10	25.0	19.2
	U2	6	25.0	11.5
	U3	16	25.0	30.8
	U4	20	25.0	38.5
	Subtotal	52	100.0	100.0
	Urban mean	13		
	Standard deviation	5.39		

Note: Standard deviation is the population standard deviation, not the sample standard deviation

Theil *L*). The within-group inequality component is the weighted average of rural and urban income inequalities with the weights being rural and urban population shares (0.6 and 0.4, respectively):

$$\begin{aligned}&(\text{pop.share})_R \times (\text{rural inequality}) + (\text{pop.share})_U \times (\text{urban inequality})\\&\quad = (0.6)(0.069) + (0.4)(0.099) = 0.081\end{aligned}$$

Table 2.9 Income distribution for 10 individuals

Location	Individual	Income	Population Share (%)	Income share (%)
Rural	R1	4	10.0	4.0
	R2	12	10.0	12.0
	R3	6	10.0	6.0
	R4	10	10.0	10.0
	R5	6	10.0	6.0
	R6	10	10.0	10.0
Urban	U1	10	10.0	10.0
	U2	6	10.0	6.0
	U3	16	10.0	16.0
	U4	20	10.0	20.0
	Total	100	100.0	100.0
	Mean income	10		
	Standard deviation	4.73		

Note: Standard deviation is the population standard deviation, not the sample standard deviation

where R and U denote rural and urban areas, respectively. How about income disparity between rural and urban areas? To obtain the rural-urban income disparity, we can use the formula given in Eq. (2.9), that is,

$$(\text{pop.share})_{\text{R}} \times \ln\left(\frac{(\text{pop.share})_{\text{R}}}{(\text{income share})_{\text{R}}}\right) + (\text{pop.share})_{\text{U}} \times \ln\left(\frac{(\text{pop.share})_{\text{U}}}{(\text{income share})_{\text{U}}}\right)$$

$$= (0.60)\ln\left(\frac{0.60}{0.48}\right) + (0.40)\ln\left(\frac{0.40}{0.52}\right) = 0.029.$$

This is the between-group inequality component.

Next, using all individuals, we can obtain overall income inequality (Table 2.9). By the Theil L index, it is 0.110, which is, in fact, the sum of the within-group and between-group inequality components, that is, equals to 0.081 + 0.029. By using a simple example, we have derived the following inequality decomposition equation by the Theil L index.

$$L = L_W + L_B$$

where L, L_W, and L_B present overall income inequality, the within-group inequality component, and the between-group inequality component, respectively.

Now, we will formally obtain inequality decomposition equations for the Theil T and L indices. Suppose that n individuals in a country are classified into m mutually exclusive and collectively exhaustive groups and group i has n_i individuals. Then, the distribution of incomes in the country can be described as a vector of m income distributions as follows:

$$\mathbf{y} = (\mathbf{y}_1, \mathbf{y}_2, \cdots, \mathbf{y}_m),$$

where $\mathbf{y}_i = \left(y_{i1}, y_{i2}, \cdots, y_{in_i}\right)$ denotes an income distribution for group i whose mean income is given by $\mu_i = \frac{1}{n_i}\sum_{j=1}^{n_i} y_{ij}$. If overall mean income is defined by $\mu = \frac{1}{n}\sum_{i=1}^{m}\sum_{j=1}^{n_i} y_{ij}$, then we have $\mu = \sum_{i=1}^{m}\frac{n_i}{n}\mu_i$ where $n = \sum_{i=1}^{m} n_i$. The Theil T and L indices are now given, respectively, by[6]

$$T = \frac{1}{n}\sum_{i=1}^{m}\sum_{j=1}^{n_i}\frac{y_{ij}}{\mu}\ln\left(\frac{y_{ij}}{\mu}\right)$$

and

$$L = \frac{1}{n}\sum_{i=1}^{m}\sum_{j=1}^{n_i}\ln\left(\frac{\mu}{y_{ij}}\right)$$

We can decompose these inequality measures into the within-group and between-group inequality components (Eqs. 2.11 and 2.12 for the Theil T and L indices, respectively).

$$T = \sum_{i=1}^{m}\frac{n_i}{n}\frac{\mu_i}{\mu}T_i + \sum_{i=1}^{m}\frac{n_i}{n}\frac{\mu_i}{\mu}\ln\left(\frac{\mu_i}{\mu}\right) = T_W + T_B \qquad (2.11)$$

where $T_i = \frac{1}{n_i}\sum_{j=1}^{n_i}\frac{y_{ij}}{\mu_i}\ln\left(\frac{y_{ij}}{\mu_i}\right)$ is the within-group inequality of group i. In Eq. (2.11), $T_W = \sum_{i=1}^{m}\frac{n_i}{n}\frac{\mu_i}{\mu}T_i$ is the within-group inequality component, which is the weighted average of within-group inequalities with the weights being income shares, while $T_B = \sum_{i=1}^{m}\frac{n_i}{n}\frac{\mu_i}{\mu}\ln\left(\frac{\mu_i}{\mu}\right)$ is the between-group inequality component.

$$L = \sum_{i=1}^{m}\frac{n_i}{n}L_i + \sum_{i=1}^{m}\frac{n_i}{n}\ln\left(\frac{\mu}{\mu_i}\right) = L_W + L_B \qquad (2.12)$$

where
$L_i = \frac{1}{n_i}\sum_{j=1}^{n_i}\ln\left(\frac{\mu_i}{y_{ij}}\right)$ is the within-group inequality of group i. In Eq. (2.12), $L_W = \sum_{i=1}^{m}\frac{n_i}{n}L_i$ is the within-group inequality component, which is the weighted average of within-group inequalities with the weights being population shares, while $L_B = \sum_{i=1}^{m}\frac{n_i}{n}\ln\left(\frac{\mu}{\mu_i}\right)$ is the between-group inequality component. The derivation of Eqs. (2.11) and (2.12) is given in Appendix 5.

Let Y_i and Y be the total income of group i and the total income of the country where $Y_i = \sum_{j=1}^{n_i} y_{ij}$ and $Y = \sum_{i=1}^{m}\sum_{j=1}^{n_i} y_{ij}$. Then, we have $n_i\mu_i = Y_i$ and $n\mu = Y$. Thus, we can rewrite Eqs. (2.11) and (2.12) as follows.

---

[6]The double summation sign $\sum_{i=1}^{m}\sum_{j=1}^{n_i} x_{ij}$ signifies that we first sum over all j ($j = 1, 2, \cdots, n_i$), holding each i constant, and then sum over all i ($i = 1, 2, \cdots, m$).

$$T = \sum_{i=1}^{m} \frac{Y_i}{Y} T_i + \sum_{i=1}^{m} \frac{Y_i}{Y} \ln \left(\frac{Y_i/Y}{n_i/n} \right) = T_W + T_B, \tag{2.13}$$

and

$$L = \sum_{i=1}^{m} \frac{n_i}{n} L_i + \sum_{i=1}^{m} \frac{n_i}{n} \ln \left(\frac{n_i/n}{Y_i/Y} \right) = L_W + L_B. \tag{2.14}$$

In other words,

$$T = \sum_{i=1}^{m} (\text{income share})_i \times T_i + \sum_{i=1}^{m} (\text{income share})_i \times \ln \left(\frac{(\text{income share})_i}{(\text{pop.share})_i} \right)$$

$$L = \sum_{i=1}^{m} (\text{pop.share})_i \times L_i + \sum_{i=1}^{m} (\text{pop.share})_i \times \ln \left(\frac{(\text{pop.share})_i}{(\text{income share})_i} \right)$$

where (pop. share)$_i$ and (income share)$_i$ are, respectively, the population and income shares of group i.

Now return to an example in Table 2.8, where there are two groups: rural and urban groups. If income inequality is measured by the Theil T index, we have

$$\begin{aligned} T &= [(0.48)(0.0646) + (0.52)(0.0899)\,] + (0.0293) = 0.0778 + 0.0293 \\ &= 0.1071. \end{aligned}$$

Rural and urban inequalities contribute, respectively, $29.0\% = \frac{(0.48)(0.0646)}{0.1071} \times 100$ and $43.6\% = \frac{(0.52)(0.0899)}{0.1071} \times 100$ of overall inequality; in total, the within-group inequality component accounts for 72.6 % (=29.0 % + 43.6%) of overall inequality. On the other hand, inequality between rural and urban sectors (between-group component) contributes $27.4\% = \frac{0.0293}{0.1071}$ of overall inequality. The result is summarized in Table 2.10.

Table 2.10 Decomposition of the Theil L and T indices and the squared coefficient of variation

	Theil L		Theil T		Squared CV		Pop. Share (%)	Income share (%)
	Value	% cont.	Value	% cont.	Value	% cont.		
Rural	0.0695	37.8	0.0647	29.0	0.1250	21.4	60.0	48.0
Urban	0.0993	36.0	0.0899	43.6	0.1716	51.8	40.0	52.0
W-group component	0.0814	73.8	0.0778	72.6	0.1640	73.2		
B-group component	0.0289	26.2	0.0293	27.4	0.0600	26.8		
Overall inequality	0.1103	100.0	0.1071	100.0	0.2240	100.0	100.0	100.0

Note: % cont. is the % contribution of each component. W-group component is within-group inequality component, while B-group component is the between-group inequality component

If income inequality is measured by the Theil L index, we have

$$L = [(0.60)(0.0695) + (0.40)(0.0993)\,] + (0.0289) = 0.0814 + 0.0289 = 0.1103$$

Rural and urban inequalities contribute, respectively, $37.8\% = \frac{(0.60)(0.0695)}{0.1103} \times 100$ and $36.0\% = \frac{(0.40)(0.0993)}{0.1103} \times 100$ of overall inequality; in total, the within-group component accounts for 73.8 % (=37.8 % + 36.0%) of overall inequality, while inequality between rural and urban areas (between-group component) contributes $26.2\% = \frac{0.0289}{0.1103}$ of overall inequality. The result is summarized in Table 2.10.

The squared coefficient of variation belongs to the generalized entropy class of measure (see Appendix 3); thus, it can also be decomposed into the within-group and between-group inequality components as follows.

$$CV^2 = \frac{1}{\mu^2}\frac{1}{n}\sum\nolimits_{i=1}^{m}\sum\nolimits_{j=1}^{n_i}\left(y_{ij} - \mu\right)^2$$

$$= \sum\nolimits_{i=1}^{m}\frac{n_i}{n}\left(\frac{\mu_i}{\mu}\right)^2 CV_i^2 + \sum\nolimits_{i=1}^{m}\frac{n_i}{n}\left(\frac{\mu_i - \mu}{\mu}\right)^2 = CV_W^2 + CV_B^2, \qquad (2.15)$$

where $CV_i^2 = \frac{1}{n_i}\sum\nolimits_{j=1}^{n_i}\left(\frac{y_{ij}-\mu_i}{\mu_i}\right)^2$ is the within-group inequality of group i. For the derivation of Eq. (2.15), please see Appendix 6. Using an example in Table 2.8, we have

$$CV^2 = [(0.384)(0.1250) + (0.676)(0.1716)\,] + (0.0600) = 0.2240.$$

Please note that the weights used in the within-group component of this decomposition equation do not sum to unity (0.384 + 0.676 $\neq$ 1), because they are

$$\frac{n_i}{n}\left(\frac{\mu_i}{\mu}\right)^2 = \left(\frac{n_i\mu_i}{n\mu}\right)\left(\frac{\mu_i}{\mu}\right) = \left(\frac{Y_i}{Y}\right)\left(\frac{Y_i/Y}{n_i/n}\right)$$

$$= (\text{income share}) \times \left(\frac{\text{income share}}{\text{population share}}\right).$$

The result is summarized in Table 2.10.

From these observations, we can conclude that about one-quarter of overall income inequality is attributable to the disparity between rural and urban areas. This suggests that if the mean incomes of rural and urban areas were the same ($\mu_R = \mu_U = \mu = 10$), then the between-group inequality component would disappear and overall income inequality would be due solely to within-group income inequalities. By the Theil L index, overall income inequality would decline to 0.0814 from 0.1103 (see Table 2.10).

We should note that the Gini coefficient cannot be decomposed in the way that the generalized entropy class of measures is decomposed, that is, it cannot generally be decomposed into the within-group and between-group inequality components (Lambert & Aronson, 1993). There is an exception, however. If there are no overlaps in the distributions of incomes between groups, then the Gini coefficient can be decomposed into the within-group and between-group components. Otherwise, the residual component appears in the decomposition equation as follows.

$$G = G_W + G_B + G_R. \tag{2.16}$$

In Eq. (2.16), $G_W = \sum_{k=1}^{m} \left(\frac{n_k}{n}\right)^2 \frac{\mu_k}{\mu} G_k$ is the within-group inequality component where $G_k = \frac{2}{n_k \mu_k} \mathrm{cov}(y_k, i(y_k))$ is the within-group Gini of group k, while G_B is the between-group Gini and $G_R \geq 0$ is the residual component.[7] In the case of the income distribution presented in Table 2.8, the largest income in rural areas (12 dollars) is larger than the smallest income in urban areas (6 dollars), indicating that there is an overlap in income distribution between rural and urban areas and thus the residual component is positive ($G_R > 0$). The following is the decomposition result for the example.

$$\begin{aligned} G &= [(0.288)(0.1944) + (0.208)(0.2308)\,] + 0.120 + 0.032 \\ &= 0.104 + 0.120 + 0.032 = 0.256 \end{aligned}$$

where $G_R = 0.032$ is the residual component.

3.2 Inequality Decomposition by Income Sources or Factor Components

Various sources of income are available for households, such as wage and salary, agricultural income, business income, interest income, government transfers, remittances, and pension benefits. Each of these income sources varies differently across households, based on the inter-household distributions of human resources, physical assets, innate abilities, and so on. One of the questions that are often addressed in the analysis of income inequality concerns the extent to which the distribution of each income source contributes to overall income inequality among households. To answer this question, the coefficient of variation and the Gini coefficient are commonly used because they are additively decomposable by income sources (Fei et al., 1978; Pyatt et al., 1980; Shorrocks, 1982).

As an example, consider a country consisting of 5 households (Fig. 2.6 and Table 2.11). For simplicity, there are two income sources: wage income (source 1) and government subsidy (source 2) so that total household income is the sum of wage income and government subsidy. Suppose first that government subsidy

[7] The between-group Gini coefficient G_B can be obtained by assuming that each individual has its group mean income, that is, G_B= Gini for (8, 8, 8, 8, 8, 8; 13, 13, 13, 13).

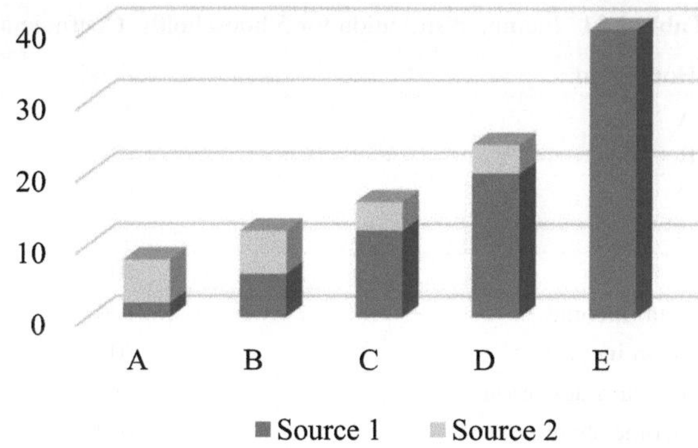

Fig. 2.6 Income distribution for 5 households: Two income sources

(source 2) is not available, that is, households have only wage income (source 1). Then, the income distribution for 5 households is given by $\boldsymbol{y_1} = (2, 6, 12, 20, 40)$. By the coefficient of variation, the income inequality is very high at 0.840. What will happen if the government decides to provide subsidy to poorer households? You can see that the distribution of subsidy $\boldsymbol{y_2} = (6, 6, 4, 4, 0)$ is highly negatively correlated with the distribution of wage income, that is, a household with a smaller amount of wage income tends to receive a larger amount of subsidy. This indicates that subsidy exerts an inequality-reducing effect. If inequality in the distribution of total household income $\boldsymbol{y} = (8, 12, 16, 24, 40)$ is measured by the coefficient of variation, then it is 0.566, much smaller than inequality in the distribution of wage income (0.840).

By the coefficient of variation, the following decomposition equation can be obtained.

$$CV = w_1\rho_1 CV_1 + w_2\rho_2 CV_2.$$

In this equation, CV is the coefficient of variation for total household income, w_k is the income share of income source k, ρ_k is the correlation coefficient between total income and income source k, and CV_k is the coefficient of variation for income source k, where $CV = \frac{\sigma}{\mu}$ and $CV_k = \frac{\sigma_k}{\mu_k}$. Using the example presented in Table 2.11, we can obtain

$$0.566 = (0.80)(0.999)(0.840) + (0.20)(-0.968)(0.548) = 0.672 + (-0.106).$$

If there are K income sources, then the decomposition equation is given by

$$CV = \sum_{k=1}^{K} w_k\rho_k CV_k. \tag{2.17}$$

Appendix 7 provides the derivation of Eq. (2.17). If we let $s_k = \rho_k \frac{CV_k}{CV}$, then Eq. (2.17) can be rewritten as

Table 2.11 Income distribution for 5 households: Coefficient of variation

Household	Total	Source 1	Source 2
A	8	2	6
B	12	6	6
C	16	12	4
D	24	20	4
E	40	40	0
Total income	100	80	20
Mean income	20	16	4
Standard deviation	11.3	13.4	2.2
Income share (w_k)	100%	80%	20%
Correlation coefficient (ρ_k)	1.000	0.999	−0.968
Coefficient of variation (CV_k)	0.566	0.840	0.548
Relative concentration coefficient (s_k)	1.000	1.484	−0.0.938
Contribution	100%	118.8%	−18.8%

Note: Standard deviation is the population standard deviation, not the sample standard deviation. The correlation coefficient is between total income and each income source

$$1 = \sum_{k=1}^{K} w_k s_k. \tag{2.18}$$

s_k is called the relative concentration coefficient of income source k. If $s_k > 1$, then income source k is an inequality-raising source. On the other hand, if $s_k < 1$, then income source k is an inequality-reducing source. Forexample, in Table 2.11, income source 1 is inequality-raising source because $s_1 = (0.999)\left(\frac{0.840}{0.566}\right) = 1.484 > 1$, while source 2 is inequality-reducing source because $s_2 = (-0.968) \times \left(\frac{0.548}{0.566}\right) = -0.938 < 1$. Using the relative concentration coefficient, we obtain:

$$1 = (0.8)(1.484) + (0.2)(-0.938) = 1.188 + (-0.188).$$

Or, in terms of percentage, we have

$$100\% = 118.8\% + (-18.8\%).$$

$w_1 s_1 = 1.188$ (or 118.8%) and $w_2 s_2 = -0.188$ (or −18.8%) are, respectively, the contributions of income sources 1 and 2 to overall inequality.

Like the coefficient of variation, the Gini coefficient can also be decomposed additively by income sources as follows.

$$G = \sum_{k=1}^{K} w_k R_k G_k, \tag{2.19}$$

In Eq. (2.19), $G = \frac{2}{n\mu}\text{cov}(\mathbf{y}, i(\mathbf{y}))$ is the Gini coefficient for total income, w_k is the income share of income source k, R_k is the rank correlation ratio for income source k, and $G_k = \frac{2}{n\mu_k}\text{cov}(\mathbf{y}_k, i(\mathbf{y}_k))$ is the Gini coefficient for income source k where $\mathbf{y} = (y_1,$

$y_2 \cdots, y_n)$ and $\boldsymbol{y}_k = (y_{1k}, y_{2k} \cdots, y_{nk})$ are, respectively, vectors of total incomes and incomes from source k for n households.[8] Appendix 7 provides the derivation of Eq. (2.19). In order to obtain Eq. (2.19), we need to introduce the concentration ratio, which is defined as

$$C_k = \frac{2}{n\mu_k} \text{cov}(\boldsymbol{y}_k, i(\boldsymbol{y})).$$

This looks like the Gini coefficient for income source k, but it is not. $\text{cov}(\boldsymbol{y}_k, i(\boldsymbol{y}))$ is the covariance between incomes from source k and the ranking of total incomes, not the ranking of incomes from source k. We should note that, unlike the Gini coefficient, the concentration ratio can take a negative value. Using the concentration ratio, R_k can be defined as

$$R_k = \frac{C_k}{G_k} = \frac{\text{cov}(\boldsymbol{y}_k, i(\boldsymbol{y}))}{\text{cov}(\boldsymbol{y}_k, i(\boldsymbol{y}_k))}.$$

R_k plays a similar role to ρ_k in Eq. (2.17).

When there are two income sources, overall Gini coefficient can be decomposed by income sources as follows.

$$G = w_1 R_1 G_1 + w_2 R_2 G_2.$$

Using the example in Table 2.11, we have (see Table 2.12)

$$0.304 = (0.80)(1.000)(0.450) + (0.20)(-1.000)(0.280) = 0.360 + (-0.056).$$

It should be noted that even if two or more individuals have the same income, different ranks should be given to these individuals when calculating the Gini coefficient. For example, when the Gini coefficient for the distribution of incomes from source 2 is calculated, individuals A and B should be given, respectively, 5 and 4 rather than 4 and 4. Similarly, individuals C and D should be given, respectively, 3 and 2 rather than 2 and 2.

If we let $g_k = R_k \frac{G_k}{G}$, then Eq. (2.19) can be rewritten as

$$1 = \sum_{k=1}^{K} w_k g_k . \tag{2.20}$$

g_k is called the relative concentration ratio of income source k. If $g_k > 1$, then income source k is an inequality-raising source. On the other hand, if $g_k < 1$, then income source k is an inequality-reducing source. For example, in Table 2.12, income source 1 is inequality-raising source because $g_1 = (1.000)\left(\frac{0.450}{0.304}\right) =$

[8] Two formulas of the Gini coefficient are presented in the previous section. Here, the second formula is employed. Please see Eq. (2.4).

Table 2.12 Income distribution for 5 households: Gini coefficient

	Total		Source 1		Source 2	
Household	Ranking	Income	Ranking	Income	Ranking	Income
A	1	8	1	2	5	6
B	2	12	2	6	4	6
C	3	16	3	12	3	4
D	4	24	4	20	2	4
E	5	40	5	40	1	0
Total income		100		80		20
Mean income		20		16		4
Income share (w_k)		100.0%		80.0%		20.0%
Rank correlation ratio (R_k)		1.000		1.000		−1.000
Gini (G_k)		0.304		0.450		0.280
Concentration ratio (C_k)		0.304		0.450		−0.280
Relative concentration ratio (g_k)		1.000		1.480		−0.921
Contribution		100.0%		118.4%		−18.4%

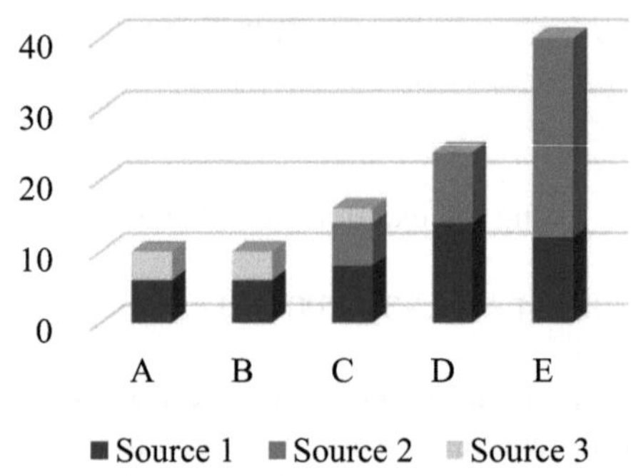

Fig. 2.7 Income distribution for 5 households: Three income sources

1.480 > 1, while source 2 is inequality-reducing source because $g_2 = (-1.000) \times \left(\frac{0.280}{0.304}\right) = -0.921 < 1$. Equation (2.20) is now given by

$$1 = (0.8)(1.480) + (0.2)(-0.921) = 1.184 + (-0.184).$$

Or, in percentage, we have

$$100\% = 118.4\% + (-18.4\%).$$

$w_1 g_1 = 1.184$ (or 118.4%) and $w_2 g_2 = -0.184$ (or −18.4%) are, respectively, the contributions of income sources 1 and 2 to overall income inequality.

Consider another distribution of incomes for 5 households (Fig. 2.7). There are now three income sources: wage income (source 1), interest income (source 2), and

Table 2.13 Income distribution for 5 households: Three income sources

	Total		Source 1		Source 2		Source 3	
Household	Rank	Income	Rank	Income	Rank	Income	Rank	Income
A	1	10	1	6	1	0	5	4
B	2	10	2	6	2	0	4	4
C	3	16	3	8	3	6	3	2
D	4	24	5	14	4	10	2	0
E	5	40	4	12	5	28	1	0
Total income		100		46		44		10
Mean income		20		9.2		8.8		2
STD		11.2		3.2		10.3		1.8
w_k		100%		46.0%		44.0%		10.0%
Coefficient of variation								
ρ_k		1.000		0.788		0.993		−0.875
CV_k		0.562		0.353		1.173		0.894
s_k		1.000		0.495		2.071		−1.392
Contribution		100.0%		22.8%		91.1%		−13.9%
Gini coefficient								
R_k		1.000		0.909		1.000		−1.000
G_k		0.296		0.191		0.600		0.480
C_k		0.296		0.174		0.600		−0.480
g_k		1.000		0.588		2.027		−1.622
Contribution		100.0%		27.0%		89.2%		−16.2%

transfer income (source 3). The result of inequality decomposition by income sources is presented in Table 2.13. The decomposition result based on the coefficient of variation is similar to the one based on the Gini coefficient. According to the coefficient of variation, the relative concentration coefficient of interest income (s_2) is much larger than one, signifying that interest income is an inequality-raising source. Due to unequal distribution of assets, interest income serves to increase overall inequality. Interest income accounts for around 90% of overall income inequality. Without interest income, overall income inequality would have been much smaller. On the other hand, the relative concentration coefficient of transfer income (s_3) is negative, meaning that transfer income is an inequality-reducing source. Since more transfers are given to poorer households, they serve to reduce income inequality.

4 Urbanization and Kuznets Process

In his seminal article, Kuznets (1955) developed the hypothesis that in the early stages of economic development, income inequality increases, but after reaching the peak, it decreases with economic development, that is, there is an inverted U-shaped

Table 2.14 Income distribution for 10 individuals: Urbanization and Kuznets process

Individual	Income (dollar)	Population Share	Mean income	Theil *L*	Theil *T*
R1	4				
R2	12				
R3	6				
R4	10				
R5	6				
R6	10				
U1	10				
U2	6				
U3	16				
U4	20				
Rural sector	48	0.60	8	0.0695	0.0647
Urban sector	52	0.40	13	0.0993	0.0899
Within-group inequality				0.0814	0.0778
Between-group inequality				0.0289	0.0293
Total	100		10	0.1103	0.1071
Urban/rural ratio			1.625		

relationship between economic development and income inequality. Kuznets argued that the process of population shift from the low-income, low-inequality traditional sector to the high-income, high-inequality modern sector is the basis for this relationship. Anand and Kanbur (1993) termed this the Kuznets process and discussed formally the Kuznets process using six inequality measures. This section discusses the Kuznets process of income inequality with respect to urbanization, that is, population shift from the rural to urban sector using the Theil indices. In order to delineate the Kuznets process, we assume that mean incomes and income inequalities remain unchanged in both rural and urban sectors. We also assume that mean income and income inequality are both larger in the urban sector than in the rural sector.

As an example, consider a country consisting of 10 individuals with the distribution of incomes presented in Table 2.8 (reproduced in Table 2.14).

Suppose first that the rural and urban sectors have the same mean income (10 dollars), that is, the between-group inequality is zero. Then, overall income inequality is equal to the within-group inequality component. Let p_U be the population share of the urban sector. By the Theil L index, the within-group inequality component can be described as a function of p_U as follows:

$$L_w = (1 - p_U)L_R + p_U L_U \geq 0, \tag{2.21}$$

where L_U and L_R are, respectively, urban and rural inequalities. This is a linear function of p_U. If $p_U = 0$, that is, all individuals are in rural areas, then $L_w = L_R$. On

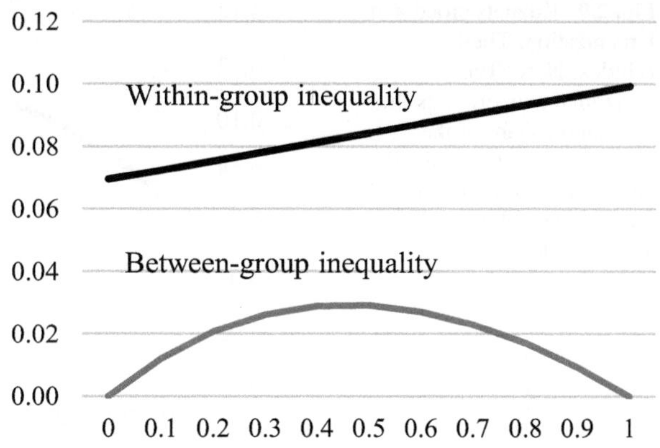

Fig. 2.8 Urbanization and Kuznets process: Theil *L* Index. Note: The horizontal axis presents the population share of the urban sector, while the vertical axis income inequality by the Theil *L* index

the other hand, If $p_U = 1$, that is, all individuals are in urban areas, then $L_w = L_U$. Using the example, we have

$$L_w = (1 - p_U)(0.0695) + p_U(0.0993).$$

If we assume that urban inequality is larger than rural inequality ($L_U > L_R$), then the within-group inequality component increases linearly with the urban population share (see Fig. 2.8).

Given the distribution of incomes presented in Table 2.14, suppose now that individuals in each group (rural or urban) have their mean group incomes, that is, the within-group inequality component is zero. Then, overall income inequality is equal to the between-group inequality component. Let δ be the urban-rural ratio of mean income $\delta = \frac{\mu_U}{\mu_R}$. Since δ is assumed to be constant, by the Theil L index, the between-group inequality component can be described as a function of p_U as follows:

$$L_B = \ln\left((1 - p_U) + \delta p_U\right) - p_U \ln(\delta) \geq 0. \tag{2.22}$$

This is a nonlinear function of p_U. If $p_U = 0$ or 1, then $L_B = 0$. Otherwise, $L_B > 0$. Using the example, we have

$$L_B = \ln\left((1 - p_U) + 1.625 p_U\right) - \ln(1.625) p_U.$$

As shown in Fig. 2.8, the between-group inequality component is a concave function.

By adding equations (2.21) and (2.22), we obtain the following equation for the Kuznets process of urbanization, which is depicted in Fig. 2.9.

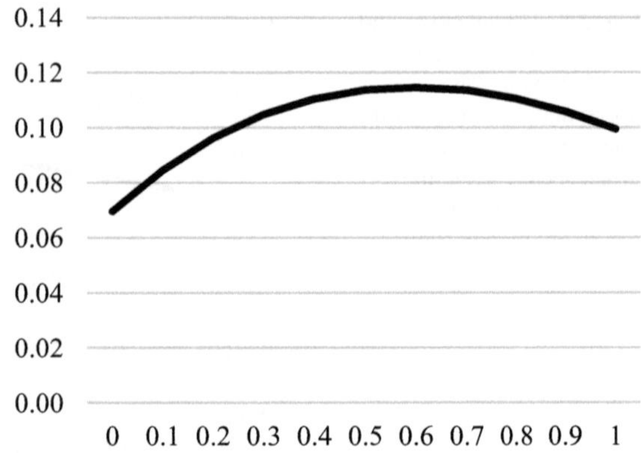

Fig. 2.9 Kuznets process of Urbanization: Theil *L* Index. Note: The horizontal axis presents the population share of the urban sector (p_U), while the vertical axis presents overall income inequality by the Theil *L* index

$$\begin{aligned} L &= L_w + L_B \\ &= [(1 - p_U)L_R + p_U L_U] + [\ln((1 - p_U) + \delta p_U) - p_U \ln(\delta)] \end{aligned} \tag{2.23}$$

Appendix 8 provides the derivation of this equation. When all individuals are in rural areas, overall inequality is equal to rural inequality. But it rises with the population shift from rural to urban areas. After reaching the peak somewhere before all individuals are in urban areas, overall inequality starts to decrease. When all individuals are in urban areas, it is equal to urban inequality. Since the current urban population share is 0.4, overall income inequality is 0.1103 by the Theil *L* index, which is smaller than the peak value of 0.1145 (see Appendix 8 to obtain the peak Theil *L* value). Under the assumption that mean income and income inequality remain constant in both rural and urban areas, this implies that further urbanization will raise overall income inequality. The peak inequality value is attained when the population share of urban areas is around 0.6.

By the Theil *T* index, the within-group and between-group inequality components can be described, respectively, as a function of p_U as follows:

$$T_W = \left[\frac{1 - p_U}{(1 - p_U) + \delta p_U}\right] T_R + \left[\frac{\delta p_U}{(1 - p_U) + \delta p_U}\right] T_U \tag{2.24}$$

$$T_B = \frac{\delta \ln(\delta) p_U}{(1 - p_U) + \delta p_U} - \ln((1 - p_U) + \delta p_U) \tag{2.25}$$

Please see Appendix 8 for the derivation of these equations. By adding Eqs. (2.24) and (2.25), we obtain the following equation for the Kuznets process of urbanization by the Theil *T* index.

$$T = \left[\left(\frac{1-p_U}{(1-p_U)+\delta p_U}\right)T_R + \left(\frac{\delta p_U}{(1-p_U)+\delta p_U}\right)T_U\right] + \left[\frac{\delta \ln(\delta) p_U}{(1-p_U)+\delta p_U} - \ln((1-p_U)+\delta p_U)\right] \quad (2.26)$$

By the Theil T index, a similar inverted U-shaped curve can be drawn for the Kuznets process of urbanization.

5 Measures of Regional Inequality

Measures of regional inequality can be classified into three broad types depending on how intra-regional income and population distributions are treated (Kanbur & Venables, 2005; Milanovic, 2005). To understand these three types, consider a country consisting of 20 individuals. The country comprises three mutually exclusive and collectively exhaustive regions: Regions 1, 2, and 3. The distribution of incomes for each region is shown in Fig. 2.10 and Table 2.15. Each region can be characterized by its mean income, income share, and population share. Region 1 is the metropolitan region, where 10 individuals live. It has the highest mean income and accounts for 62.5% of total income. Regions 2 and 3 are smaller than Region 1 in population size, each having 5 individuals. Region 2 is a city, having the second highest mean income. It accounts for 25% of total income. Region 3 is a village and has the smallest mean income.

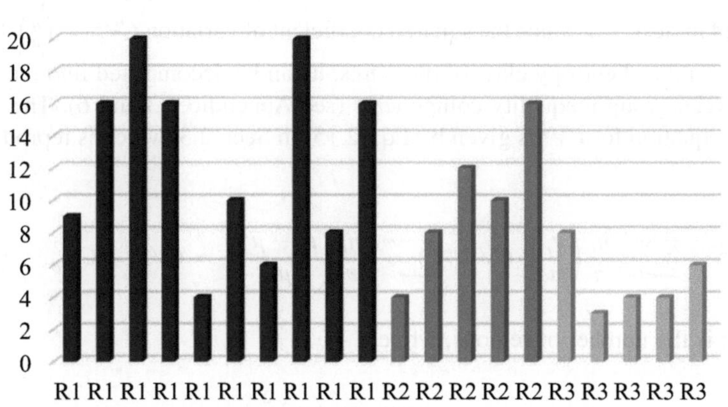

Fig. 2.10 Distribution of individual incomes by region. Note: R1, R2, and R3 refer to Regions 1, 2, and 3, respectively

Table 2.15 Distribution of individual incomes by region

Descriptive statistics	Region 1	Region 2	Region 3	Total
	9	4	8	
	16	8	3	
	20	12	4	
	16	10	4	
	4	16	6	
	10			
	6			
	20			
	8			
	16			
Total income	125	50	25	200
Population share	50.0%	25.0%	25.0%	100%
Income share	62.5%	25.0%	12.5%	100%
Mean income (μ)	12.5	10.0	5.0	10.0
Standard deviation (σ)	5.5	4.0	1.8	5.4
Coefficient of variation (CV)	0.440	0.400	0.358	0.541

5.1 Contribution of Between-region Inequality to Overall Interpersonal Income Inequality (Type 1 Measure)

How can we measure regional inequality in this situation? One way is to use the decomposition method of interpersonal income inequality by population subgroups discussed in Sect. 2.3. Since the squared coefficient of variation $CV^2 = \left(\frac{\sigma}{\mu}\right)^2$ belongs to the generalized entropy class of measures, it can be decomposed into the within- and between-group inequality components (see Appendices 3 and 6). The decomposition equation for CV^2 is given by Eq. (2.15) in Sect. 2.3, which is reproduced as follows.

$$CV^2 = \sum\nolimits_{i=1}^{m} \frac{n_i}{n} \left(\frac{\mu_i}{\mu}\right)^2 CV_i^2 + \sum\nolimits_{i=1}^{m} \frac{n_i}{n} \left(\frac{\mu_i - \mu}{\mu}\right)^2 = CV_W^2 + CV_B^2, \quad (2.27)$$

where m is the number of regions, while

$$CV_W^2 = \sum\nolimits_{i=1}^{m} \frac{n_i}{n} \left(\frac{\mu_i}{\mu}\right)^2 CV_i^2$$

and

$$CV_B^2 = \sum_{i=1}^{m} \frac{n_i}{n} \left(\frac{\mu_i - \mu}{\mu} \right)^2 = \frac{1}{\mu^2} \sum_{i=1}^{m} \frac{n_i}{n} (\mu_i - \mu)^2$$

are, respectively, the within- and between-region inequality components. $\frac{n_i}{n}$ and μ_i are, respectively, the population share and mean income of region i. Based on this decomposition equation, the first type of regional income inequality calculates the contribution of the between-region inequality component $\left(CV_B^2\right)$ to overall interpersonal income inequality (CV^2). This assesses the extent of regional income variation in the interpersonal distribution of incomes.

For the distribution of incomes presented in Table 2.15, interpersonal income inequality for the whole country is 0.541 by the coefficient of variation (CV). Among the three regions, region 1 has the largest interpersonal income inequality at 0.440, which is followed by region 2 (0.400) and region 3 (0.358). Using Eq. (2.27), the within-region inequality component is thus given by:

$$CV_W^2 = (0.50)\left(\frac{12.5}{10}\right)^2 (0.440)^2 + (0.25)\left(\frac{10}{10}\right)^2 (0.400)^2 + (0.25)\left(\frac{5}{10}\right)^2 (0.358)^2$$
$$= 0.151 + 0.040 + 0.008 = 0.199.$$

On the other hand, the between-region inequality component is given by:

$$CV_B^2 = (0.5)\left(\frac{12.5 - 10}{10}\right)^2 + (0.25)\left(\frac{10 - 10}{10}\right)^2 + (0.25)\left(\frac{5 - 10}{10}\right)^2$$
$$= 0.031 + 0.00 + 0.063 = 0.094.$$

The sum of the within- and between-region inequality components should be equal to overall interpersonal income inequality $(0.541)^2 = 0.293$. The following provides the decomposition result for the example.

$$0.293 = 0.199 + 0.094.$$

According to Table 2.16, which presents the inequality decomposition result, the contribution of the between-region inequality component to overall interpersonal income inequality is $32.0\% = \frac{0.094}{0.293} \times 100$, meaning that if the regional mean incomes are the same, that is, the between-region inequality component is zero, then overall interpersonal inequality would be reduced by 32%.

A number of studies have been conducted to examine regional income or expenditure inequality using the inequality decomposition method. They include Anand (1983), Glewwe (1986), Mishra and Parikh (1992), Tsakloglou (1993), Estudillo (1997), Akita and Lukman (1999), Akita et al. (1999), Kanbur and Zhang (1999), Liu (2001), Tadjoeddin et al. (2001), Eastwood and Lipton (2004),

Table 2.16 Inequality decomposition by regions: Squared coefficient of variation

	Squared *CV*	Contribution (%)	Population share	Mean income
Region 1	0.194	51.6	50.0%	12.5
Region 2	0.160	13.7	25.0%	10.0
Region 3	0.128	2.7	25.0%	5.0
Within-region component	0.199	68.0		
Between-region component	0.094	32.0		
Overall interpersonal inequality	0.293	100.0	100%	10.0

Shorrocks and Wan (2005), Motonishi (2006), Zaman and Akita (2012), Yusuf et al. (2014), and Chongvilaivan and Kim (2016).

5.2 *Population-Weighted Coefficient of Variation (Type 2 Measure)*

In order to introduce the second type of regional inequality, consider a hypothetical income distribution where individuals in each region have their regional mean income, that is, individuals in regions 1, 2, and 3 have 12.5, 10.0, and 5.0, respectively (see Table 2.15). Since there are no income variations across individuals within each region, the within-region inequality component vanishes in the inequality decomposition equation.

The second type of regional inequality is concerned with the between-region inequality component, $CV_B^2 = \frac{1}{\mu^2}\sum_{i=1}^{m}\frac{n_i}{n}(\mu_i - \mu)^2$. The square root of this component is, in fact, the population-weighted coefficient of variation introduced by Williamson (1965). For the income distribution in Table 2.15, the population-weighted coefficient of variation (*WCV*) is

$$WCV = \sqrt{CV_B^2} = \frac{1}{\mu}\sqrt{\sum_{i=1}^{3}\frac{n_i}{n}(\mu_i - \mu)^2} = \sqrt{0.094} = 0.306. \tag{2.28}$$

It should be noted that when *WCV* is calculated, the mean income μ is used. It is the weighted average of regional mean incomes with the weights being the population shares, that is,

$$\mu = \sum_{i=1}^{m}\left(\frac{n_i}{n}\right)\mu_i = \frac{Y}{n}, \tag{2.29}$$

where m is the number of regions and Y is total income. This is different from the simple average of regional mean incomes, which is defined by:

$$\mu^* = \frac{1}{m}\sum_{i=1}^{m}\mu_i. \tag{2.30}$$

In general, we have $\mu^* \neq \mu$. If the simple average $\mu^* = \frac{1}{3}(12.5 + 10 + 5) = 9.167$ is used, then the population-weighted coefficient of variation is

$$\begin{aligned} WCV^* &= \frac{1}{\mu^*}\sqrt{\sum_{i=1}^{3}\frac{n_i}{n}(\mu_i - \mu^*)^2} \\ &= \frac{1}{9.167}\sqrt{(0.5)(12.5-9.167)^2+(0.25)(10-9.167)^2+(0.25)(5-9.167)^2} = 0.346. \end{aligned} \tag{2.31}$$

This value is larger than the one based on the population-weighted average μ (see Eq. (2.28)).

Since the seminal article by Williamson (1965), a number of studies have been conducted to investigate regional income inequality using the population-weighted coefficient of variation. But, most of them have used data from the regional economic accounts such as regional GDP (Gross Domestic Product) rather than personal income data from national household surveys. Some of these studies are Mathur (1983), Lyons (1991), Tsui (1991), Akita and Lukman (1995), Chen and Fleisher (1996), Tsui (1996), Shankar and Shah (2003), Ezcurra and Rapún (2006), Hill et al. (2008), Portnov and Felsenstein (2010), Rodríguez-Pose and Ezcurra (2010), Lessmann (2014), and Hill and Vidyattama (2016). In these studies, μ and μ_i are, respectively, national GDP per capita and GDP per capita of ith region.

To illustrate how the population-weighted coefficient of variation is calculated using regional GDP and population data, consider a country comprising 5 regions. Table 2.17 presents their GDP and population. To obtain the population-weighted coefficient of variation (*WCV*), we first calculate

$$\sum_{i=1}^{5}\frac{n_i}{n}(\mu_i - \mu)^2$$

$$= (0.15)(200 - 300)^2 + (0.1)(250 - 300)^2 + (0.25)(300 - 300)^2$$

Table 2.17 Regional GDP and population (5 Regions)

Region	GDP	Population	GDP per capita	Population share (%)
Region 1	3000	15	200	15
Region 2	2500	10	250	10
Region 3	7500	25	300	25
Region 4	1000	10	100	10
Region 5	16,000	40	400	40
Total	30,000	100	300	100

$$+(0.1)(100-300)^2+(0.4)(400-300)^2=9,750.$$

Using Eq. (2.28), we now obtain

$$WCV=\frac{1}{300}\sqrt{9,750}=0.329.$$

If the intra-regional distribution of individual incomes is unknown for each region, then it is reasonable to assume that individuals in each region have their regional mean incomes. However, since regions vary in terms of population size, it is legitimate to consider regional differences in population size if we want to measure the extent of regional variation in interpersonal income inequality. This is the basic idea behind the second type of regional inequality.

In the example presented in Table 2.17, individuals in each region are assumed to receive their region's GDP per capita, that is, individuals in region 1 receive 200, individuals in region 2 receive 250, and so on. Since there is no inequality within each region, within-region inequalities are all zero. That is, the second type of regional inequality focuses on the between-region inequality component in the decomposition equation of interpersonal income inequality. As pointed out by Gluschenko (2018), the second type of regional inequality does not measure regional inequality; it tries to measure interpersonal income inequality. But due to unavailability of individual incomes, it assumes that individuals in each region have their regional mean incomes and weighs each region with its population share.

5.3 Population-Unweighted Coefficient of Variation (Type 3 Measure)

The third type of regional inequality compares regions in terms of their mean incomes, but without considering their population size. It is defined as

$$UWCV=\frac{1}{\mu}\sqrt{\frac{1}{m}\sum\nolimits_{i=1}^{m}(\mu_i-\mu)^2}. \tag{2.32}$$

If Eqs. (2.28) and (2.32) are compared, we can see that $\frac{n_i}{n}$ is replaced by $\frac{1}{m}$. This is called the population-unweighted coefficient of variation (*UWCV*) introduced by Williamson (1965). *UWCV* for the income distribution in Table 2.15 is:

$$UWCV = \frac{1}{10}\sqrt{\frac{1}{3}\left((12.5-10)^2+(10-10)^2+(5.0-10)^2\right)}$$
$$= \frac{1}{10}\sqrt{\frac{1}{3}(6.25+0+25.0)} = 0.323.$$

In Eq. (2.32), $\sqrt{\frac{1}{m}\sum_{i=1}^{m}(\mu_i-\mu)^2}$ looks like the standard deviation of regional mean incomes; but, it is not. μ is the weighted average of regional mean incomes defined by Eq. (2.29), not the simple average μ^* defined by Eq. (2.30). If μ is replaced by μ^*, then the unweighted coefficient of variation is:

$$UWCV^* = \frac{1}{9.167}\sqrt{\frac{1}{3}\left((12.5-9.167)^2+(10-9.167)^2+(5.0-9.167)^2\right)}$$
$$= \frac{1}{9.167}\sqrt{\frac{1}{3}(11.11+0.694+17.36)} = 0.340.$$

In the case of the third type, each region is treated as a single observation regardless of its population size.

Using the GDP and population data in Table 2.17, the population-unweighted coefficient of variation is:

$$UWCV = \frac{1}{300}\sqrt{\frac{1}{5}\left((-100)^2+(-50)^2+(0)^2+(-200)^2+(100)^2\right)} = 0.373$$

If the simple average $\mu^* = 250$ is used instead of the population-weighted average $\mu = 300$, the population-unweighted coefficient of variation is:

$$UWCV^* = \frac{1}{250}\sqrt{\frac{1}{5}\left((-50)^2+(0)^2+(50)^2+(-150)^2+(150)^2\right)} = 0.400.$$

This is the ratio between the standard deviation and the simple average.

In this example, the population-unweighted coefficient of variation (0.373) and the population-weighted coefficient of variation (0.329) are within the range of 0.3–0.4. However, we can have a situation where there is a large difference between these two measures. To see this, consider another example presented in Fig. 2.11 and Table 2.18. There are now 10 regions. One of them (Region 10) is a very rich enclave whose GDP per capita (1000) is 20 times the smallest (Region 9), though it has a population share of 0.5%.

For this data set, the population-weighted coefficient of variation (*WCV*) is 0.527, while the population-unweighted coefficient of variation (*UWCV*) is 1.287. There is a huge difference between them. The main reason is that the rich enclave (region 10) constitutes only 0.5% of the total population thus its contribution to *WCV* is not large even though it has a very large GDP per capita. In the equation for *WCV*, the term

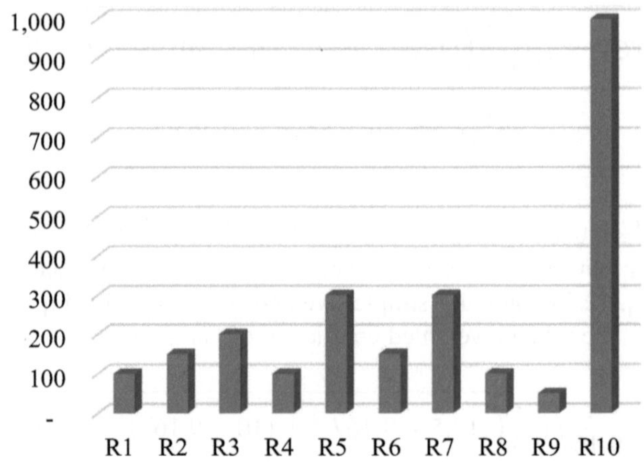

Fig. 2.11 GDP per capita (10 Regions)

Table 2.18 GDP per capita and population (10 Regions)

Region	Population	GDP per capita	Population share (%)
Region 1	100	100	10.0
Region 2	50	150	5.0
Region 3	100	200	10.0
Region 4	100	100	10.0
Region 5	250	300	25.0
Region 6	50	150	5.0
Region 7	200	300	20.0
Region 8	100	100	10.0
Region 9	45	50	4.5
Region 10	5	1000	0.5
Total	1000	207	100.0

corresponding to region 10 is $(0.005)(1{,}000 - 207)^2 = 3{,}142$, accounting for 26% of the sum of the population-weighted squared differences. On the other hand, in Eq. (2.32) for *UWCV*, it is $(0.1)(1{,}000 - 207)^2 = 62{,}845$, and this accounts for 88% of the sum of the squared differences, showing that region 10 contributes a lot to *UWCV*. *UWCV* of 1.287 indicates a very large regional inequality in GDP per capita, and this corresponds very closely to our observation of the pattern exhibited in Fig. 2.11 and Table 2.18.

As discussed above, *WCV* essentially measures interpersonal inequality by focusing on the between-region component of the inequality decomposition equation for interpersonal income inequality (see Eq. 2.27). Therefore, we should be very careful when *WCV* is used as a measure of regional inequality. On the other hand, *UWCV* compares regions in terms of their mean incomes or GDP per capita without considering their population sizes. It really measures regional inequality.

5.4 Theil Indices as Measures of Regional Inequality

As discussed in Sect. 2.2, the Theil indices (Theil T and L indices) belong to the generalized entropy class of measures. Like the squared coefficient of variation, they are decomposable by population subgroups, that is, they can be decomposed into the within- and between-group components (see Sect. 2.3). The decomposition equations for the Theil T and L indices (Eqs. 2.13 and 2.14 in Sect. 2.3) are reproduced, respectively, as follows:

$$T = \sum_{i=1}^{m} \frac{Y_i}{Y} T_i + \sum_{i=1}^{m} \frac{Y_i}{Y} \ln \left(\frac{Y_i/Y}{n_i/n} \right) = T_W + T_B, \tag{2.33}$$

and

$$L = \sum_{i=1}^{m} \frac{n_i}{n} L_i + \sum_{i=1}^{m} \frac{n_i}{n} \ln \left(\frac{n_i/n}{Y_i/Y} \right) = L_W + L_B, \tag{2.34}$$

where m is the number of regions.

The first type of regional inequality can be obtained by using these decomposition equations. The decomposition result for the income distribution given in Table 2.15 is presented in Table 2.19. By the Theil L index, overall interpersonal income inequality is 0.161, which is the sum of 0.099 (within-region component) and 0.062 (between-region component). Since the ratio of the between-region component to overall inequality is

$$\frac{0.062}{0.161} = 0.384,$$

Table 2.19 Inequality decomposition by regions: Theil indices

	Theil L		Theil T			
	Value	Contribution (%)	Value	Contribution (%)	Population share	Income share
Region 1	0.119	37.0	0.103	44.2	50.0%	62.5%
Region 2	0.097	15.1	0.085	14.5	25.0%	25.0%
Region 3	0.061	9.5	0.061	5.2	25.0%	12.5%
Within-region component	0.099	61.6	0.094	63.9		
Between-region component	0.062	38.4	0.053	36.1		
Overall interpersonal inequality	0.161	100.0	0.146	100.0	100.0%	100.0%

the between-region component contributes 38.4% of overall inequality. This implies that if all regions have the same mean income, then overall interpersonal income inequality will be reduced by 38.4% by the Theil L index.

The second type of regional inequality can be obtained by assuming that individuals in each region have their regional mean income, that is, 12.5, 10, and 5 for Regions 1, 2, and 3, respectively (see Table 2.15). Because the within-region inequality component vanishes, the second type of regional inequality is equal to the between-region inequality component of interpersonal inequality, that is,

$$WT = T_B = \sum_{i=1}^{m} \frac{Y_i}{Y} \ln\left(\frac{Y_i/Y}{n_i/n}\right) = \sum_{i=1}^{m} \frac{n_i}{n}\frac{\mu_i}{\mu} \ln\left(\frac{\mu_i}{\mu}\right), \tag{2.35}$$

$$WL = L_B = \sum_{i=1}^{m} \frac{n_i}{n} \ln\left(\frac{n_i/n}{Y_i/Y}\right) = \sum_{i=1}^{m} \frac{n_i}{n} \ln\left(\frac{\mu}{\mu_i}\right), \tag{2.36}$$

where m is the number of regions. Since the population share $\left(\frac{n_i}{n}\right)$ is included in these equations, they can be called the population-weighted Theil T and L indices, respectively. For the income distribution given in Table 2.15, we have $WT = 0.053$ and $WL = 0.062$.

Using regional GDP and population data in Table 2.18, WT and WL are calculated, respectively, as follows.

$$\begin{aligned} WT &= (0.1)\left(\frac{100}{207}\right)\ln\left(\frac{100}{207}\right) + (0.05)\left(\frac{150}{207}\right)\ln\left(\frac{150}{207}\right) + \cdots + (0.005) \\ &\times \left(\frac{1000}{207}\right)\ln\left(\frac{1000}{207}\right) \\ &= 0.131 \end{aligned}$$

$$WL = (0.1)\ln\left(\frac{207}{100}\right) + (0.05)\ln\left(\frac{207}{150}\right) + \cdots + (0.005)\ln\left(\frac{207}{1000}\right) = 0.144.$$

Like WCV, WT, and WL essentially measure interpersonal inequality by focusing on the between-region component of the decomposition equation for interpersonal income inequality.

What is the third type of regional inequality? In other words, what is the population-unweighted Theil indices? By replacing the population shares $\left(\frac{n_i}{n}\right)$ with $\left(\frac{1}{m}\right)$ in the equations for WT and WL, we can obtain the population-unweighted Theil T and L indices as follows.

$$UWT = \frac{1}{m}\sum_{i=1}^{m} \frac{\mu_i}{\mu} \ln\left(\frac{\mu_i}{\mu}\right), \tag{2.37}$$

$$UWL = \frac{1}{m}\sum\nolimits_{i=1}^{m} \ln\left(\frac{\mu}{\mu_i}\right), \tag{2.38}$$

where μ is the weighted average of regional mean incomes defined by Eq. (2.29), not the simple average μ^* defined by Eq. (2.30). If μ is replaced by μ^*, then the population-unweighted Theil T and L indices are given, respectively, by

$$UWT^* = \frac{1}{m}\sum\nolimits_{i=1}^{m} \frac{\mu_i}{\mu^*} \ln\left(\frac{\mu_i}{\mu^*}\right), \tag{2.39}$$

$$UWL^* = \frac{1}{m}\sum\nolimits_{i=1}^{m} \ln\left(\frac{\mu^*}{\mu_i}\right). \tag{2.40}$$

Using regional GDP and population data in Table 2.18, *UWT* and *UWL* are calculated, respectively, as follows.

$$\begin{aligned} UWT &= (0.1)\left(\frac{100}{207}\right)\ln\left(\frac{100}{207}\right) + (0.1)\left(\frac{150}{207}\right)\ln\left(\frac{150}{207}\right) + \cdots + (0.1) \\ &\quad \times \left(\frac{1,000}{207}\right)\ln\left(\frac{1,000}{207}\right) \\ &= 0.676 \end{aligned}$$

$$UWL = (0.1)\ln\left(\frac{207}{100}\right) + (0.1)\ln\left(\frac{207}{150}\right) + \cdots + (0.1)\ln\left(\frac{207}{1,000}\right) = 0.198.$$

The population-unweighted Theil T (*UWT*) is much larger than the population-weighted Theil T (*WT*) (0.676 vs. 0.131). This is due mainly to the very large contribution of the rich enclave (region 10) in *UWT*. In the equation of *UWT*, region 10 has $0.759 = (0.1)\left(\frac{1,000}{207}\right)\ln\left(\frac{1,000}{207}\right)$, while in the equation of *WT*, it has only $0.038 = (0.005)\left(\frac{1,000}{207}\right)\ln\left(\frac{1,000}{207}\right)$. The rich enclave (region 10) contributes a lot to *UWT*. On the other hand, while the population-unweighted Theil L (*UWL*) is larger than the population-weighted Theil L (*WL*), the difference is not large (0.198 vs. 0.144). This is due to the fact that the poorest region (region 9) does not contribute much to *UWL*. If we look at the term for region 9, it is $0.142 = (0.1)\ln\left(\frac{207}{50}\right)$, while the term for region 10 is $-0.157 = (0.1)\ln\left(\frac{207}{1000}\right)$. The sum of these two terms is negative.

6 Regional Convergence

Since the pioneering work of Barro and Sala-i-Martin (1991), regional convergence has attracted considerable attention among researchers in regional economic growth. According to the neoclassical growth model, among regions that share the same

Table 2.20 GDP per capita in 2010 and 2020 for 5 regions (Example 1)

	GDP per capita		
	2010	2020	Growth rate
Region 1	100	180	5.9%
Region 2	400	550	3.2%
Region 3	150	300	6.9%
Region 4	50	120	8.8%
Region 5	300	450	4.1%
Average (μ)	200	320	4.7%
Variance of log income	0.626	0.341	
Coefficient of variation	0.652	0.504	

steady state, poor regions should grow faster than rich regions (Solow, 1956).[9] This is related to the concept of so-called β-convergence. There are however two concepts of convergence in the literature on economic growth: β-convergence and σ-convergence (Barro & Sala-i-Martin, 1991, 1992, 2004). In a cross section of regional economies, if there is a negative relationship between the growth rate of income per capita and the initial level of income per capita, that is, if poor regions grow faster than rich regions, then there is β-convergence among them. On the other hand, if the dispersion of income per capita across regions tends to decrease over time, then there is σ-convergence. The previous section discussed measures of regional inequality, and they are related to σ-convergence. This section will discuss the concept of β-convergence among regional economies and its relationship with the concept of σ-convergence.

To understand the concepts of β-convergence and σ-convergence, consider a country consisting of 5 regions whose real GDP per capita in 2010 and 2020 are given in Table 2.20. Figure 2.12 plots a region's GDP per capita in 2010 (horizontal axis) against the region's growth rate from 2010 to 2020 (vertical axis). It reveals a strong negative relationship between the two variables; the coefficient of correlation is -0.927. Poor regions (regions 1 and 4) grew faster on average than rich regions (regions 2 and 5), indicating the existence of β-convergence among these 5 regions. On the other hand, the dispersion of GDP per capita across 5 regions in 2010 and 2020 can be measured by the variance of log income defined by

$$\sigma^2 = \frac{1}{n}\sum\nolimits_{i=1}^{n}(\ln(y_i) - \ln(\mu))^2,$$

where n, y_i, and $\mu = \frac{1}{n}\sum\nolimits_{i=1}^{n} y_i$ are, respectively, the number of regions, GDP per capita of region i, and average GDP per capita.[10] The variance of log income decreased substantially from 0.626 in 2010 to 0.341 in 2020, indicating that there

[9] Appendix 9 presents Solow's neoclassical growth model.

[10] The variance of log income is one of relative inequality measures. Please see Appendix 4 for its definition.

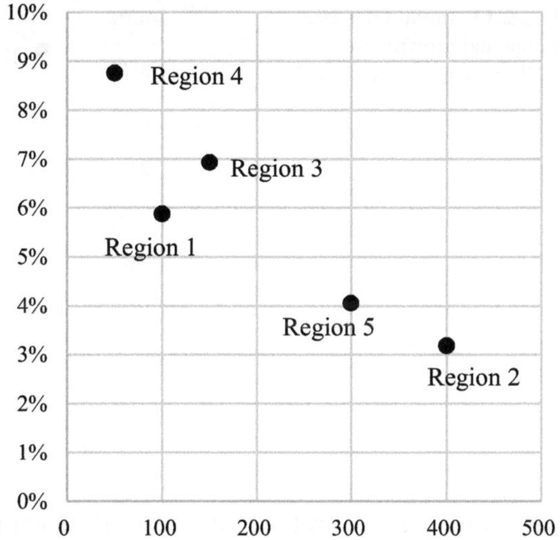

Fig. 2.12 Initial GDP per capita and growth rate of GDP per capita (Example 1)

Table 2.21 GDP per capita in 2010 and 2020 for 5 Regions (Example 2)

	GDP per capita		
	2010	2020	Growth rate
Region 1	100	200	6.9%
Region 2	400	400	0.0%
Region 3	150	200	2.9%
Region 4	50	2000	36.9%
Region 5	300	350	1.5%
Average (μ)	200	630	11.5%
Variance of log income	0.626	0.904	
Coefficient of variation	0.652	1.095	

is also σ-convergence. In sum, among the 5 regions presented in Table 2.20, there are both β-convergence and σ-convergence.

But, this is not always the case. Consider another country consisting of 5 regions (Table 2.21). In 2010, the distribution of GDP per capita among these 5 regions is the same as the one for the country exhibited in Table 2.20. But, the growth rates from 2010 to 2020 are completely different. Particularly, the poorest region (region 4) grew very rapidly at an annual average rate of 36.9% due, for example, to the development of a large-scale industrial estate. Meanwhile, the GDP per capita of the richest region (region 2) remained constant. In 2020, region 4 became the richest region by surpassing all other regions. Figure 2.13 presents the initial GDP per capita and the growth rate from 2010 to 2020. It reveals that poor regions tend to grow faster than rich regions. The coefficient of correlation between the initial GDP per capita and the growth rate is −0.690, showing that there is a negative relationship between these two variables. This indicates β-convergence among the 5 regions. How about σ-convergence? The variance of log income in 2010 was 0.626, but increased prominently to 0.904, indicating that there is no σ-convergence in this

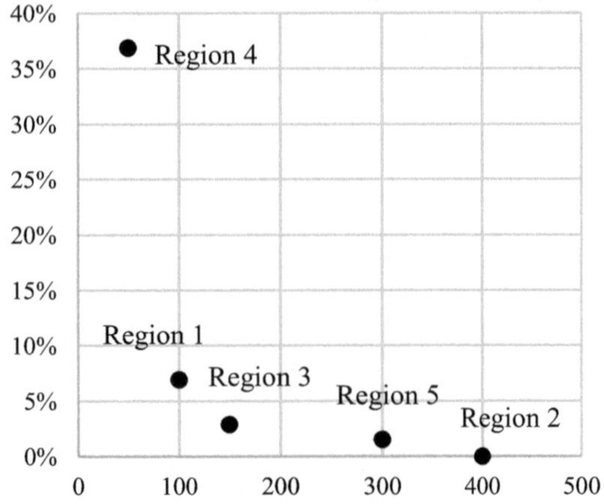

Fig. 2.13 Initial GDP per capita and growth rate of GDP per capita (Example 2)

case. This suggests that β-convergence does not guarantee σ-convergence. In other words, β-convergence is a necessary, but not a sufficient condition for σ-convergence.

To formally test whether there is β-convergence in a cross section of regional economies, we estimate the following regression equation, where the subscript i refers to region i.

$$\frac{1}{T}\ln\left(\frac{y_{iT}}{y_{i0}}\right) = \alpha + \beta\ln(y_{i0}) + u_i. \tag{2.41}$$

In this equation, y_{i0}, y_{iT}, and u_i are, respectively, GDP per capita in the initial year, GDP per capita in the terminal year, and error term, while $\frac{1}{T}\ln\left(\frac{y_{iT}}{y_{i0}}\right)$ is the annual average growth rate of GDP per capita.[11] If we conduct a simple regression analysis for a cross section of regional economies using Eq.(2.41) and find that β is significantly negative, then we can say that there is *absolute* β-convergence among them. The reason why we say *absolute* convergence is that Eq. (2.41) includes only initial GDP per capita and does not include any other variables. If we conduct a multiple regression analysis with a model including initial GDP per capita and some other independent variables that may affect the growth rate of GDP per capita and find that β is significantly negative, then the regional economies exhibit *conditional* β-convergence.

If regions in a country have similar preferences, savings rates, technologies, and institutions, they are likely to have similar steady states and converge in the absolute sense. On the other hand, if regions have different preferences, savings rates, technologies, and institutions, then they are likely to have different steady states.

[11]If per capita GDP grows exponentially at an annual average rate of g, then we have $y_{iT} = y_{i0}e^{gT}$. Thus, we obtain $g = \frac{1}{T}\ln\left(\frac{y_{iT}}{y_{i0}}\right)$.

Table 2.22 Regression analysis

	Example 1		Example 2	
	Coefficient	Standard error	Coefficient	Standard error
Intercept	0.1842***	0.0262	0.8853*	0.2874
Log (initial GDP per capita)	−0.0251**	0.0051	−0.1564*	0.0564
Adjusted R Square	0.8515		0.6261	
Number of observations	5		5	

Note: ***significant at 1% level, **significant at 5% level, *significant at 10% level

To test β-convergence in this case, we need to estimate the following multiple regression model.

$$\frac{1}{T}\ln\left(\frac{y_{iT}}{y_{i0}}\right) = \alpha + \beta\ln(y_{i0}) + \gamma_1 x_{i1} + \gamma_2 x_{i2} + \cdots + \gamma_m x_{im} + u_i, \tag{2.42}$$

where $x_{i1}, x_{i2}, \cdots, x_{im}$ are conditioning variables which may affect the growth rate of GDP per capita and are supposed to represent the steady-state level of GDP per capita of region i. If β is found to be significantly negative after controlling for the effects of the conditioning variables, then we can say that the regions exhibit *conditional* β-convergence.

Using data in Tables 2.20 and 2.21, a simple regression analysis is conducted. The result is presented in Table 2.22. The coefficient associated with initial GDP per capita is negative and significant either at the 5% or 10% significance level. In this regression analysis, no conditioning variables are included. Therefore, both examples 1 and 2 exhibit *absolute* β-convergence.

7 Some Useful Stata Commands

Many researchers use Stata to analyze inequality and poverty. Stata is a statistical software package for Windows and Macintosh. This section introduces some useful Stata commands for the measurement of inequality. We should note that you may need to search Stata files including these Stata commands using the **`search`** command and install them. For the basics of Stata, please see, for example, Hamilton (2012) and Daniels and Minot (2019).

1. **`inequal`** calculates the following inequality measures: relative mean deviation, coefficient of variation, standard deviation of logs, Gini index, Mehran index, Piesch index, Kakwani index, Theil entropy index (Theil *T* index), and mean log deviation (Theil *L* index).

    - **`inequal`** `varname [`**`if`** `exp] [fweights]`
      (Example) The following is the Stata output of **`inequal`** using the income data of Distribution 2 in Table 2.1.

```
-------------------------------------------------------------
relative mean deviation              .28
coefficient of variation             .77136243
standard deviation of logs           .91154552
Gini coefficient                     .376
Mehran measure                       .5328
Piesch measure                       .2976
Kakwani measure                      .1334245
Theil entropy measure                .23802128
Theil mean log deviation measure     .28743334
-------------------------------------------------------------
```

(Note) The value of the coefficient of variation differs from the one in Tables 2.1 and 2.6 since **inequal** uses the sample standard deviation rather than the population standard deviation.

2. **ineqerr** calculates the following inequality measures: Gini coefficient, Theil entropy measure (Theil *T* index), and variance of logs. In addition to the point estimates of these inequality measures, it provides bootstrap estimates of their sampling variances.

   - **ineqerr** varlist [weight] [**if** exp]
     (Example) The following is the Stata output of **ineqerr** using the income data of Distribution 2 in Table 2.1.

```
-----------------------------------------------------------------
Variable |  Reps  Observed     Bias  Std. Err.  [95% Conf. Interval]
-----------------------------------------------------------------
    Gini |   100      .376 -.0564489 .0992497 .1790671 .5729329  (N)
         |                                    .1103448       .5  (P)
         |                                    .2197183 .5212121 (BC)
-----------------------------------------------------------------
   Theil |   100  .2380213 -.0284062 .1121721 .0154474 .4605951  (N)
         |                                    .0339965 .4700759  (P)
         |                                    .0741265 .5435063 (BC)
-----------------------------------------------------------------
 Varlogs |   100  .6647321   -.11063 .3168739 .0359856 1.293479  (N)
         |                                    .0552789 1.164877  (P)
         |                                    .1204966 1.206208 (BC)
-----------------------------------------------------------------
                      N = normal, P = percentile, BC = bias-corrected
```

3. **geivars** calculates the generalized entropy class of inequality measures, including GE(0), GE(1), and GE(2), where GE(0) $= E_0$ is the Theil *L* index (mean logarithmic deviation), GE(1) $= E_1$ is the Theil *T* index, and GE(2) $= E_2$ is half of the squared coefficient of variation.

   - **geivars** varname [weight] [**if** exp]
     (Example) The following is the Stata output of **geivars** using the income data of Distribution 2 in Table 2.1.

```
------------------------------------------------------------------
Generalized entropy inequality measures, GE(a), with asym. s.e.s
------------------------------------------------------------------
  a      |    -1          0          1          2
------------------------------------------------------------------
GE(a)    |   0.43990    0.28743    0.23802    0.23800

Var0     |   0.16834    0.16618    1.37198    0.19158
s.e.0    |   0.41030    0.40766    1.17131    0.43770
asym. t  |   1.07215    0.70509    0.20321    0.54375
P > |t|  |   0.34403    0.51965    0.84889    0.61550

delta1   |  -0.10160   -0.14373   -1.35690   -0.17307
Var1     |   0.06674    0.02246    0.01508    0.01851
s.e.1    |   0.25834    0.14985    0.12279    0.13606
asym. t  |   1.70281    1.91811    1.93844    1.74926
P > |t|  |   0.16382    0.12755    0.12460    0.15515

delta2   |   0.00000    0.00000    0.00000    0.00000
Var2     |   0.06674    0.02246    0.01508    0.01851
s.e.2    |   0.25834    0.14985    0.12279    0.13606
asym. t  |   1.70281    1.91811    1.93844    1.74926
P > |t|  |   0.16382    0.12755    0.12460    0.15515
------------------------------------------------------------------
```

4. **lorenz** draws the Lorenz curve of income distribution.
   - **lorenz** varname [**if** exp] [fweights]
     (Example) Fig. 2.14 is the Stata output of **lorenz** using the income data of the Household Income and Expenditure Survey of a country.
5. **sumdist** estimates distributional summary statistics commonly used by income distribution analysts (for example, income or expenditure shares of decile groups).
   - **sumdist** varname [weight] [**if** exp]
     (Example) The following is the Stata output of **sumdist** using the income data of the Household Income and Expenditure Survey of a country.

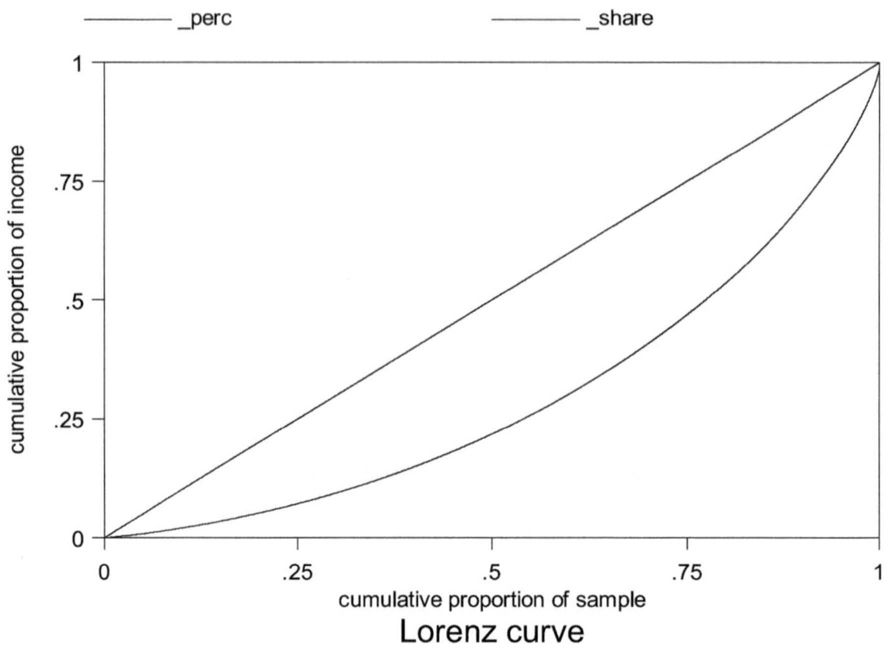

Fig. 2.14 Stata output of Lorenz curve

Quantile group	Quantile	% of median	Share, %	L(p), %	GL(p)
1	5007.00	40.94	2.01	2.01	333.51
2	6824.00	55.80	3.59	5.60	927.60
3	8506.00	69.55	4.65	10.25	1697.63
4	10172.67	83.18	5.64	15.89	2632.38
5	12230.00	100.00	6.75	22.65	3751.37
6	14506.00	118.61	8.07	30.72	5088.83
7	17654.00	144.35	9.60	40.32	6678.67
8	22780.00	186.26	12.07	52.39	8678.42
9	33307.29	272.34	16.47	68.86	11407.27
10			31.14	100.00	16565.70

Share = quantile group share of total per capita income;
L(p)=cumulative group share; GL(p)=L(p)*mean(per capita income)

6. **ineqdeco** conducts an inequality decomposition analysis by population subgroup using the generalized entropy class of inequality measures and the Atkinson inequality indices.

- **ineqdeco** varname [weight] [**if** exp] , **by**(groupvar)
  (Example) The following is the Stata output of **ineqdeco** using income data in Table 2.8, where income inequality is decomposed by urban and rural locations.

```
-------------------------------------------------------------------
Percentile ratios for distribution of income: all valid obs.
-------------------------------------------------------------------
p90/p10  p90/p50  p10/p50  p75/p25  p75/p50  p25/p50
-------------------------------------------------------------------
  3.600    1.800    0.500    2.000    1.200    0.600

Generalized Entropy indices GE(a), where a = income difference
sensitivity parameter, and Gini coefficient

-------------------------------------------------------------------
 All obs |    GE(-1)      GE(0)      GE(1)      GE(2)       Gini
---------+---------------------------------------------------------
         |   0.12292    0.11033    0.10711    0.12444    0.25600
-------------------------------------------------------------------

Atkinson indices, A(e), where e > 0 is the inequality aversion
parameter

------------------------------------------
 All obs |    A(0.5)       A(1)       A(2)
---------+--------------------------------
         |   0.05311    0.10446    0.19732
------------------------------------------

Subgroup summary statistics, for each subgroup k = 1,...,K:

-------------------------------------------------------------------
urban | Pop. share       Mean   Rel.mean  Income share   log(mean)
------+------------------------------------------------------------
    0 |    0.60000    8.00000    0.80000       0.48000     2.07944
    1 |    0.40000   13.00000    1.30000       0.52000     2.56495
-------------------------------------------------------------------

Subgroup indices: GE_k(a) and Gini_k

-----------------------------------------------------------
   urban |   GE(-1)     GE(0)     GE(1)     GE(2)      Gini
---------+-------------------------------------------------
       0 |  0.07778   0.06946   0.06466   0.06250   0.19444
       1 |  0.11615   0.09928   0.08991   0.08580   0.23077
-----------------------------------------------------------
```

Within-group inequality, GE_W(a)

All obs	GE(-1)	GE(0)	GE(1)	GE(2)
	0.09407	0.08139	0.07779	0.08200

Between-group inequality, GE_B(a):

All obs	GE(-1)	GE(0)	GE(1)	GE(2)
	0.02885	0.02894	0.02932	0.03000

Subgroup Atkinson indices, A_k(e)

urban	A(0.5)	A(1)	A(2)
0	0.03307	0.06710	0.13462
1	0.04636	0.09451	0.18850

Within-group inequality, A_W(e)

All obs	A(0.5)	A(1)	A(2)
	0.03998	0.08136	0.16264

Between-group inequality, A_B(e)

All obs	A(0.5)	A(1)	A(2)
	0.01368	0.02515	0.04142

(Note)
GE(0) = Theil L index,
GE(1) = Theil T index, and
GE(2) = half of the squared coefficient of variation.

7. **descogini** conducts an inequality decomposition analysis by income sources using the Gini coefficient.

   - **descogini** varlist [**if** exp]

The first variable in `varlist` should be total per capita household income. The other variables in `varlist` are the household income components in per capita household income.

(Example) The following is the Stata output of **descogini** using income data in Table 2.11 (and Table 2.12), where household income inequality is decomposed by income sources.

```
---------------------------------------------------------------
Total Income Variable: total
---------------------------------------------------------------
Source          Sk        Gk          Rk       Share    % Change
---------------------------------------------------------------
Source 1     0.8000    0.4500     1.0000     1.1842     0.3842
Source 2     0.2000    0.2800    -1.0000    -0.1842    -0.3842
Total income           0.3040
---------------------------------------------------------------
```

(Note)

Sk = income share of source *k*;

Gk = Gini coefficient of source *k*;

Rk = Rank correlation ratio of source *k*; and

Share = contribution of source *k* to overall inequality.

8. **ineqfac** conducts an inequality decomposition analysis by income sources using the coefficient of variation.

- **ineqfac** `facvars [weight] [`**if**` exp]`

  The variables in the `facvars` are the household income components in per capita household income. Unlike **descogini**, you do not need to include total per capita household income in `facvars`.

  (Example) The following is the Stata output of **ineqfac** using income data in Table 2.11 (and Table 2.12), where household income inequality is decomposed by income sources.

```
---------------------------------------------------------------
Factor    |   100*s_f     S_f    100*m_f/m    CV_f  CV_f/CV(Total)
----------+----------
Source 1  |  118.7500  0.7510    80.0000    0.9396     1.4856
Source 2  |  -18.7500  0.1186    20.0000    0.6124     0.9682
----------+----------------------------------------------------
Total     |  100.0000  0.6325   100.0000    0.6325     1.0000
---------------------------------------------------------------
Note: The proportionate contribution of factor f to inequality of
Total,
   s_f = rho_f*sd(f)/sd(Total). S_f = s_f*CV(Total).
   m_f = mean(f). sd(f) = std.dev. of f. CV_f = sd(f)/m_f.
---------------------------------------------------------------
```

(Note)
CV(Total) = CV for overall inequality,
CV_f = CV for inequality of each income source,
100*s_f = contribution of each income source to overall inequality (in %),
S_f = (s_f) × CV(Total),
100*m_f/m = income share (in %) of each income source, and
CV_f/CV(Total) = ratio between inequality of each income source and overall inequality by CV.

Appendix 1: Geometric Definition of the Gini Coefficient (Eq. 2.3)

To derive Eq. 2.3, consider the area below the Lorenz curve between individuals i and $i + 1$. This area is a trapezoid so that using cumulative population and income shares, it is given by $\frac{1}{2}(F_{i+1} - F_i)(H_{i+1} + H_i)$. Therefore, total area below the Lorenz curve and above the horizontal axis is $\frac{1}{2}\sum_{i=0}^{n-1}(F_{i+1} - F_i)(H_{i+1} + H_i)$. On the other hand, the area below the 45° line and above the horizontal axis is a triangle, and thus it is given by $\frac{1}{2}$. Since the area between the 45° line and the Lorenz curve (A) is given by $\frac{1}{2} - \frac{1}{2}\sum_{i=0}^{n-1}(F_{i+1} - F_i)(H_{i+1} + H_i)$, we obtain the following formula by dividing this area (A) by the area of the triangle (A + B),

$$G_1 = \frac{\mathrm{A}}{\mathrm{A} + \mathrm{B}} = 1 - \sum_{i=0}^{n-1}(F_{i+1} - F_i)(H_{i+1} + H_i).$$

Appendix 2: Some Properties of the Natural Logarithm Function

The natural logarithm function is given by $y = \ln(x)$, whose graph is depicted in Fig. 2.15 where x is on the horizontal axis and y is on the vertical axis. It is defined over $x > 0$. The natural logarithm function is the inverse of the exponential function with the base $e \equiv \lim_{n\to\infty}\left(1 + \frac{1}{n}\right)^n \cong 2.71828$, that is, we have

$$y = \ln(x) \leftrightarrow x = e^y.$$

The derivative of the natural logarithm function is given by:

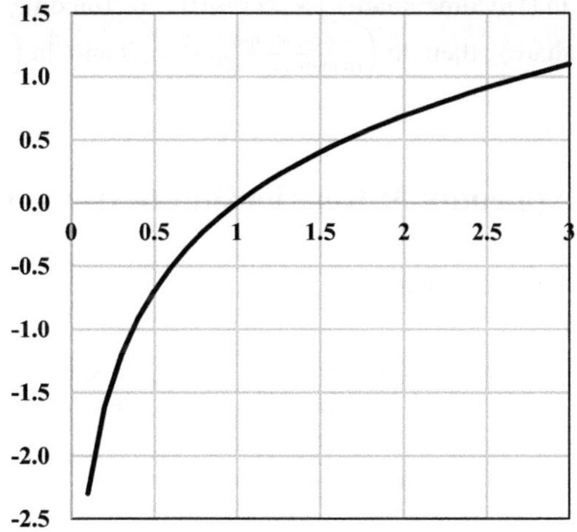

Fig. 2.15 Natural logarithm function

$$\frac{\mathrm{d}y}{\mathrm{d}x} = \frac{1}{x} > 0 \text{ for } x > 0.$$

Thus, the natural logarithm function is a monotonically increasing function (see Fig. 2.15). Some of the useful properties are:

$$y = \ln(x) < 0 \text{ if } 0 < \mathrm{x} < 1,$$

$$y = \ln(x) = 0 \text{ if } \mathrm{x} = 1,$$

$$y = \ln(x) > 0 \text{ if } \mathrm{x} > 1,$$

$$\ln(e^a) = a,$$

$$\ln(1) = \ln\left(e^0\right) = 0,$$

$$\ln(x^a) = a \ln(x),$$

$$\ln(a \cdot b) = \ln(a) + \ln(b),$$

and

$$\ln\left(\frac{a}{b}\right) = \ln(a) - \ln(b).$$

For more details, see, for example, Chiang and Wainwright (2005) and Simon and Blume (1994).

In the equation for the Theil T index, if (income share)$_i$ is larger (smaller) than (pop. share)$_i$, then $\ln\left(\frac{(\text{income share})_i}{(\text{pop. share})_i}\right) = \ln\left((\text{income share})_i\right) - \ln\left((\text{pop.share})_i\right) > 0\ (< 0)$. In the equation for the Theil L index, if (income share)$_i$ is larger (smaller) than (pop. share)$_i$, then $\ln\left(\frac{(\text{pop. share})_i}{(\text{income share})_i}\right) = \ln\left((\text{pop.share})_i\right) -$

$\ln\left((\text{income share})_i\right) < 0\ (> 0)$. If (income share)$_i$ is the same as (population share)$_i$, then $\ln\left(\frac{(\text{income share})_i}{(\text{population share})_i}\right) = 0$ and $\ln\left(\frac{(\text{population share})_i}{(\text{income share})_i}\right) = 0$.

Appendix 3: Relationship Between E_2 and CV^2 (Eq. 2.10)

First, we have

$$CV^2 = \frac{1}{\mu^2}\left[\frac{1}{n}\sum\nolimits_{i=1}^{n}(y_i - \mu)^2\right] = \frac{1}{n}\sum\nolimits_{i=1}^{n}\left(\frac{y_i - \mu}{\mu}\right)^2 = \frac{1}{n}\sum\nolimits_{i=1}^{n}\left[\left(\frac{y_i}{\mu}\right) - 1\right]^2$$
$$= \frac{1}{n}\sum\nolimits_{i=1}^{n}\left[\left(\frac{y_i}{\mu}\right)^2 - 1\right].$$

On the other hand, when $\alpha = 2$, the generalized entropy class of measures is given by

$$E_2 = \frac{1}{2}\frac{1}{n}\sum\nolimits_{i=1}^{n}\left[\left(\frac{y_i}{\mu}\right)^2 - 1\right]$$

Therefore, the generalized entropy class of measures when $\alpha = 2$ is one-half of the squared coefficient of variation.

$$E_2 = \frac{1}{2}CV^2.$$

Appendix 4: Other Relative Inequality Measures

Consider an income distribution for n individuals, $\mathbf{y} = (y_1, y_2, \ldots, y_n)$, with the mean income given by μ.

1. The Range.

   The range is the ratio of the difference between the largest and the smallest of incomes to the mean income, that is,

$$D = \frac{\text{Max}(y_i) - \text{Min}(y_i)}{\mu} \tag{2.43}$$

   This index runs from 0 (perfect equality) to n (perfect inequality).

2. The Relative Mean Deviation.

   The relative mean deviation is the average of all the absolute differences between incomes and the mean income divided by the mean income, that is,

$$M = \frac{1}{n}\sum_{i=1}^{n}\frac{|y_i - \mu|}{\mu} \tag{2.44}$$

This index runs from 0 (perfect equality) to $\frac{2(n-1)}{n}$ (perfect inequality)

3. The Variance of Log Income.

   The variance of log income is given by:

$$V = \frac{1}{n}\sum_{i=1}^{n}(\ln(y_i) - \ln(\mu))^2. \tag{2.45}$$

   In the case of perfect equality, $V = 0$.

4. The Atkinson Class of Inequality Measures.

   The Atkinson class of inequality measures is given by:

$$A_\varepsilon = 1 - \left[\frac{1}{n}\sum_{i=1}^{n}\left(\frac{y_i}{\mu}\right)^{\varepsilon}\right]^{1/\varepsilon} \text{ for } \varepsilon < 1 \text{ and } \varepsilon \neq 0 \tag{2.46}$$

   and

$$A_0 = 1 - \prod_{i=1}^{n}\left(\frac{y_i}{\mu}\right)^{1/n}. \tag{2.47}$$

   The Atkinson class of inequality measures ranges between 0 (perfect equality) and 1 (perfect inequality).

   When $\varepsilon < 1$ and $\varepsilon \neq 0$, we have the following relationship between the Atkinson class of measures A_ε and the generalized entropy class of measures E_ε.

$$\begin{aligned}
A_\varepsilon &= 1 - \left[\frac{1}{n}\sum_{i=1}^{n}\left(\frac{y_i}{\mu}\right)^{\varepsilon}\right]^{1/\varepsilon} = 1 - \left[\frac{1}{n}\left[\sum_{i=1}^{n}\left(\frac{y_i}{\mu}\right)^{\varepsilon} - n\right] + 1\right]^{1/\varepsilon} \\
&= 1 - \left[\frac{1}{n}\sum_{i=1}^{n}\left[\left(\frac{y_i}{\mu}\right)^{\varepsilon} - 1\right] + 1\right]^{1/\varepsilon} \\
&= 1 - \left[\varepsilon(\varepsilon - 1)\frac{1}{\varepsilon(\varepsilon - 1)}\frac{1}{n}\sum_{i=1}^{n}\left[\left(\frac{y_i}{\mu}\right)^{\varepsilon} - 1\right] + 1\right]^{1/\varepsilon} \\
&= 1 - [\varepsilon(\varepsilon - 1)E_\varepsilon + 1]^{1/\varepsilon}
\end{aligned}$$

   where $E_\varepsilon = \frac{1}{\varepsilon(\varepsilon-1)}\frac{1}{n}\sum_{i=1}^{n}\left[\left(\frac{y_i}{\mu}\right)^{\varepsilon} - 1\right]$ is the generalized entropy class of measures with parameter ε. Since we have $\frac{\partial A_\varepsilon}{\partial E_\varepsilon} = (1 - \varepsilon)[\varepsilon(\varepsilon - 1)E_\varepsilon + 1]^{(1-\varepsilon)/\varepsilon} > 0$ for $\varepsilon < 1$ and $\varepsilon \neq 0$, the Atkinson class of measures is a monotonic transformation of the generalized entropy class of measures.

Next, we consider $A_0 = 1 - \prod_{i=1}^{n}\left(\frac{y_i}{\mu}\right)^{1/n}$. Since $1 - A_0 = \prod_{i=1}^{n}\left(\frac{y_i}{\mu}\right)^{1/n}$, taking the natural logarithm on both sides, we obtain

$$\ln(1 - A_0) = \frac{1}{n}\sum_{i=1}^{n} \ln\left(\frac{y_i}{\mu}\right) = -\frac{1}{n}\sum_{i=1}^{n} \ln\left(\frac{\mu}{y_i}\right) = -E_0 \text{ or } A_0$$
$$= 1 - \exp(-E_0).$$

Since we have $\frac{\partial A_0}{\partial E_0} = \exp(-E_0) > 0$, the Atkinson class of measures with $\varepsilon = 0$ is a monotonic transformation of the Theil L index.

From these relationships, we can conclude that the inequality ranking of income distributions by the Atkinson class of measures and the corresponding generalized entropy class of measures are equivalent.

Appendix 5: Inequality Decomposition by Population Subgroups

1. Theil T Index (Eq. 2.11)

$$T = \frac{1}{n}\sum_{i=1}^{m}\sum_{j=1}^{n_i} \frac{y_{ij}}{\mu} \ln\left(\frac{y_{ij}}{\mu}\right) = \sum_{i=1}^{m} \frac{n_i}{n}\frac{\mu_i}{\mu}\frac{1}{n_i}\sum_{j=1}^{n_i} \frac{y_{ij}}{\mu_i} \ln\left(\frac{y_{ij}}{\mu_i}\frac{\mu_i}{\mu}\right)$$
$$= \sum_{i=1}^{m} \frac{n_i}{n}\frac{\mu_i}{\mu}\frac{1}{n_i}\sum_{j=1}^{n_i} \frac{y_{ij}}{\mu_i}\left[\ln\left(\frac{y_{ij}}{\mu_i}\right) + \ln\left(\frac{\mu_i}{\mu}\right)\right]$$
$$= \sum_{i=1}^{m} \frac{n_i}{n}\frac{\mu_i}{\mu}\left[\frac{1}{n_i}\sum_{j=1}^{n_i} \frac{y_{ij}}{\mu_i} \ln\left(\frac{y_{ij}}{\mu_i}\right)\right] + \sum_{i=1}^{m} \frac{n_i}{n}\frac{\mu_i}{\mu} \ln\left(\frac{\mu_i}{\mu}\right)\left(\frac{1}{n_i}\sum_{j=1}^{n_i} \frac{y_{ij}}{\mu_i}\right)$$
$$= \sum_{i=1}^{m} \frac{n_i}{n}\frac{\mu_i}{\mu}T_i + \sum_{i=1}^{m} \frac{n_i}{n}\frac{\mu_i}{\mu} \ln\left(\frac{\mu_i}{\mu}\right) = T_W + T_B \text{ since } \frac{1}{n_i}\sum_{j=1}^{n_i} \frac{y_{ij}}{\mu_i} = \frac{\mu_i}{\mu_i}$$
$$= 1.$$

2. Theil L Index (Eq. 2.12)

$$L = \frac{1}{n}\sum_{i=1}^{m}\sum_{j=1}^{n_i} \ln\left(\frac{\mu}{y_{ij}}\right) = \sum_{i=1}^{m} \frac{n_i}{n}\frac{1}{n_i}\sum_{j=1}^{n_i} \ln\left(\frac{\mu_i}{y_{ij}}\frac{\mu}{\mu_i}\right)$$
$$= \sum_{i=1}^{m} \frac{n_i}{n}\frac{1}{n_i}\sum_{j=1}^{n_i}\left[\ln\left(\frac{\mu_i}{y_{ij}}\right) + \ln\left(\frac{\mu}{\mu_i}\right)\right]$$
$$= \sum_{i=1}^{m} \frac{n_i}{n}\left[\frac{1}{n_i}\sum_{j=1}^{n_i} \ln\left(\frac{\mu_i}{y_{ij}}\right)\right] + \sum_{i=1}^{m} \frac{n_i}{n} \ln\left(\frac{\mu}{\mu_i}\right)\left[\frac{1}{n_i}\sum_{j=1}^{n_i}(1)\right]$$
$$= \sum_{i=1}^{m} \frac{n_i}{n}L_i + \sum_{i=1}^{m} \frac{n_i}{n} \ln\left(\frac{\mu}{\mu_i}\right) = L_W + L_B \text{ since } \frac{1}{n_i}\sum_{j=1}^{n_i}(1) = 1.$$

Appendix 6: Decomposition by Population Subgroups: Generalized Entropy Class of Measures

The generalized entropy class of inequality measures is defined by:

$$E_\alpha(\boldsymbol{y}) = \frac{1}{\alpha(\alpha-1)}\frac{1}{n}\sum\nolimits_{i=1}^{m}\sum\nolimits_{j=1}^{n_i}\left[\left(\frac{y_{ij}}{\mu}\right)^\alpha - 1\right], \tag{2.48}$$

where $\boldsymbol{y} = (y_1, y_2, \cdots, y_n)$, $n = \sum_{i=1}^{m} n_i$, and $\mu = \sum_{i=1}^{m}\frac{n_i}{n}\mu_i$. Equation (2.48) can be decomposed into the within- and between-group components as follows.

$$\begin{aligned} E_\alpha(\boldsymbol{y}) &= \sum\nolimits_{i=1}^{m}\frac{n_i}{n}\left(\frac{\mu_i}{\mu}\right)^\alpha E_\alpha(\boldsymbol{y}_i) + \frac{1}{\alpha(\alpha-1)}\sum\nolimits_{i=1}^{m}\frac{n_i}{n}\left[\left(\frac{\mu_i}{\mu}\right)^\alpha - 1\right] \\ &= E_W + E_B \end{aligned} \tag{2.49}$$

In Eq. (2.49), $E_\alpha(\boldsymbol{y}_i) = \frac{1}{\alpha(\alpha-1)}\frac{1}{n_i}\sum_{j=1}^{n_i}\left[\left(\frac{y_{ij}}{\mu_i}\right)^\alpha - 1\right]$ is the within-group inequality of group i, where $\boldsymbol{y}_i = (y_{i1}, y_{i2}, \cdots, y_{in_i})$. In this equation, $E_W = \sum_{i=1}^{m}\frac{n_i}{n}\left(\frac{\mu_i}{\mu}\right)^\alpha E_\alpha(\boldsymbol{y}_i)$ is the within-group inequality component, which is the weighted sum of within-group inequalities, while $E_B = \frac{1}{\alpha(\alpha-1)}\sum_{i=1}^{m}\frac{n_i}{n}\left[\left(\frac{\mu_i}{\mu}\right)^\alpha - 1\right]$ is the between-group inequality component.

When $\alpha = 2$, we have

$$E_2(\boldsymbol{y}) = \sum\nolimits_{i=1}^{m}\frac{n_i}{n}\left(\frac{\mu_i}{\mu}\right)^2 E_2(\boldsymbol{y}_i) + \frac{1}{2}\sum\nolimits_{i=1}^{m}\frac{n_i}{n}\left[\left(\frac{\mu_i}{\mu}\right)^2 - 1\right] \tag{2.50}$$

Since $E_2(\boldsymbol{y}) = \frac{1}{2}CV(\boldsymbol{y})^2$ and $E_2(\boldsymbol{y}_i) = \frac{1}{2}CV(\boldsymbol{y}_i)^2$, this decomposition equation can be rewritten as

$$CV(\boldsymbol{y})^2 = \sum\nolimits_{i=1}^{m}\frac{n_i}{n}\left(\frac{\mu_i}{\mu}\right)^2 CV(\boldsymbol{y}_i)^2 + \sum\nolimits_{i=1}^{m}\frac{n_i}{n}\left(\frac{\mu_i-\mu}{\mu}\right)^2 = CV_W^2 + CV_B^2. \tag{2.51}$$

where $CV(\boldsymbol{y}_i)^2 = \frac{1}{n_i}\sum_{j=1}^{n_i}\left(\frac{y_{ij}-\mu_i}{\mu_i}\right)^2$ is the within-group inequality of group i. Equation (2.51) is the inequality decomposition equation for the squared coefficient of variation. $CV_W^2 = \sum_{i=1}^{m}\frac{n_i}{n}\left(\frac{\mu_i}{\mu}\right)^2 CV(\boldsymbol{y}_i)^2$ is the within-group inequality component and $CV_B^2 = \sum_{i=1}^{m}\frac{n_i}{n}\left(\frac{\mu_i-\mu}{\mu}\right)^2$ is the between-group inequality component.

Appendix 7: Inequality Decomposition by Income Sources

Consider the distribution of total incomes for n households, $\mathbf{y} = (y_1, y_2, \ldots, y_n)$. Suppose that total household income is composed of K income sources or components, then we have

$$y_i = \sum_{k=1}^{K} y_{ik} \text{ and } \mu = \sum_{k=1}^{K} \mu_k,$$

where y_{ik} and μ_k are, respectively, income from source k of household i and mean income from source k.

1. The Coefficient of Variation (Eq. 2.17).

   To obtain inequality decomposition equation by the coefficient of variation, we start with the variance of the distribution of total incomes, which is given by

$$\sigma^2 = \frac{1}{n} \sum_{i=1}^{n} (y_i - \mu)^2.$$

   Substituting $y_i = \sum_{k=1}^{K} y_{ik}$ and $\mu = \sum_{k=1}^{K} \mu_k$ into the equation above, we have

$$\sigma^2 = \frac{1}{n} \sum_{i=1}^{n} \left(\sum_{k=1}^{K} y_{ik} - \sum_{k=1}^{K} \mu_k \right) (y_i - \mu) = \frac{1}{n} \sum_{i=1}^{n} \sum_{k=1}^{K} (y_{ik} - \mu_k)(y_i - \mu)$$
$$= \sum_{k=1}^{K} \left[\frac{1}{n} \sum_{i=1}^{n} (y_{ki} - \mu_k)(y_i - \mu) \right] = \sum_{k=1}^{K} \text{cov}_k,$$

   where $\text{cov}_k = \frac{1}{n} \sum_{i=1}^{n} (y_{ki} - \mu_k)(y_i - \mu)$ is covariance between total income and income from source k. By substituting $\sigma^2 = \sum_{k=1}^{K} \text{cov}_k$ into $CV^2 = \frac{\sigma^2}{\mu^2}$, we obtain

$$CV^2 = \frac{\sigma^2}{\mu^2} = \sum_{k=1}^{K} \frac{\text{cov}_k}{\mu^2} = \sum_{k=1}^{K} \left(\frac{\mu_k}{\mu} \right) \frac{\text{cov}_k}{\mu_k \mu} = \sum_{k=1}^{K} w_k \frac{\text{cov}_k}{\mu_k \mu},$$

   where $w_k = \frac{\mu_k}{\mu}$ is the income share of source k.

   Since the coefficient of correlation between the distribution of incomes from source k and the distribution of total incomes is defined by $\rho_k = \frac{\text{cov}_k}{\sigma_k \sigma}$, we have

$$CV^2 = \sum_{k=1}^{K} w_k \rho_k \left(\frac{\sigma_k}{\mu_k} \right) \left(\frac{\sigma}{\mu} \right) = \sum_{k=1}^{K} w_k \rho_k (CV_k)(CV).$$

   By dividing both sides by CV, we obtain the following inequality decomposition equation for the coefficient of variation (Eq. 2.17).

$$CV = \sum_{k=1}^{K} w_k \rho_k CV_k \,. \tag{2.52}$$

2. The Gini Coefficient (Eq. 2.19).

The Gini coefficient is defined by $G = \frac{2}{n\mu}\text{cov}(y, i(y))$ (Eq. 2.4). Since $\text{cov}(y, i(y)) = \frac{1}{n}\sum_{i=1}^{n}(y_i - \mu)(i - \bar{i})$ by definition, we have

$$\begin{aligned} G &= \frac{2}{n\mu}\text{cov}(y, i(y)) = \frac{2}{n\mu}\left[\frac{1}{n}\sum_{i=1}^{n}(y_i - \mu)(i - \bar{i})\right] \\ &= \frac{2}{n\mu}\left[\frac{1}{n}\sum_{i=1}^{n}((y_{1i} + y_{2i} + \cdots + y_{Ki}) - (\mu_1 + \mu_2 + \cdots + \mu_K))(i - \bar{i})\right] \\ &= \frac{2}{n\mu}\left[\frac{1}{n}\sum_{i=1}^{n}(y_{1i} - \mu_1)(i - \bar{i}) + \cdots + \frac{1}{n}\sum_{i=1}^{n}(y_{Ki} - \mu_K)(i - \bar{i})\right] \\ &= \frac{2}{n\mu}[\text{cov}(y_1, i(y)) + \cdots + \text{cov}(y_K, i(y))] = \sum_{k=1}^{K}\left(\frac{\mu_k}{\mu}\right)\left[\frac{2}{n\mu_k}\text{cov}(y_k, i(y))\right] \\ &= \sum_{k=1}^{K} w_k C_k, \end{aligned}$$

where $y_k = (y_{1k}, y_{2k}, \cdots, y_{nk})$ and $C_k = \frac{2}{n\mu_k}\text{cov}(y_k, i(y))$ is called the concentration ratio. Let $R_k = \frac{C_k}{G_k} = \frac{\text{cov}(y_k, i(y))}{\text{cov}(y_k, i(y_k))}$ be the rank correlation ratio. Then, we obtain the following inequality decomposition equation for the Gini coefficient (Eq. 2.19).

$$G = \sum_{k=1}^{K} w_k R_k G_k. \tag{2.53}$$

Appendix 8: Kuznets Process of Urbanization (Eqs. 2.23 and 2.26)

By the Theil L index, the within-group inequality component is given by

$$L_W = p_R L_R + p_U L_U = (1 - p_U)L_R + p_U L_U.$$

On the other hand, since $\mu = \mu_R p_R + \mu_U p_U$ and $\delta = \frac{\mu_U}{\mu_R}$, the between-group inequality component is given by:

$$
\begin{aligned}
L_B &= p_R \ln\left(\frac{\mu}{\mu_R}\right) + p_U \ln\left(\frac{\mu}{\mu_U}\right) \\
&= p_R \ln\left(\frac{\mu_R p_R + \mu_U p_U}{\mu_R}\right) + p_U \ln\left(\frac{\mu_R p_R + \mu_U p_U}{\mu_U}\right) \\
&= (1-p_U)\ln\left((1-p_U)+\delta p_U\right) + p_U \ln\left(\frac{1-p_U}{\delta} + p_U\right) \\
&= (1-p_U)\ln\left((1-p_U)+\delta p_U\right) + p_U \ln\left((1-p_U)+\delta p_U\right) - p_U \ln(\delta) \\
&= \ln\left((1-p_U)+\delta p_U\right) - p_U \ln(\delta).
\end{aligned}
$$

By adding these two equations, we obtain the equation for the Kuznets process of urbanization by the Theil L index.

$$
\begin{aligned}
L &= L_w + L_B \\
&= [(1-p_U)L_R + p_U L_U] + [\ln\left((1-p_U)+\delta p_U\right) - p_U \ln(\delta)]
\end{aligned}
\tag{2.54}
$$

By differentiating Eq. (2.54) with respect to p_U, we have

$$
\frac{\partial L}{\partial p_U} = (L_U - L_R) + \frac{(\delta-1) - ((1-p_U)+\delta p_U)\ln(\delta)}{(1-p_U)+\delta p_U}.
$$

The peak value is obtained by setting this equation to 0 and solving for p_U. Let p_U^* denote the urban population share that achieves the peak Theil L value. Then, we have

$$
p_U^* = \frac{(L_U - L_R) + (\delta - 1) - \ln(\delta)}{(\delta-1)(\ln(\delta) - (L_U - L_R))}. \tag{2.55}
$$

By substituting the value of p_U^* into Eq. (2.54), we obtain the peak Theil L value. By the Theil T index, the within-group inequality component is given by:

$$
\begin{aligned}
T_W &= \frac{n_R}{n}\frac{\mu_R}{\mu} T_R + \frac{n_U}{n}\frac{\mu_U}{\mu} T_U = p_R \frac{\mu_R}{\mu_R p_R + \mu_U p_U} T_R + p_U \frac{\mu_U}{\mu_R p_R + \mu_U p_U} T_U \\
&= \left[\frac{1-p_U}{(1-p_U)+\delta p_U}\right] T_R + \left[\frac{\delta p_U}{(1-p_U)+\delta p_U}\right] T_U.
\end{aligned}
$$

since $\mu = \mu_R p_R + \mu_U p_U$ and $\delta = \frac{\mu_U}{\mu_R}$. On the other hand, the between-group inequality component is given by:

$$
\begin{aligned}
T_B &= \frac{n_R}{n}\frac{\mu_R}{\mu}\ln\left(\frac{\mu_R}{\mu}\right) + \frac{n_U}{n}\frac{\mu_U}{\mu}\ln\left(\frac{\mu_U}{\mu}\right) \\
&= p_R \frac{\mu_R}{\mu_R p_R + \mu_U p_U}\ln\left(\frac{\mu_R}{\mu_R p_R + \mu_U p_U}\right) \\
&\quad + p_U \frac{\mu_U}{\mu_R p_R + \mu_U p_U}\ln\left(\frac{\mu_U}{\mu_R p_R + \mu_U p_U}\right) \\
&= \frac{1-p_U}{(1-p_U)+\delta p_U}\ln\left(\frac{1}{(1-p_U)+\delta p_U}\right) \\
&\quad + \frac{\delta p_U}{(1-p_U)+\delta p_U}\ln\left(\frac{\delta}{(1-p_U)+\delta p_U}\right) \\
&= \frac{\delta \ln(\delta) p_U}{(1-p_U)+\delta p_U} - \ln\left((1-p_U)+\delta p_U\right).
\end{aligned}
$$

By adding these two equations, we obtain the following equation for the Kuznets process of urbanization by the Theil T index.

$$
\begin{aligned}
T = &\left[\left(\frac{1-p_U}{(1-p_U)+\delta p_U}\right)T_R + \left(\frac{\delta p_U}{(1-p_U)+\delta p_U}\right)T_U\right] \\
&+ \left[\frac{\delta \ln(\delta) p_U}{(1-p_U)+\delta p_U} - \ln\left((1-p_U)+\delta p_U\right)\right] \qquad (2.56)
\end{aligned}
$$

Appendix 9: Neoclassical Growth Model (Solow Growth Model)

To obtain Solow's neoclassical growth model in a closed economy, we first assume that the production function has the following Cobb-Douglas form.

$$
Y = AK^{\alpha}L^{1-\alpha}, \qquad (2.57)
$$

where Y, K, and L are, respectively, output, capital, and labor. In this equation, A is an exogenously given technology parameter, while α is a parameter ranging between 0 and 1. Next, we let I be gross investment and assume that capital stock depreciates at a constant proportion in each time period. Then, the capital accumulation equation is given by

$$
\dot{K} = I - \delta K,
$$

where δ is a constant depreciation rate. In this equation, $\dot{K}$ is the continuous time version of the change in capital stock, $\Delta K = K_{t+1} - K_t$. We use "dot" notation to denote a derivative with respect to time, that is, $\dot{K} = {}^{dK}\!/_{dt}$. The change in capital stock is the amount of gross investment less the amount of depreciation that occurs during the production process. In a closed economy, investment is financed wholly by a constant proportion of output, so that we have

$$I = sY,$$

where s is a constant savings ratio. Substituting this equation into the capital accumulation equation results in

$$\dot{K} = sY - \delta K.$$

By dividing this equation by K, we have

$$\frac{\dot{K}}{K} = s\frac{Y}{K} - \delta. \tag{2.58}$$

Next, dividing Eq. (2.57) by L, we have

$$\frac{Y}{L} = A\frac{K^{\alpha}L^{1-\alpha}}{L} = A\left(\frac{K}{L}\right)^{\alpha}$$

If we let $y = \frac{Y}{L}$ and $k = \frac{K}{L}$ be, respectively, output per labor and capital per labor, then the production function is rewritten as

$$y = Ak^{\alpha}. \tag{2.59}$$

That is, output per labor is a function of capital per labor. On the other hand, taking the natural logarithm of both sides of $k = \frac{K}{L}$ yields $\ln(k) = \ln(K) - \ln(L)$. If this is differentiated with respect to time, then we have $\frac{\dot{k}}{k} = \frac{\dot{K}}{K} - \frac{\dot{L}}{L}$. If we assume that labor changes at a constant rate, n, then we have $\frac{\dot{k}}{k} = \frac{\dot{K}}{K} - n$. By substituting Eq. (2.58) into this equation, we obtain

$$\frac{\dot{k}}{k} = s\frac{y}{k} - (\delta + n), \tag{2.60}$$

since $\frac{Y}{K} = \frac{Y/L}{K/L} = \frac{y}{k}$. This now yields the capital accumulation equation in per labor terms as follows.

$$\dot{k} = sy - (\delta + n)k, \tag{2.61}$$

where $y = Ak^{\alpha}$. Equations (2.60) or (2.61) is the basic Solow growth model. It should be noted that since $y = Ak^{\alpha}$, we have $\frac{\dot{y}}{y} = \alpha\frac{\dot{k}}{k}$.

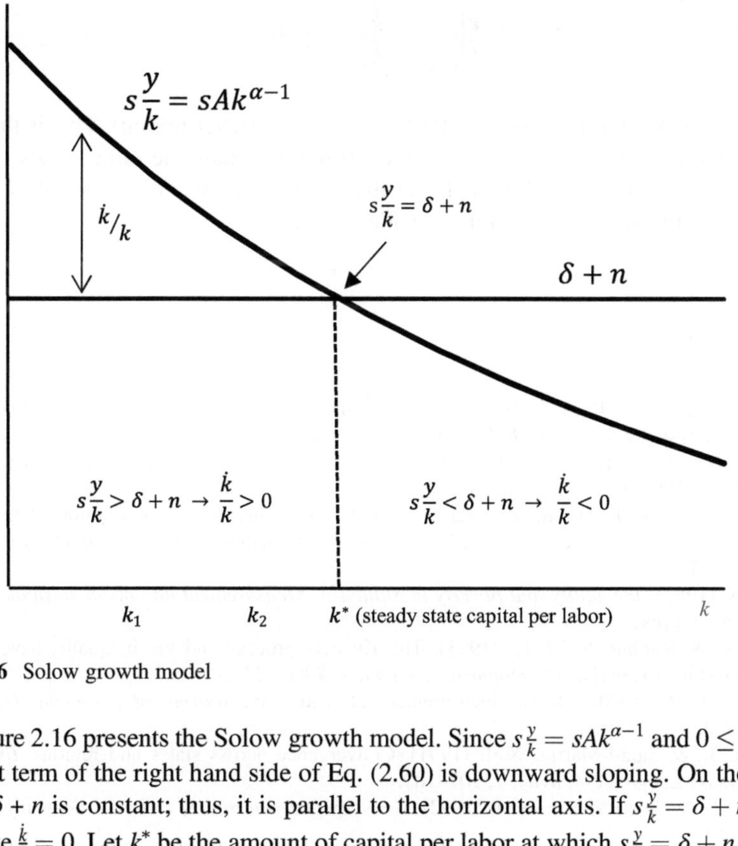

Fig. 2.16 Solow growth model

Figure 2.16 presents the Solow growth model. Since $s\frac{y}{k} = sAk^{\alpha-1}$ and $0 \leq \alpha \leq 1$, the first term of the right hand side of Eq. (2.60) is downward sloping. On the other hand, $\delta + n$ is constant; thus, it is parallel to the horizontal axis. If $s\frac{y}{k} = \delta + n$, then we have $\frac{\dot{k}}{k} = 0$. Let k^* be the amount of capital per labor at which $s\frac{y}{k} = \delta + n$. Then, we have, using $y = Ak^{\alpha}$,

$$k^* = \left(\frac{\delta + n}{sA}\right)^{1/\alpha-1} \tag{2.62}$$

At this point, capital per labor remains constant, and we call such a point a *steady state*. If $s\frac{y}{k} > \delta + n$, then $\frac{\dot{k}}{k} > 0$, that is, capital per labor increases, and thus output per labor increases since we have $\frac{\dot{y}}{y} = \alpha\frac{\dot{k}}{k}$. On the other hand, if $s\frac{y}{k} < \delta + n$, then $\frac{\dot{k}}{k} < 0$, that is, capital per labor decreases, and thus output per labor decreases.

Consider a country consisting of two regions (regions 1 and 2), which are assumed to follow the Solow growth model shown in Fig. 2.16. If region 1's capital per labor is k_1, then capital per labor increases at a growth rate of $\left.\frac{\dot{k}}{k}\right|_{k=k_1} > 0$. On the other hand, if region 2's capital per labor is $k_2 > k_1$, then capital per labor increases at a growth rate of $\left.\frac{\dot{k}}{k}\right|_{k=k_2} > 0$. Since we have

$$\left.\frac{\dot{k}}{k}\right|_{k=k_1} > \left.\frac{\dot{k}}{k}\right|_{k=k_2} > 0,$$

region 1 (poorer region) grows faster than region 2 (richer region). This is the basic idea behind the concept of β-convergence. If regions share the same steady state k^*, then poorer regions should grow faster than richer regions. Therefore, they should converge to the steady state in the absolute sense.

References

Akita, T., & Lukman, R. A. (1995). Interregional inequalities in Indonesia: A sectoral decomposition analysis for 1975-92. *Bulletin of Indonesian Economic Studies, 31*, 61–81.

Akita, T., & Lukman, R. A. (1999). Spatial patterns of expenditure inequalities in Indonesia: 1987, 1990, and 1993. *Bulletin of Indonesian Economic Studies, 35*, 65–88.

Akita, T., Lukman, R. A., & Yamada, Y. (1999). Inequality in the distribution of household expenditures in Indonesia: A Theil decomposition analysis. *The Developing Economies, 37*(2), 197–221.

Anand, S. (1983). *Inequality and poverty in Malaysia: Measurement and decomposition*. Oxford University Press.

Anand, S., & Kanbur, S. M. R. (1993). The Kuznets process and the inequality-development relationship. *Journal of Development Economics, 40*(1), 25–52.

Atkinson, A. B. (1970). On the measurement of inequality. *Journal of Economic Theory, 2*, 244–263.

Barro, R. J., & Sala-i-Martin, X. I. (1991). Convergence across states and regions. *Brookings Papers on Economic Activity, 1*, 107–182.

Barro, R. J., & Sala-i-Martin, X. I. (1992). Convergence. *Journal of Political Economy, 100*(2), 223–251.

Barro, R. J., & Sala-i-Martin, X. I. (2004). *Economic growth* (2nd ed.). McGraw Hill.

Bourguignon, F. (1979). Decomposable income inequality measures. *Econometrica, 47*(4), 901–920.

Chen, J., & Fleisher, B. M. (1996). Regional income inequality and economic growth in China. *Journal of Comparative Economic, 22*(2), 141–164.

Chiang, A. C., & Wainwright, K. (2005). *Fundamental methods of mathematical economics* (4th ed.). McGraw-Hill/Irwin.

Chongvilaivan, A., & Kim, J. (2016). Individual income inequality and its drivers in Indonesia: A Theil decomposition reassessment. *Social Indicators Research, 126*, 79–98.

Daniels, L., & Minot, N. W. (2019). *An introduction to statistics and data analysis using stata: From research design to final report*. Sage Publications Inc.

Eastwood, R., & Lipton, M. (2004). Rural and urban income inequality and poverty: Does convergence between sectors offset divergence within them? In G. A. Cornia (Ed.), *Inequality, growth, and poverty in an era of liberalization and globalization* (pp. 112–141). Oxford University Press.

Estudillo, J. (1997). Income inequality in the Philippines, 1961–91. *The Developing Economies, 35*(1), 68–95.

Ezcurra, R., & Rapún, M. (2006). Regional disparities and national development revisited: The case of Western Europe. *European Urban and Regional Studies, 13*(4), 355–369.

Fei, J. C. H., Ranis, G., & Kuo, S. W. Y. (1978). Growth and the family distribution of income by factor components. *Quarterly Journal of Economics, 92*(1), 17–53.

Fields, G. S. (2001). *Distribution and development*. MIT Press.

Glewwe, P. (1986). The distribution of income in Sri Lanka in 1969–70 and 1980–81: A decomposition analysis. *Journal of Development Economics, 24*(2), 255–274.

Gluschenko, K. (2018). Measuring regional inequality: To weight or not to weight? *Spatial Economic Analysis, 13*(1), 36–59.

Hamilton, L. C. (2012). *Statistics with Stata: Version 12*. Duxbury Press.

Hill, H., Resosudarmo, B. P., & Vidyattama, Y. (2008). Indonesia's changing economic geography. *Bulletin of Indonesian Economic Studies, 44*, 407–435.

Hill, H., & Vidyattama, Y. (2016). Regional development dynamics In Indonesia before and after the 'Big Bang' decentralization. *The Singapore Economic Review, 61*(2), 1–26.

Kanbur, R., & Venables, A. J. (2005). Spatial inequality and development. In R. Kanbur & A. J. Venables (Eds.), *Spatial inequality and development* (pp. 3–11). Oxford University Press.

Kanbur, R., & Zhang, X. (1999). Which regional inequality? The evolution of rural–urban and inland–coastal inequality in China from 1983 to 1995. *Journal of Comparative Economics, 27*(4), 686–701.

Kuznets, S. S. (1955). Economic growth and income inequality. *American Economic Review, 45*(1), 1–28.

Lambert, P. J., & Aronson, J. R. (1993). Inequality decomposition analysis and the Gini coefficient revisited. *The Economic Journal, 103*(420), 1221–1227.

Lessmann, C. (2014). Spatial inequality and development—is there an inverted-U relationship? *Journal of Development Economics, 106*, 35–51.

Liu, A. Y. C. (2001). Markets, inequality and poverty in Vietnam. *Asian Economic Journal, 15*(2), 217–235.

Lorenz, M. O. (1905). Methods of measuring the concentration of wealth. *Publications of the American Statistical Association*, 9 (70), 209-219.

Lyons, T. P. (1991). Interprovincial disparities in China: Output and consumption, 1952-1987. *Economic Development and Cultural Change, 39*(3), 471–506.

Mathur, A. (1983). Regional development and income disparities in India: A sectoral Analysis. *Economic Development and Cultural Change, 31*(3), 475–505.

Milanovic, B. (2005). Half a world: regional inequality in five great federations. *Journal of the Asia and Pacific Economy, 10*(4), 408–445.

Mishra, P., & Parikh, A. (1992). Household consumer expenditure inequalities in India: A decomposition analysis. *Review of Income and Wealth, 38*(2), 225–236.

Motonishi, T. (2006). Why has income inequality in Thailand increased?: An analysis using surveys from 1975 to 1998. *Japan and the World Economy, 18*(4), 464–487.

Portnov, B. A., & Felsenstein, D. (2010). On the suitability of income inequality measures for regional analysis: Some evidence from simulation analysis and bootstrapping tests. *Socio-Economic Planning Sciences, 44*(4), 212–219.

Pyatt, G., Chen, C. N., & Fei, J. (1980). The distribution of income by factor components. *Quarterly Journal of Economics, 95*(3), 451–474.

Ray, D. (1998). *Development economics*. Princeton Press.

Rodríguez-Pose, A., & Ezcurra, R. (2010). Does decentralization matter for regional disparities? A cross-country analysis. *Journal of Economic Geography, 10*(5), 619–644.

Sen, A. (1997). *On economic inequality*. Oxford University Press.

Shankar, R., & Shah, A. (2003). Bridging the economic divide within countries: A scorecard on the performance of regional policies in reducing regional income disparities. *World Development, 31*(8), 1421–1441.

Shorrocks, A. (1980). The class of additively decomposable inequality measures. *Econometrica, 48*(3), 613–625.

Shorrocks, A. (1982). Inequality decomposition by factor components. *Econometrica, 50*(1), 193–211.

Shorrocks, A., & Wan, G. (2005). Spatial decomposition of inequality. *Journal of Economic Geography, 5*(1), 59–81.

Simon, C. P., & Blume, L. (1994). *Mathematics for economists*. Norton & Company.

Solow, R. M. (1956). A contribution to the theory of economic growth. *The Quarterly Journal of Economics, 70*(1), 65–94.

Tadjoeddin, M. Z., Suharyo, W. I., & Mishra, S. (2001). Regional disparity and vertical conflict in Indonesia. *Journal of the Asia Pacific Economy, 6*(3), 283–304.

Theil, H. (1967). *Economics and information theory*. North Holland.

Tsakloglou, P. (1993). Aspects of inequality in Greece: Measurement, decomposition and intertemporal change, 1974, 1982. *Journal of Development Economics, 40*(1), 53–74.

Tsui, K. Y. (1991). China's regional inequality, 1952–1985. *Journal of Comparative Economics, 15*(1), 1–21.

Tsui, K. Y. (1996). Economic reform and interprovincial inequalities in China. *Journal of Development Economics, 50*(2), 353–368.

Williamson, J. G. (1965). Regional inequality and the process of national development: A description of the patterns. *Economic Development and Cultural Change, 13*, 3–45.

World Bank. (2020). *World development indicators*. World Bank.

Yusuf, A. A., Sumner, A., & Rum, I. A. (2014). Twenty years of expenditure inequality in Indonesia, 1993-2013. *Bulletin of Indonesian Economic Studies, 50*(2), 243–254.

Zaman, K. A., & Akita, T. (2012). Spatial dimensions of income inequality and poverty in Bangladesh: An analysis of the 2005 and 2010 Household Income and Expenditure Survey Data. *Bangladesh Development Studies, 35*(3), 19–51.

Chapter 3
Analysis of Regional Inequality

Abstract This chapter introduces some analytical methods for regional income inequality. It first presents a bidimensional inequality decomposition method. Using the squared coefficient of variation (squared *CV*), income inequality can be decomposed not only by population subgroups but also by factor components. Using data on GDP by industrial sectors, the method combines these properties to explore the determinants of inter-provincial income inequality. Using data on GDP by industrial sectors, the squared *CV* can also be decomposed into variation and covariation components. This chapter also discusses this sectoral inequality decomposition method where one can analyze the roles of spatial covariations between industrial sectors in inter-provincial income inequality. Next, the chapter presents a two-stage nested hierarchical Theil decomposition method. Like the squared *CV*, the Theil indices can be decomposed by population subgroups. Using this decomposition property in the three-level hierarchical structure of a country (region-province-district), the method decomposes overall income inequality into three components: the between-region, between-province, and within-province components to explore the determinants of income inequality across districts. Finally, this chapter introduces a factor decomposition method. This method considers labor in addition to GDP and population and expresses GDP per capita as the product of labor productivity and labor participation rate. After linearizing this product, it additively decomposes regional income inequality into three components: inequality in labor productivity, inequality in labor participation rate, and residual component. The first two components are regional inequalities measured by the Theil index and take nonnegative values, while the residual component represents the interaction between labor productivity and labor participation rate, which can take negative values.

Keywords Bidimensional inequality decomposition method · Sectoral inequality decomposition method · Two-stage nested hierarchical Theil decomposition method · Factor decomposition method

---

This chapter is written jointly by Takahiro Akita and Mitsuhiko Kataoka.

T. Akita, M. Kataoka, *Regional Inequality and Development*, New Frontiers in Regional Science: Asian Perspectives 63,
https://doi.org/10.1007/978-981-19-2968-7_3

1 Introduction

This chapter introduces some analytical methods that could be used to investigate the determinants of regional income inequality. The next section presents a bidimensional inequality decomposition method developed by Akita and Miyata (2010). To implement the method, provincial data on population and GDP by industrial sectors are required and all the provinces need to be grouped into mutually exclusive and collectively exhaustive regions. Using the squared coefficient of variation, the method first decomposes overall inequality in GDP per capita across provinces into the within-region and between-region inequality components. Next, it decomposes inter-provincial inequality within each region and inequality between regions by GDP components. Lastly, the method calculates the contribution of each component to overall inter-provincial inequality in a unified framework.

Using provincial data on population and GDP by industrial sectors, the squared coefficient of variation can also be decomposed into variation and covariation components. Section 3.3 introduces this sectoral inequality decomposition method. Unlike the bidimensional inequality decomposition method, covariation components appear in this decomposition method; thus, one can analyze the roles of spatial covariations between industrial sectors in overall inter-provincial inequality in per capita GDP.

Section 3.4 presents a two-stage nested hierarchical Theil decomposition method developed by Akita (2003). Like the squared coefficient of variation, the Theil indices belong to the generalized entropy class of inequality measures and thus can be decomposed into the within-group and between-group inequality components. Using this decomposition property in the three-level hierarchical structure of a country (region-province-district), the method decomposes overall income inequality into three components: the between-region, between-province, and within-province inequality components. The method uses a district as the underlying regional unit to measure income inequality rather than a province and thus can examine the contributions of within-province inequalities as well as between-province and between-region inequalities to overall income inequality in a coherent framework.

The final section of this chapter presents a factor decomposition method for regional income inequality developed by Cheng and Li (2006). Unlike the inequality decomposition methods in the previous sections, Cheng and Li's method considers labor in addition to GDP and population and expresses GDP per capita as the product of labor productivity and labor participation rate. After linearizing this product using the natural logarithm, it additively decomposes regional inequality in per capita GDP into three components: regional inequality in labor productivity, regional inequality in labor participation rate, and residual component. The first two components in the decomposition equation are regional inequalities measured by the Theil index and take nonnegative values. On the other hand, the residual component represents the interaction between labor productivity and labor participation rate, which can be positive, negative, or zero if the two element variables are positively, negatively, or not correlated, respectively.

2 Bidimensional Inequality Decomposition Analysis

As discussed in Chap. 2, the squared coefficient of variation belongs to the generalized entropy class of inequality measures and satisfies four principles as a measure of inequality, that is, anonymity, income homogeneity, population homogeneity, and the Pigou-Dalton principle of transfers. Furthermore, the squared coefficient of variation can be decomposed into the within-group and between-group inequality components (method 1: decomposition by population subgroups). It can also be expressed as the sum of the contributions associated with different income components (method 2: decomposition by income components).

To analyze the determinants of inter-provincial income inequality for a country, Akita and Miyata (2010) developed the bidimensional inequality decomposition method by combining the two decomposition methods discussed above.[1] The method requires provincial data on population and GDP by industrial sectors (see Table 3.1). By classifying all the provinces into mutually exclusive and collectively exhaustive regions, the method first decomposes overall inter-provincial inequality in GDP per capita into the within-region and between-region inequality components. Next, it decomposes inter-provincial inequality within each region by GDP components. It also decomposes the between-region inequality by GDP components. Lastly, the method calculates the contribution of each component to overall inter-provincial inequality in a unified framework.

The result of this bidimensional inequality decomposition analysis for a hypothetical example can be presented in a matrix format as shown in Table 3.2, where there are three regions and three industrial sectors (e.g., agriculture, industry, and services). Values in the table are % contributions to overall inter-provincial inequality in GDP per capita. For example, values in the row corresponding to "Inequality within region 1" are the % contributions of inter-provincial inequalities for three industrial sectors in region 1. In total, region 1 contributes 20% to overall inter-provincial inequality. The total contribution of the within-region inequality component is 80%, which is the sum of the contributions of regions 1, 2, and 3 (20% + 30% + 30%). On the other hand, the contribution of the between-region inequality component is 20%. Sector 2 (industry) is the main contributor by accounting for 50% of overall inter-provincial inequality (40% due to inter-provincial inequality within three regions and 10% due to disparity between three regions).

[1]There are some studies that employed the bidimensional inequality decomposition method. They include Akita et al. (2011) and Alisjahbana and Akita (2020).

Table 3.1 Provincial data on population and GDP by industrial sector

	Population	GDP			
		Sector 1	Sector 2	…	Sector K
Province 1	POP_1	GDP_{11}	GDP_{12}	…	GDP_{1K}
Province 2	POP_2	GDP_{21}	GDP_{22}	…	GDP_{2K}
⋮					
Province p	POP_p	GDP_{p1}	GDP_{p2}	…	GDP_{pK}

Note: p is the number of provinces, while K is the number of industrial sectors

Table 3.2 Result of bidimensional inequality decomposition analysis: A hypothetical example (% contribution to overall inter-provincial inequality in GDP per capita)

	Sector 1 Agriculture	Sector 2 Industry	Sector 3 Services	Total
Inequality within region 1	5	5	10	20
Inequality within region 2	5	15	10	30
Inequality within region 3	5	20	5	30
Within-region inequality	15	40	25	80
Between-region inequality	5	10	5	20
Total inequality	20	50	30	100

If we obtain the decomposition result for 2 years, say, 2010 and 2020, then we could investigate the effects of the changes in industrial and spatial structures on inter-provincial income inequality for the period from 2010–2020. It should be noted that Akita and Miyata (2010) used the population-weighted coefficient of variation rather than the coefficient of variation to develop the bidimensional inequality decomposition method. But, we first develop the method using the coefficient of variation.

2.1 *Decomposition of the Squared Coefficient of Variation by Regions*

To illustrate the method, consider a country consisting of 10 provinces, which are divided into 2 regions. Regions 1 and 2 consist of 6 and 4 provinces, respectively. Table 3.3 presents GDP and population data for these provinces, while Fig. 3.1 exhibits GDP per capita. Let y_{ij}, p_i, p, and μ be, respectively, GDP per capita of province j in region i, the number of provinces in region i, the total number of provinces in the country, and the simple average of GDP per capita for all provinces, where $p = \sum_{i=1}^{2} p_i$ and $\mu = \frac{1}{p}\sum_{i=1}^{2}\sum_{j=1}^{p_i} y_{ij}$.[2] Then, by the squared coefficient of

[2]The double summation in the definition of the simple average of GDP per capita for all provinces is given by:

Table 3.3 GDP and population for 10 provinces

		GDP		Population		GDP per capita	
	Province	Variable	Value	Variable	Value	Variable	Value
Region 1	1	Y_{11}	300	N_{11}	20	y_{11}	15.0
	2	Y_{12}	200	N_{12}	10	y_{12}	20.0
	3	Y_{13}	300	N_{13}	15	y_{13}	20.0
	4	Y_{14}	100	N_{14}	20	y_{14}	5.0
	5	Y_{15}	500	N_{15}	20	y_{15}	25.0
	6	Y_{16}	300	N_{16}	15	y_{16}	20.0
Subtotal or simple average		Y_1	1700	N_1	100	μ_1	17.5
Region 2	1	Y_{21}	400	N_{21}	10	y_{21}	40.0
	2	Y_{22}	600	N_{22}	30	y_{22}	20.0
	3	Y_{23}	5000	N_{23}	50	y_{23}	100.0
	4	Y_{24}	300	N_{24}	10	y_{24}	30.0
Subtotal or simple average		Y_2	6300	N_2	100	μ_2	47.5
Total or simple average		Y	8000	N	200	μ	29.5

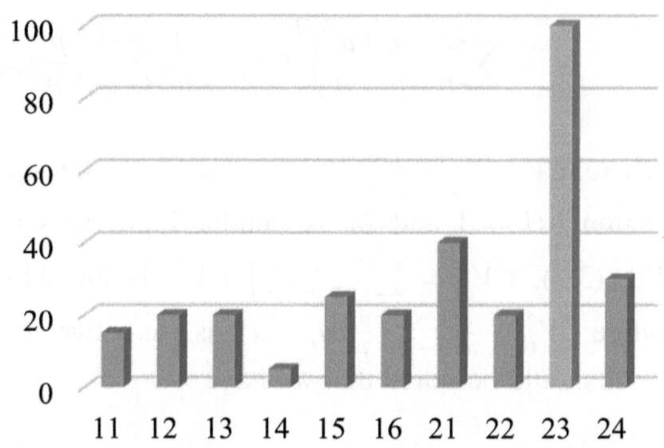

Fig. 3.1 GDP per capita for 10 provinces

variation, overall inter-provincial inequality in GDP per capita is calculated as follows ($m = 2$ regions):

$\sum_{i=1}^{2}\sum_{j=1}^{p_i} y_{ij} = (y_{11} + y_{12} + y_{13} + y_{14} + y_{15} + y_{16}) + (y_{21} + y_{22} + y_{23} + y_{24})$ since $p_1 = 6$ and $p_2 = 4$.

$$\begin{aligned} CV^2 &= \frac{1}{\mu^2}\frac{1}{p}\sum_{i=1}^{m}\sum_{j=1}^{p_i}\left(y_{ij}-\mu\right)^2 \\ &= \frac{1}{(29.5)^2}\frac{1}{10}\Big[(15-29.5)^2+(20-29.5)^2+(20-29.5)^2+(5-29.5)^2 \\ &\quad +(25-29.5)^2+(20-29.5)^2+(40-29.5)^2+(20-29.5)^2+(100 \\ &\quad -29.5)^2+(30-29.5)^2\Big] \\ &= \frac{1}{(29.5)^2}\frac{1}{10}(6,273) = 0.7208 \end{aligned} \tag{3.1}$$

As mentioned above, the squared coefficient of variation can be decomposed into the within-region and between-region inequality components. Let μ_i be the simple average of GDP per capita for provinces in region i, where $\mu_i = \frac{1}{p_i}\sum_{j=1}^{p_i} y_{ij}$. Then, the decomposition equation is given by

$$\begin{aligned} CV^2 &= \frac{1}{\mu^2}\frac{1}{p}\sum_{i=1}^{2}\sum_{j=1}^{p_i}\left(y_{ij}-\mu\right)^2 \\ &= \sum_{i=1}^{2}\frac{p_i}{p}\left(\frac{\mu_i}{\mu}\right)^2 CV_i^2 + \frac{1}{\mu^2}\sum_{i=1}^{2}\frac{p_i}{p}(\mu_i-\mu)^2 = CV_W^2 + CV_B^2, \end{aligned} \tag{3.2}$$

where $CV_i^2 = \frac{1}{(\mu_i)^2}\frac{1}{p_i}\sum_{j=1}^{p_i}\left(y_{ij}-\mu_i\right)^2$ is the squared coefficient of variation for region i ($i = 1$ and 2). Appendix 1 provides the derivation of this equation. In Eq. (3.2), $CV_W^2 = \sum_{i=1}^{2}\frac{p_i}{p}\left(\frac{\mu_i}{\mu}\right)^2 CV_i^2$ is the within-region inequality component, while $CV_B^2 = \frac{1}{\mu^2}\sum_{i=1}^{2}\frac{p_i}{p}(\mu_i-\mu)^2$ is the between-region inequality component.

It should be noted that we have

$$\begin{aligned} \mu &= \frac{1}{p}\sum_{i=1}^{2}\sum_{j=1}^{p_i} y_{ij} = \frac{p_1}{p}\left(\frac{1}{p_1}\sum_{j=1}^{p_1} y_{1j}\right) + \frac{p_2}{p}\left(\frac{1}{p_2}\sum_{j=1}^{p_2} y_{2j}\right) \\ &= \frac{p_1}{p}\mu_1 + \frac{p_2}{p}\mu_2, \end{aligned} \tag{3.3}$$

since $\mu_i = \frac{1}{p_i}\sum_{j=1}^{p_i} y_{ij}$. Using data in Table 3.3, we have the following relationship between μ and μ_i ($i = 1$ and 2).

$$\mu = \frac{p_1}{p}\mu_1 + \frac{p_2}{p}\mu_2 \Rightarrow 29.5 = \frac{6}{10}(17.5) + \frac{4}{10}(47.5).$$

Next, to obtain the within-region inequality component, CV_1^2 and CV_2^2 need to be calculated. For region 1, we have

$$\begin{aligned} CV_1^2 &= \frac{1}{(\mu_1)^2}\frac{1}{p_1}\sum\nolimits_{j=1}^{p_1}(y_{1j}-\mu_1)^2 \\ &= \frac{1}{(17.5)^2}\frac{1}{6}\left[(15-17.5)^2+(20-17.5)^2+(20-17.5)^2+(5-17.5)^2\right. \\ &\quad \left.+(25-17.5)^2+(20-17.5)^2\right] \\ &= \frac{1}{(17.5)^2}\frac{1}{6}(238) = 0.1293. \end{aligned} \tag{3.4}$$

For region 2, we have

$$\begin{aligned} CV_2^2 &= \frac{1}{(\mu_2)^2}\frac{1}{p_2}\sum\nolimits_{j=1}^{p_2}(y_{2j}-\mu_2)^2 \\ &= \frac{1}{(47.5)^2}\frac{1}{4} \\ &\quad \times\left[(40-47.5)^2+(20-47.5)^2+(100-47.5)^2+(30-47.5)^2\right] \\ &= \frac{1}{(47.5)^2}\frac{1}{4}(3,875) = 0.4294. \end{aligned} \tag{3.5}$$

Now, the within-region inequality component is calculated as follows.

$$\begin{aligned} CV_W^2 &= \sum\nolimits_{i=1}^{2}\frac{p_i}{p}\left(\frac{\mu_i}{\mu}\right)^2 CV_i^2 = \frac{6}{10}\left(\frac{17.5}{29.5}\right)^2(0.1293)+\frac{4}{10}\left(\frac{47.5}{29.5}\right)^2(0.4294) \\ &= 0.4726. \end{aligned}$$

On the other hand, inequality in GDP per capita between regions 1 and 2 (between-region inequality component) is given by

$$\begin{aligned} CV_B^2 &= \frac{1}{\mu^2}\sum\nolimits_{i=1}^{2}\frac{p_i}{p}(\mu_i-\mu)^2 \\ &= \frac{1}{(29.5)^2}\left[\frac{6}{10}(17.5-29.5)^2+\frac{4}{10}(47.5-29.5)^2\right] = \frac{1}{(29.5)^2}(216) \\ &= 0.2482. \end{aligned} \tag{3.6}$$

Sum of the within-region and between-region inequality components should be equal to overall inter-provincial inequality in GDP per capita, that is,

$$CV_W^2 + CV_B^2 = CV^2 \Rightarrow 0.4726 + 0.2482 = 0.7208.$$

By dividing both sides of this equation by overall inter-provincial inequality, we can obtain the contributions of the within-region and between-region inequality components to overall inter-provincial inequality. The contribution of the within-region component is $\frac{0.4726}{0.7208} \times 100 = 65.6\%$, while the contribution of the between-region component is $\frac{0.2482}{0.7208} \times 100 = 34.4\%$. This indicates that if there is no disparity in GDP per capita between regions 1 and 2, then overall inter-provincial inequality would be lowered by 34.4% by the squared coefficient of variation.

2.2 *Decomposition of the Squared Coefficient of Variation by GDP Components*

Suppose that total GDP consists of two components: GDP from agriculture (sector 1) and GDP from industry and services (sector 2). Then, GDP per capita of province *j* in region *i* can be written as:

$$y_{ij} = y_{ij1} + y_{ij2}, \tag{3.7}$$

where y_{ij1} and y_{ij2} are GDP per capita of province *j* in region *i* for sectors 1 and 2, respectively. Let μ_{i1} and μ_{i2} be, respectively, the simple averages of GDP per capita for sectors 1 and 2 in region *i*. Then, the following relationship can be obtained since $\mu_i = \frac{1}{p_i}\sum_{j=1}^{p_i} y_{ij} = \frac{1}{p_i}\sum_{j=1}^{p_i} y_{ij1} + \frac{1}{p_i}\sum_{j=1}^{p_i} y_{ij2}$.

$$\mu_i = \mu_{i1} + \mu_{i2}\ (i = 1, 2). \tag{3.8}$$

Using data in Table 3.4, we have for industrial sectors 1 and 2

$$\mu_{11} = \frac{1}{p_1}\sum_{j=1}^{p_1} y_{1j1} = \frac{1}{6}(10 + 10 + 5 + 2.5 + 2.5 + 10) = 6.7,$$

$$\mu_{21} = \frac{1}{p_2}\sum_{j=1}^{p_2} y_{2j1} = \frac{1}{4}(5 + 5 + 10 + 10) = 7.5,$$

$$\mu_{12} = \frac{1}{p_1}\sum_{j=1}^{p_1} y_{1j2} = \frac{1}{6}(5 + 10 + 15 + 2.5 + 22.5 + 10) = 10.8,$$

$$\mu_{22} = \frac{1}{p_2}\sum_{j=1}^{p_2} y_{2j2} = \frac{1}{4}(35 + 15 + 90 + 20) = 40.0.$$

From these results, we can see the following relationship (Eq. 3.8).

Table 3.4 GDP by industrial sectors for 10 provinces

		GDP				GDP per capita		
	Province	Total	Sector 1	Sector 2	Population	Total	Sector 1	Sector 2
Region 1	1	300	200	100	20	15.0	10.0	5.0
	2	200	100	100	10	20.0	10.0	10.0
	3	300	75	225	15	20.0	5.0	15.0
	4	100	50	50	20	5.0	2.5	2.5
	5	500	50	450	20	25.0	2.5	22.5
	6	300	150	150	15	20.0	10.0	10.0
Subtotal or simple average		1700	625	1075	100	μ_1=17.5	$\mu_{11}=6.7$	$\mu_{12}=10.8$
Region 2	7	400	50	350	10	40.0	5.0	35.0
	8	600	150	450	30	20.0	5.0	15.0
	9	5000	500	4500	50	100.0	10.0	90.0
	10	300	100	200	10	30.0	10.0	20.0
Subtotal or simple average		6300	800	5500	100	μ_2=47.5	μ_{21}=7.5	$\mu_{22}=40.0$
Total or simple average		8000	1425	6575	200	μ=29.5	$\mu_{\cdot 1}$=7.0	$\mu_{\cdot 2}=22.5$

$$\mu_1 = \mu_{11} + \mu_{12} \Rightarrow 17.5 = 6.7 + 10.8,$$
$$\mu_2 = \mu_{21} + \mu_{22} \Rightarrow 47.5 = 7.5 + 40.0.$$

Now, the squared coefficient of variation for region i can be decomposed by GDP components (GDP for industrial sectors) as follows.

$$CV_i^2 = \frac{1}{(\mu_i)^2}\frac{1}{P_i}\sum\nolimits_{j=1}^{P_i}(y_{ij} - \mu_i)^2 = v_{i1}\left(\frac{\text{cov}_{i1}}{\mu_{i1}\mu_i}\right) + v_{i2}\left(\frac{\text{cov}_{i2}}{\mu_{i2}\mu_i}\right). \tag{3.9}$$

In Eq. (3.9), $v_{ik} = \frac{\mu_{ik}}{\mu_i}$ is the share of industrial sector k in region i in terms of GDP per capita, while $\text{cov}_{ik} = \frac{1}{P_i}\sum\nolimits_{j=1}^{P_i}(y_{ijk} - \mu_{ik})(y_{ij} - \mu_i)$ is the covariance between GDP component k and total GDP in region i. Appendix 2 provides the derivation of Eq. (3.9).

Using data in Table 3.4, the squared coefficient of variation for regions 1 and 2 can be decomposed by GDP components as follows.

For region 1,

$$CV_1^2 = v_{11}\left(\frac{\text{cov}_{11}}{\mu_{11}\mu_1}\right) + v_{12}\left(\frac{\text{cov}_{12}}{\mu_{12}\mu_1}\right) \Rightarrow 0.1293$$

$$= (0.381)\left(\frac{4.167}{(6.67)(17.5)}\right) + (0.619)\left(\frac{35.417}{(10.83)(17.5)}\right) = 0.0136 + 0.1157.$$

For region 2,

$$CV_2^2 = v_{21}\left(\frac{\text{cov}_{21}}{\mu_{21}\mu_2}\right) + v_{22}\left(\frac{\text{cov}_{22}}{\mu_{22}\mu_2}\right) \Rightarrow 0.4294$$

$$= (0.158)\left(\frac{43.75}{(7.50)(47.5)}\right) + (0.842)\left(\frac{925.00}{(40.00)(47.5)}\right) = 0.0194 + 0.4100.$$

Similarly, the squared coefficient of variation for the between-region inequality component can be decomposed by GDP components (GDP for industrial sectors) as follows (see Appendix 2).

$$CV_B^2 = \frac{1}{\mu^2}\sum_{i=1}^{2}\frac{p_i}{p}(\mu_i - \mu)^2 = v_1\left(\frac{\text{cov}_1}{\mu_{\cdot 1}\mu}\right) + v_2\left(\frac{\text{cov}_2}{\mu_{\cdot 2}\mu}\right), \tag{3.10}$$

where $\mu_{\cdot k} = \frac{1}{p}\sum_{i=1}^{2}\sum_{j=1}^{p_i} y_{ijk} = \sum_{i=1}^{2}\frac{p_i}{p}\mu_{ik}$ is the simple average of sector k's GDP per capita for all provinces in the country. In Eq. (3.10), $v_k = \frac{\mu_{\cdot k}}{\mu}$ is the share of industrial sector k in the country in terms of GDP per capita while $\text{cov}_k = \sum_{i=1}^{2}\frac{p_i}{p}(\mu_{ik} - \mu_{\cdot k})(\mu_i - \mu)$ is the covariance between GDP component k and total GDP in the whole country.

We should note that we have

$$\mu = \mu_{\cdot 1} + \mu_{\cdot 2}, \tag{3.11}$$

where $\mu = \frac{p_1}{p}\mu_1 + \frac{p_2}{p}\mu_2$ and $\mu_{\cdot k} = \frac{p_1}{p}\mu_{1k} + \frac{p_2}{p}\mu_{2k}$. Using data in Table 3.4, we have

$$\mu_{\cdot 1} = \frac{p_1}{p}\mu_{11} + \frac{p_2}{p}\mu_{21} = \frac{6}{10}(6.7) + \frac{4}{10}(7.5) = 7.0,$$

$$\mu_{\cdot 2} = \frac{p_1}{p}\mu_{12} + \frac{p_2}{p}\mu_{22} = \frac{6}{10}(10.8) + \frac{4}{10}(40.0) = 22.5.$$

Thus, we can see the following relationship (Eq. 3.11).

$$\mu = \mu_{\cdot 1} + \mu_{\cdot 2} \Rightarrow 29.5 = 7.0 + 22.5.$$

Now, using data in Table 3.4, the squared coefficient of variation for the between-region component can be decomposed by GDP components as follows.

$$CV_B^2 = v_1\left(\frac{\text{cov}_1}{\mu_{\cdot 1}\mu}\right) + v_2\left(\frac{\text{cov}_2}{\mu_{\cdot 2}\mu}\right) \Rightarrow 0.2482$$

$$= (0.237)\left(\frac{6.0}{(7.0)(29.5)}\right) + (0.763)\left(\frac{210.0}{(22.5)(29.5)}\right) = 0.0069 + 0.2413.$$

2.3 *Bidimensional Inequality Decomposition Equation based on the Coefficient of Variation*

By substituting Eqs. (3.9) and (3.10) into Eq. (3.2), the following bidimensional inequality decomposition equation is obtained.

$$\begin{aligned}CV^2 &= \sum\nolimits_{i=1}^{2}\frac{p_i}{p}\left(\frac{\mu_i}{\mu}\right)^2 CV_i^2 + \frac{1}{\mu^2}\sum\nolimits_{i=1}^{2}\frac{p_i}{p}(\mu_i-\mu)^2\\ &= \frac{p_1}{p}\left(\frac{\mu_1}{\mu}\right)^2\left[v_{11}\left(\frac{\text{cov}_{11}}{\mu_{11}\mu_1}\right) + v_{12}\left(\frac{\text{cov}_{12}}{\mu_{12}\mu_1}\right)\right] \text{(Within region 1)}\\ &+ \frac{p_2}{p}\left(\frac{\mu_2}{\mu}\right)^2\left[v_{21}\left(\frac{\text{cov}_{21}}{\mu_{21}\mu_2}\right) + v_{22}\left(\frac{\text{cov}_{22}}{\mu_{22}\mu_2}\right)\right] \text{(Within region 2)}\\ &+ \left[v_1\left(\frac{\text{cov}_1}{\mu_{\cdot 1}\mu}\right) + v_2\left(\frac{\text{cov}_2}{\mu_{\cdot 2}\mu}\right)\right] \text{(Between – region).}\end{aligned} \tag{3.12}$$

Using data in Table 3.4, we can now conduct a bidimensional inequality decomposition analysis, the result of which can be summarized in Table 3.5. In Table 3.5, values in the rows corresponding to "Inequality within region 1" and "Inequality within region 2" are obtained as follows.

Table 3.5 Result of bidimensional inequality decomposition analysis based on the coefficient of variation (using data in Table 3.4)

	Sector 1		Sector 2		Total	
	Value	Contribution (%)	Value	Contribution (%)	Value	Contribution (%)
Inequality within region 1	0.0029	0.4	0.0244	3.4	0.0273	3.8
Inequality within region 2	0.0201	2.8	0.4252	59.0	0.4453	61.8
Within-region inequality	0.0230	3.2	0.4496	62.4	0.4726	65.6
Between-region inequality	0.0069	1.0	0.2413	33.5	0.2482	34.4
Total inequality	0.0299	4.1	0.6909	95.9	0.7208	100.0

For region 1,

$$\frac{p_1}{p}\left(\frac{\mu_1}{\mu}\right)^2\left[v_{11}\left(\frac{\text{cov}_{11}}{\mu_{11}\mu_1}\right)\right] \Rightarrow \frac{6}{10}\left(\frac{17.5}{29.5}\right)^2(0.0136) = 0.0029 \text{ (Sector 1)}$$

$$\frac{p_1}{p}\left(\frac{\mu_1}{\mu}\right)^2\left[v_{12}\left(\frac{\text{cov}_{12}}{\mu_{12}\mu_1}\right)\right] \Rightarrow \frac{6}{10}\left(\frac{17.5}{29.5}\right)^2(0.1157) = 0.0244.\text{(Sector 2)}$$

For region 2,

$$\frac{p_2}{p}\left(\frac{\mu_2}{\mu}\right)^2\left[v_{21}\left(\frac{\text{cov}_{21}}{\mu_{21}\mu_2}\right)\right] \Rightarrow \frac{4}{10}\left(\frac{47.5}{29.5}\right)^2(0.0194) = 0.0201 \text{ (Sector 1)}$$

$$\frac{p_2}{p}\left(\frac{\mu_2}{\mu}\right)^2\left[v_{22}\left(\frac{\text{cov}_{22}}{\mu_{22}\mu_2}\right)\right] \Rightarrow \frac{4}{10}\left(\frac{47.5}{29.5}\right)^2(0.4100) = 0.4252. \text{ (Sector 2)}$$

On the other hand, values in the row corresponding to "Between-region inequality" are calculated as follows.

$$v_1\left(\frac{\text{cov}_1}{\mu_{\cdot 1}\mu}\right) \Rightarrow (0.237)\left(\frac{6.0}{(7.0)(29.5)}\right) = 0.0069 \text{ (Sector 1)}$$

$$v_2\left(\frac{\text{cov}_2}{\mu_{\cdot 2}\mu}\right) \Rightarrow (0.763)\left(\frac{210.0}{(22.5)(29.5)}\right) = 0.2413.\text{(Sector 2)}$$

Next, the contribution of each component is obtained by dividing the corresponding value by overall inter-provincial inequality (0.7208). According to the result, inter-provincial inequality in sector 2 (industry and services) of region 2 is the major contributor to overall inter-provincial inequality by accounting for 59.0%; its squared coefficient of variation is very large at 0.5547.

If there are m regions and K industrial sectors, the bidimensional inequality decomposition equation is given by

$$CV^2 = \sum_{i=1}^{m}\frac{p_i}{p}\left(\frac{\mu_i}{\mu}\right)^2\left[\sum_{k=1}^{K}v_{ik}\left(\frac{\text{cov}_{ik}}{\mu_{ik}\mu_i}\right)\right] + \sum_{k=1}^{K}v_k\left(\frac{\text{cov}_k}{\mu_{\cdot k}\mu}\right). \quad (3.13)$$

Dividing Eq. (3.13) by CV^2 yields

$$1 = \sum_{i=1}^{m}\sum_{k=1}^{K}c_{ik} + \sum_{k=1}^{K}c_k. \quad (3.14)$$

c_{ik} is the contribution of region i's inter-provincial inequality for sector k, whereas c_k is the contribution of between-region inequality for sector k. Since the country consists of m regions and K industrial sectors, there are $(m + 1) \times k$ components. Appendix 3 provides the derivation of Eqs. (3.13) and (3.14).

2.4 Bi-dimensional Inequality Decomposition Equation based on the Population-weighted Coefficient of Variation

As mentioned before, Akita and Miyata (2010) used the population-weighted coefficient of variation rather than the coefficient of variation to develop the bidimensional inequality decomposition method. This subsection formulates the method based on the population-weighted coefficient of variation. To obtain the method, consider a country consisting of p provinces. These provinces are divided into m regions where region i contains p_i provinces. Let N, N_{ij}, y, and y_{ij} be, respectively, population of the whole country, population of province j in region i, GDP per capita of the whole country, and GDP per capita of province j in region i. Then, by the squared population-weighted coefficient of variation, overall income inequality can be measured by

$$WCV^2 = \frac{1}{y^2}\sum\nolimits_{i=1}^{m}\sum\nolimits_{j=1}^{p_i}\frac{N_{ij}}{N}\left(y_{ij} - y\right)^2, \tag{3.15}$$

where $y = \frac{1}{N}\sum\nolimits_{i=1}^{m}\sum\nolimits_{j=1}^{p_i}N_{ij}y_{ij}$.

When Eq. (3.15) is compared with Eq. (3.1), two differences can be observed. First, μ is replaced by y where $\mu = \frac{1}{p}\sum\nolimits_{i=1}^{m}\sum\nolimits_{j=1}^{p_i}y_{ij}$ (simple average of GDP per capita for all provinces) and $y = \sum\nolimits_{i=1}^{m}\sum\nolimits_{j=1}^{p_i}\frac{N_{ij}}{N}y_{ij}$ (population-weighted average of GDP per capita for all provinces). Second, $\frac{1}{p}$ is replaced by $\frac{N_{ij}}{N}$ where $p = \sum\nolimits_{i=1}^{m}p_i$ (total number of provinces) and $N = \sum\nolimits_{i=1}^{m}\sum\nolimits_{j=1}^{p_i}N_{ij}$ (total population). We should note that WCV^2 does not measure inter-provincial inequality in GDP per capita, but measures interpersonal income inequality by assuming that individuals in each province have their provincial GDP per capita.

Next, let N_i and y_i be, respectively, population and GDP per capita of region i where $N_i = \sum\nolimits_{j=1}^{p_i}N_{ij}$ and $y_i = \sum\nolimits_{j=1}^{p_i}\frac{N_{ij}}{N_i}y_{ij}$. Then, WCV^2 can be decomposed into the within-region and between-region inequality components as follows.

$$\begin{aligned} WCV^2 &= \sum\nolimits_{i=1}^{m}\frac{N_i}{N}\left(\frac{y_i}{y}\right)^2 WCV_i^2 + \frac{1}{y^2}\sum\nolimits_{i=1}^{m}\frac{N_i}{N}\left(y_i - y\right)^2 \\ &= WCV_W^2 + WCV_B^2, \end{aligned} \tag{3.16}$$

where $WCV_i^2 = \frac{1}{y_i^2}\sum_{j=1}^{p_i}\frac{N_{ij}}{N_i}\left(y_{ij}-y_i\right)^2$ is the squared population-weighted coefficient of variation for region i (i = 1, 2, …, m). In Eq. (3.16), $WCV_W^2 = \sum_{i=1}^{m}\frac{N_i}{N}\left(\frac{y_i}{y}\right)^2 WCV_i^2$ is the within-region inequality component, while $WCV_B^2 = \frac{1}{y^2}\sum_{i=1}^{m}\frac{N_i}{N}(y_i - y)^2$ is the between-region inequality component. Appendix 4 provides the derivation of Eq. (3.16).

Suppose next that total GDP consists of K GDP components. Then, $WCV_i^2 = \frac{1}{y_i^2}\sum_{j=1}^{p_i}\frac{N_{ij}}{N_i}\left(y_{ij}-y_i\right)^2$ can be decomposed by GDP components as follows.

$$WCV_i^2 = \sum_{k=1}^{K} w_{ik}\left(\frac{\mathrm{wcov}_{ik}}{y_{ik}y_i}\right), \tag{3.17}$$

where $y_{ik} = \sum_{j=1}^{p_i}\frac{N_{ij}}{N_i}y_{ijk}$ is GDP per capita for sector k of region i. In Eq. (3.17), $w_{ik} = \frac{y_{ik}}{y_i}$ is the GDP share of industrial sector k in region i and $\mathrm{wcov}_{ik} = \sum_{j=1}^{p_i}\frac{N_{ij}}{N_i}\left(y_{ijk}-y_{ik}\right)\left(y_{ij}-y_i\right)$ is the population-weighted covariance between GDP component k and total GDP in region i. Similarly, $WCV_B^2 = \frac{1}{y^2}\sum_{i=1}^{m}\frac{N_i}{N}(y_i - y)^2$ can be decomposed by GDP components as follows.

$$WCV_B^2 = \sum_{k=1}^{K} w_k\left(\frac{\mathrm{wcov}_k}{y_{\cdot k}y}\right), \tag{3.18}$$

where $y_{\cdot k} = \sum_{i=1}^{m}\frac{N_i}{N}y_{ik}$ is GDP per capita for sector k of the country. In Eq. (3.18), $w_k = \frac{y_{\cdot k}}{y}$ is the GDP share of sector k in the country while $\mathrm{wcov}_k = \sum_{i=1}^{m}\frac{N_i}{N} \times (y_{ik} - y_{\cdot k})(y_i - y)$ is the population-weighted covariance between GDP component k and total GDP in the country. Appendix 4 provides the derivation of Eqs. (3.17) and (3.18).

Substituting Eqs. (3.17) and (3.18) into Eq. (3.16), we obtain the following bidimensional inequality decomposition equation based on the squared population-weighted coefficient of variation.

$$WCV^2 = \sum_{i=1}^{m}\frac{N_i}{N}\left(\frac{y_i}{y}\right)^2\left[\sum_{k=1}^{K} w_{ik}\left(\frac{\mathrm{wcov}_{ik}}{y_{ik}y_i}\right)\right] + \sum_{k=1}^{K} w_k\left(\frac{\mathrm{wcov}_k}{y_{\cdot k}y}\right). \tag{3.19}$$

Since the country consists of m regions and K industrial sectors, there are $(m + 1) \times K$ components in Eq. (3.19).

When the country consists of 2 regions and 2 industrial sectors, Eq. (3.19) is written as

Table 3.6 Result of bi-dimensional inequality decomposition analysis based on the population-weighted coefficient of variation (using data in Table 3.4)

	Sector 1		Sector 2		Total	
	Value	Contribution (%)	Value	Contribution (%)	Value	Contribution (%)
Inequality within region 1	0.0012	0.1	0.0132	1.7	0.0144	1.8
Inequality within region 2	0.0237	3.0	0.4141	52.9	0.4378	55.9
Within-region inequality	0.0249	3.2	0.4273	54.6	0.4522	57.8
Between-region inequality	0.0126	1.6	0.3180	40.6	0.3306	42.2
Total inequality	0.0375	4.8	0.7453	95.2	0.7828	100.0

$$
\begin{aligned}
WCV^2 &= \sum_{i=1}^{2} \frac{N_i}{N}\left(\frac{y_i}{y}\right)^2 WCV_i^2 + \frac{1}{y^2}\sum_{i=1}^{2}\frac{N_i}{N}(y_i - y)^2 \\
&= \frac{N_1}{N}\left(\frac{y_1}{y}\right)^2\left[w_{11}\left(\frac{\text{wcov}_{11}}{y_{11}y_1}\right) + w_{12}\left(\frac{\text{wcov}_{12}}{y_{12}y_1}\right)\right] \text{ (Within region 1)} \\
&\quad + \frac{N_2}{N}\left(\frac{y_2}{y}\right)^2\left[w_{21}\left(\frac{\text{wcov}_{21}}{y_{21}y_2}\right) + w_{22}\left(\frac{\text{wcov}_{22}}{y_{22}y_2}\right)\right] \text{ (Within region 2)} \\
&\quad + \left[w_1\left(\frac{\text{wcov}_1}{y_{\cdot 1}y}\right) + w_2\left(\frac{\text{wcov}_2}{y_{\cdot 2}y}\right)\right]. \text{(Between} - \text{region)}
\end{aligned} \tag{3.20}
$$

Applying Eq. (3.20) to data in Table 3.4, we can conduct a bidimensional inequality decomposition analysis based on the population-weighted coefficient of variation. The result is presented in Table 3.6.

To obtain the result, inter-provincial inequalities within regions 1 and 2 are first decomposed by GDP components as follows.

For region 1,

$$
\begin{aligned}
WCV_1^2 &= w_{11}\left(\frac{\text{wcov}_{11}}{y_{11}y_1}\right) + w_{12}\left(\frac{\text{wcov}_{12}}{y_{12}y_1}\right) \Rightarrow 0.1592 \\
&= (0.368)\left(\frac{3.75}{(6.25)(17.0)}\right) + (0.632)\left(\frac{42.25}{(10.75)(17.0)}\right) = 0.0130 + 0.1462.
\end{aligned}
$$

For region 2,

$$WCV_2^2 = w_{21}\left(\frac{\mathrm{wcov}_{21}}{y_{21}y_2}\right) + w_{22}\left(\frac{\mathrm{wcov}_{22}}{y_{22}y_2}\right) \Rightarrow 0.3530$$
$$= (0.127)\left(\frac{76.00}{(8.0)(63.0)}\right) + (0.873)\left(\frac{1325.00}{(55.0)(63.0)}\right) = 0.0191 + 0.3338.$$

Then, values in the rows corresponding to "Inequality within region 1" and "Inequality within region 2" in Table 3.6 are obtained as follows.

For region 1,

$$\frac{N_1}{N}\left(\frac{y_1}{y}\right)^2\left[w_{11}\left(\frac{\mathrm{wcov}_{11}}{y_{11}y_1}\right)\right] \Rightarrow \frac{100}{200}\left(\frac{17.0}{40.0}\right)^2(0.0130) = 0.0012 \quad \text{(Sector 1)}$$

$$\frac{N_1}{N}\left(\frac{y_1}{y}\right)^2\left[w_{12}\left(\frac{\mathrm{wcov}_{12}}{y_{12}y_1}\right)\right] \Rightarrow \frac{100}{200}\left(\frac{17.0}{40.0}\right)^2(0.1462) = 0.0132.\text{(Sector 2)}$$

For region 2,

$$\frac{N_2}{N}\left(\frac{y_2}{y}\right)^2\left[w_{21}\left(\frac{\mathrm{wcov}_{21}}{y_{21}y_2}\right)\right] \Rightarrow \frac{100}{200}\left(\frac{63.0}{40.0}\right)^2(0.0191) = 0.0237 \quad \text{(Sector 1)}$$
$$\frac{N_2}{N}\left(\frac{y_2}{y}\right)^2\left[w_{22}\left(\frac{\mathrm{wcov}_{22}}{y_{22}y_2}\right)\right] \Rightarrow \frac{100}{200}\left(\frac{63.0}{40.0}\right)^2(0.3338) = 0.4141.\text{(Sector 2)}$$

The within-region inequality component is the sum of these four values, that is,

$$WCV_W^2 = \sum\nolimits_{i=1}^{2}\frac{N_i}{N}\left(\frac{y_i}{y}\right)^2\left[\sum\nolimits_{k=1}^{2} w_{ik}\left(\frac{\mathrm{wcov}_{ik}}{y_{ik}y_i}\right)\right]$$
$$= 0.0012 + 0.0132 + 0.0237 + 0.4141 = 0.4522.$$

On the other hand, the between-region inequality is decomposed by GDP components as follows.

$$WCV_B^2 = w_1\left(\frac{\mathrm{wcov}_1}{y_{\cdot 1}y}\right) + w_2\left(\frac{\mathrm{wcov}_2}{y_{\cdot 2}y}\right) \Rightarrow 0.3306$$
$$= (0.178)\left(\frac{20.1}{(7.12)(40.0)}\right) + (0.822)\left(\frac{508.9}{(32.88)(40.0)}\right) = 0.0126 + 0.3180.$$

The values on the right-hand side of this equation appear in the row corresponding to "Between-region inequality" in Table 3.6.

The sum of the within-region and between-region inequality components should be equal to overall inter-provincial inequality.

$$WCV^2 = WCV_W^2 + WCV_B^2 = 0.4522 + 0.3306 = 0.7828.$$

To check this, overall inter-provincial inequality in GDP per capita is calculated using Eq. (3.15). First, the population-weighted variance is obtained by

$$\begin{aligned}\sum_{i=1}^{2}\sum_{j=1}^{p_i}\frac{N_{ij}}{N}(y_{ij}-y)^2 &= \frac{20}{200}(15-40)^2+\frac{10}{200}(20-40)^2+\frac{15}{200}(20-40)^2\\ &\quad+\frac{20}{200}(5-40)^2+\frac{20}{200}(25-40)^2+\frac{15}{200}(20-40)^2\\ &\quad+\frac{10}{200}(40-40)^2+\frac{30}{200}(20-40)^2\\ &\quad+\frac{50}{200}(100-40)^2+\frac{10}{200}(30-40)^2\\ &= 62.5+20+30+122.5+22.5+30+0+60\\ &\quad+900+5\\ &= 1,232.5.\end{aligned}$$

Then, overall inter-provincial inequality is given by

$$WCV^2 = \frac{1}{y^2}\sum_{i=1}^{2}\sum_{j=1}^{p_i}\frac{N_{ij}}{N}(y_{ij}-y)^2 = \frac{1}{(40)^2}(1,232.5) = 0.7828.$$

This is the same as the value obtained above.

The decomposition analysis based on the population-weighted coefficient of variation provides a similar result to the one based on the coefficient of variation qualitatively (see Tables 3.5 and 3.6). We should note however that the population-weighted coefficient of variation measures interpersonal income inequality under the assumption that individuals in each province have their provincial GDP per capita.

3 Sectoral Inequality Decomposition Analysis

Based on provincial data on population and GDP by industrial sectors over the period from 1975 to 1992, Akita and Lukman (1995) explored the determinants of inter-provincial income inequality in Indonesia by using a sectoral inequality decomposition method. This section first discusses the method using the squared coefficient of variation and then the method using the squared population-weighted coefficient of variation.

To illustrate the method, consider a country comprising 10 provinces ($p = 10$). Table 3.7 presents GDP and population data, while Fig. 3.2 shows GDP per capita for three industrial sectors. Let y_i and μ be, respectively, GDP per capita of province i and the simple average of GDP per capita, where $\mu = \frac{1}{p}\sum_{i=1}^{p} y_i$. Then, by the

Table 3.7 Population and GDP by industrial sectors for 10 provinces

Province	GDP				Population	GDP per capita			
	Total	Sector 1	Sector 2	Sector 3		Total	Sector 1	Sector 2	Sector 3
1	700	50	300	350	20	35.0	2.5	15.0	17.5
2	500	100	200	200	20	25.0	5.0	10.0	10.0
3	300	50	100	150	25	12.0	2.0	4.0	6.0
4	500	100	100	300	25	20.0	4.0	4.0	12.0
5	1000	100	450	450	25	40.0	4.0	18.0	18.0
6	400	100	100	200	25	16.0	4.0	4.0	8.0
7	600	100	200	300	40	15.0	2.5	5.0	7.5
8	800	100	200	500	20	40.0	5.0	10.0	25.0
9	4000	400	2000	1600	80	50.0	5.0	25.0	20.0
10	1200	100	500	600	20	60.0	5.0	25.0	30.0
Total or simple average	10,000	1200	4150	4650	300	$\mu = 31.3$	$\mu_1 = 3.9$	$\mu_2 = 12.0$	$\mu_3 = 15.4$

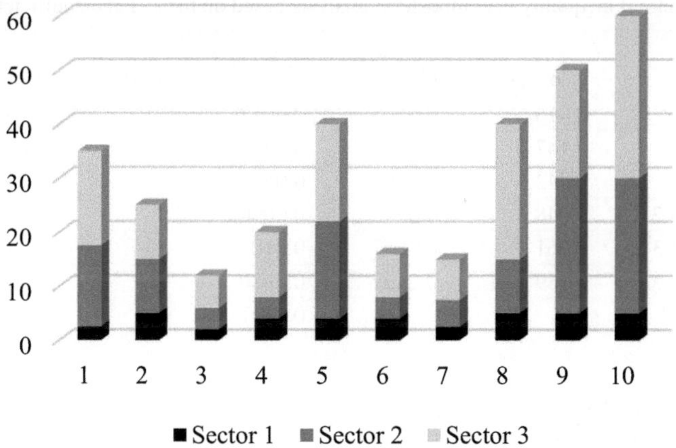

Fig. 3.2 GDP per capita by three industrial sectors for 10 provinces

squared coefficient of variation, overall inter-provincial inequality in GDP per capita is given by

$$\begin{aligned} CV^2 &= \frac{1}{\mu^2}\frac{1}{p}\sum\nolimits_{i=1}^{p}(y_i-\mu)^2 \\ &= \frac{1}{(31.3)^2}\frac{1}{10}\Big[(35-31.3)^2+(25-31.3)^2+(12-31.3)^2+(20 \\ &\quad -31.3)^2+(40-31.3)^2+(16-31.3)^2+(15-31.3)^2+(40-31.3)^2 \\ &\quad +(50-31.3)^2+(60-31.3)^2\Big] \\ &= 0.2427. \end{aligned} \tag{3.21}$$

Suppose next that total GDP consists of three components: GDP from agriculture (sector 1); GDP from manufacturing (sector 2); and GDP from services (sector 3). Then, GDP per capita of province i can be written as

$$y_i = y_{i1} + y_{i2} + y_{i3},$$

where y_{i1}, y_{i2}, and y_{i3} are, respectively, GDP per capita for sectors 1, 2, and 3 of province i. Let μ_1, μ_2, and μ_3 be, respectively, the simple averages of GDP per capita for sectors 1, 2, and 3. Then, we have

$$\mu = \mu_1 + \mu_2 + \mu_3.$$

Now, the squared coefficient of variation can be decomposed into variation and covariation terms as follows.

Table 3.8 Sectoral inequality decomposition analysis based on the squared coefficient of variation

Component	v_k^2 or $v_k v_j$	CV_k^2 or COV_{kj}	$v_k^2 CV_k^2$ or $2v_k v_j COV_{kj}$	Contribution (%)
Sector 1	0.016	0.0815	0.0012	0.5
Sector 2	0.147	0.4389	0.0645	26.6
Sector 3	0.242	0.2462	0.0596	24.6
Sectors 1 and 2	0.048	0.0940	0.0090	3.7
Sectors 1 and 3	0.061	0.0847	0.0104	4.3
Sectors 2 and 3	0.189	0.2597	0.0980	40.4
Total			0.2427	100.0

$$\begin{aligned} CV^2 &= \frac{1}{\mu^2}\frac{1}{p}\sum\nolimits_{i=1}^{p}(y_i-\mu)^2 \\ &= v_1^2CV_1^2+v_2^2CV_2^2+v_3^2CV_3^2+2v_1v_2COV_{12}+2v_1v_3COV_{13} \\ &\quad +2v_2v_3COV_{23}. \end{aligned} \tag{3.22}$$

This is the sectoral inequality decomposition equation for a country consisting of 3 industrial sectors. In Eq. (3.22), $v_k=\frac{\mu_k}{\mu}$ is the share of sector k in terms of GDP per capita ($k=1,2,3$). On the other hand, $CV_k^2=\frac{1}{\mu_k^2}\frac{1}{p}\sum_{i=1}^{p}(y_{ik}-\mu_k)^2$ is the squared coefficient of variation for sector k, while $COV_{kj}=\frac{1}{\mu_k\mu_j}\frac{1}{p}\sum_{i=1}^{p}(y_{ik}-\mu_k)(y_{ij}-\mu_j)$ is the coefficient of covariation between sectors k and j ($k,j=1,2,3; j\neq k$). Appendix 5 presents the derivation of Eq. (3.22).

Using data in Table 3.7, the squared coefficient of variation is decomposed into variation and covariation terms as follows (see Table 3.8).

$$\begin{aligned} CV^2 &= v_1^2CV_1^2+v_2^2CV_2^2+v_3^2CV_3^2+2v_1v_2COV_{12}+2v_1v_3COV_{13}+2v_2v_3COV_{23} \\ &\Rightarrow 0.2427 \\ &= (0.125)^2(0.0815)+(0.383)^2(0.4389)+(0.492)^2(0.2462)+2(0.125) \\ &\quad \times(0.383)(0.0940)+2(0.125)(0.492)(0.0847)+2(0.383)(0.492) \\ &\quad \times(0.2597) \\ &= (0.0012+0.0645+0.0596)+(0.0090+0.0104+0.0980). \end{aligned}$$

Dividing both sides by $CV^2=0.2427$ results in the contribution of each component to overall inter-provincial inequality (in %).

$$100\% = (0.5\%+26.6\%+24.6\%)+(3.7\%+4.3\%+40.4\%).$$

This result shows that the term associated with CV_2^2 contributes 26.6% of overall inter-provincial inequality, while the term associated with CV_3^2 contributes 24.6%. It also shows that the term associated with COV_{23} contributes 40.4% of overall inequality. A large coefficient of covariation between sectors 2 and 3 implies that service activities are developed concomitantly with manufacturing. These observations indicate that the geographical distribution of manufacturing activities together with the concomitant distribution of service activities determines overall inter-provincial inequality.

We should note that Eq. (3.22) is different from the decomposition of the squared coefficient of variation by GDP components developed in the previous section (Eqs. 3.9 and 3.10). In the bidimensional inequality decomposition method, the squared coefficient of variation given by Eq. (3.21) is decomposed by GDP components as follows.

$$CV^2 = \frac{1}{\mu^2}\frac{1}{p}\sum\nolimits_{i=1}^{p}(y_i-\mu)^2 = v_1\left(\frac{\text{cov}_1}{\mu_1\mu}\right) + v_2\left(\frac{\text{cov}_2}{\mu_2\mu}\right) + v_3\left(\frac{\text{cov}_3}{\mu_3\mu}\right)$$
$$= v_1 COV_1 + v_2 COV_2 + v_3 COV_3. \quad (3.23)$$

where $\text{cov}_k = \frac{1}{p}\sum_{i=1}^{p}(y_{ik}-\mu_k)(y_i-\mu)$ is the covariance in GDP per capita between sector k and the whole country. In Eq. (3.23), $COV_k = \frac{\text{cov}_k}{\mu_k\mu}$ is the coefficient of covariation between sector k and the whole country. Unlike Eq. (3.22), there are no variation terms in this decomposition equation. Using data in Table 3.7, Eq. (3.23) is given by

$$\begin{aligned} CV^2 &= v_1 COV_1 + v_2 COV_2 + v_3 COV_3 \Rightarrow 0.2427 \\ &= (0.125)(0.0879) + (0.383)(0.3078) + (0.492)(0.2313) \\ &= 0.0110 + 0.1180 + 0.1138. \end{aligned}$$

We can see from this result that sectors 2 and 3 (manufacturing and services) are the main contributors and contribute equally to overall inter-provincial inequality. Eq. (3.23) is simpler than Eqs. (3.22), since Eq. (3.23) does not contain covariation terms between two industrial sectors. However, it does not enable us to analyze spatial interdependence between two industrial sectors.

Akita and Lukman (1995) employed the population-weighted coefficient of variation rather than the coefficient of variation. But, as discussed before, the population-weighted coefficient of variation measures interpersonal income inequality by assuming that individuals in each province receive their provincial GDP per capita. With this caveat in mind, this section develops the sectoral inequality decomposition method using the squared population-weighted coefficient of variation.

Consider a country consisting of 10 provinces ($p = 10$) whose GDP and population are presented in Table 3.7. Let N, N_i, y and y_i be, respectively, population of the whole country, population of province i, GDP per capita of the country, and GDP per capita of province i, where $y = \frac{1}{N}\sum_{i=1}^{p}N_i y_i$. Then, by the squared population-weighted coefficient of variation, overall income inequality is given by

Table 3.9 Sectoral inequality decomposition analysis based on the squared population-weighted coefficient of variation

Component	w_k^2 or $w_k w_j$	WCV_k^2 or $WCOV_{kj}$	$w_k^2 WCV_k^2$ or $2w_k w_j WCOV_{kj}$	Contribution (%)
Sector 1	0.014	0.0781	0.0011	0.5
Sector 2	0.172	0.4162	0.0717	31.2
Sector 3	0.216	0.2081	0.0450	19.6
Sectors 1 and 2	0.050	0.1175	0.0117	5.1
Sectors 1 and 3	0.056	0.0874	0.0098	4.2
Sectors 2 and 3	0.193	0.2351	0.0907	39.4
Total			0.2300	100.0

$$\begin{aligned} WCV^2 &= \frac{1}{y^2}\sum_{i=1}^{p}\frac{N_i}{N}(y_i - y)^2 \\ &= \frac{1}{(33.3)^2}\frac{1}{300}\Big[20(35-33.3)^2 + 20(25-33.3)^2 + 25(12-33.3)^2 \\ &\quad + 25(20-33.3)^2 + 25(40-33.3)^2 + 25(16-33.3)^2 + 40(15-33.3)^2 \\ &\quad + 20(40-33.3)^2 + 80(50-33.3)^2 + 20(60-33.3)^2\Big] \\ &= 0.2300. \end{aligned} \tag{3.24}$$

Suppose next that total GDP consists of 3 GDP components (GDP from three industrial sectors: agriculture; manufacturing; and services). Let y_{ik} and $y_{\cdot k}$ be, respectively, GDP per capita for sector k of province i and GDP per capita for sector k in the country, where $y_{\cdot k} = \frac{1}{N}\sum_{i=1}^{p} N_i y_{ik}$. Since we have $y_i = \sum_{k=1}^{3} y_{ik}$ and $y = \sum_{k=1}^{3} y_{\cdot k}$, WCV^2 in Eq. (3.23) can be decomposed by GDP components as follows.

$$\begin{aligned} WCV^2 = {} & w_1^2 WCV_1^2 + w_2^2 WCV_2^2 + w_3^2 WCV_3^2 + 2w_1 w_2 WCOV_{12} \\ & + 2w_1 w_3 WCOV_{13} + 2w_2 w_3 \mathrm{WCOV}_{23}, \end{aligned} \tag{3.25}$$

where $w_k = \frac{y_{\cdot k}}{y}$ is the GDP share of sector k ($k = 1, 2, 3$). In Eq. (3.25), $WCV_k^2 = \frac{1}{y_{\cdot k}^2}\sum_{i=1}^{p}\frac{N_i}{N}(y_{ik} - y_{\cdot k})^2$ is the squared population-weighted coefficient of variation for sector k, while $WCOV_{kj} = \frac{1}{y_{\cdot k} y_{\cdot j}}\sum_{i=1}^{p}\frac{N_i}{N}(y_{ik} - y_{\cdot k})(y_{ij} - y_{\cdot j})$ is the population-weighted coefficient of covariation between sectors k and j ($k, j = 1, 2, 3; j \neq k$).

Appendix 5 presents the derivation of Eq. (3.25).

Using data in Table 3.7, the squared population-weighted coefficient of variation is decomposed into variation and covariation terms as follows (see Table 3.9).

$$
\begin{aligned}
WCV^2 &= w_1^2 WCV_1^2 + w_2^2 WCV_2^2 + w_3^2 WCV_3^2 + 2w_1 w_2 WCOV_{12} + 2w_1 w_3 WCOV_{13} \\
&\quad + 2w_2 w_3 \mathrm{WCOV}_{23} \\
&\Rightarrow 0.2300 \\
&= (0.120)^2(0.0781) + (0.415)^2(0.4162) + (0.465)^2(0.2081) + 2(0.120) \\
&\quad \times (0.415)(0.1175) + 2(0.120)(0.465)(0.0674) + 2(0.415)(0.465) \\
&\quad \times (0.2351) \\
&= (0.0011 + 0.0717 + 0.0450) + (0.0117 + 0.0098 + 0.0907).
\end{aligned}
$$

Dividing both sides by $WCV^2 = 0.2300$ results in the contribution of each component to overall inter-provincial inequality (in %).

$$100\% = (0.5\% + 31.2\% + 19.6\%) + (5.1\% + 4.2\% + 39.5\%).$$

This result is similar to the one based on the squared coefficient of variation (compare Tables 3.8 and 3.9).

4 Two-stage Nested Theil Decomposition Analysis

Like the squared coefficient of variation, the Theil indices (Theil L and T) belong to the generalized entropy class of inequality measures and satisfy four principles as a measure of inequality, that is, anonymity, income homogeneity, population homogeneity, and the Pigou-Dalton principle of transfers. Furthermore, they can be decomposed additively by population subgroup. Using this decomposition property in the three-level hierarchical structure of a country, region-province-district, Akita (2003) developed the two-stage nested hierarchical Theil decomposition method to examine the determinants of income inequality.[3] The method is analogous to a two-stage nested design in the analysis of variance. It uses a district as the underlying regional unit rather than a province and decomposes overall income inequality into three components: the between-region, between-province, and within-province inequality components.

To illustrate the method, consider a country comprising 20 districts whose GDP and population are given in Table 3.10. Let N and Y be, respectively, the population and GDP of the country and N_{ijk} and Y_{ijk} be, respectively, the population and GDP of district k in province j of region i. Then, by the Theil T index, overall income inequality is measured by

[3]There are some studies that used the method, which include Akita and Alisjahbana (2002), Paredes et al. (2014), Akita and Miyata (2018), Wu et al. (2018).

Table 3.10 GDP and population for 20 districts

Region	Province	District	GDP	Population	GDP per capita
Region 1	Province 1	District 1	1200	40	30
		District 2	1500	30	50
		District 3	900	30	30
		District 4	500	20	25
	Province 2	District 5	800	20	40
		District 6	300	30	10
		District 7	1400	70	20
	Province 3	District 8	250	25	10
		District 9	1600	40	40
		District 10	1000	50	20
		District 11	150	10	15
		District 12	450	45	10
Region 2	Province 4	District 13	100	10	10
		District 14	600	30	20
		District 15	9000	60	150
		District 16	1600	80	20
		District 17	450	30	15
	Province 5	District 18	1200	20	60
		District 19	15,000	60	250
		District 20	2000	100	20
Total			40,000	800	50

$$T = \sum_i \sum_j \sum_k \frac{Y_{ijk}}{Y} \ln\left(\frac{Y_{ijk}/Y}{N_{ijk}/N}\right). \tag{3.26}$$

If y and y_{ijk} denote, respectively, GDP per capita of the whole country and district k in province j of region i, then Eq. (3.26) can be rewritten as

$$T = \sum_i \sum_j \sum_k \left(\frac{N_{ijk}}{N}\right)\left(\frac{y_{ijk}}{y}\right) \ln\left(\frac{y_{ijk}}{y}\right), \tag{3.27}$$

since $Y = Ny$ and $Y_{ijk} = N_{ijk}y_{ijk}$. This is the population-weighted Theil T index; thus, Eq. (3.26) measures interpersonal income inequality by assuming that individuals in each district receive the per capita GDP of their district. By contrast, the unweighted counterpart is given by

$$UWT = \frac{1}{K}\sum_i \sum_j \sum_k \left(\frac{y_{ijk}}{y}\right) \ln\left(\frac{y_{ijk}}{y}\right), \tag{3.28}$$

where K is the total number of districts in the country.

Using GDP and population data in Table 3.10, overall income inequality, as measured by Eq. (3.26), is given by

$$
\begin{aligned}
T &= \sum_i \sum_j \sum_k \frac{Y_{ijk}}{Y} \ln\left(\frac{Y_{ijk}/Y}{N_{ijk}/N}\right) \\
&= \sum_i \sum_j \sum_k (\text{income share})_{ijk} \ln\left(\frac{(\text{income share})_{ijk}}{(\text{population share})_{ijk}}\right) \\
&= (0.030)\ln\left(\frac{0.030}{0.050}\right) + (0.038)\ln\left(\frac{0.038}{0.038}\right) + (0.023)\ln\left(\frac{0.023}{0.038}\right) + \cdots \\
&\quad + (0.050)\ln\left(\frac{0.050}{0.125}\right) \\
&= -0.015 + 0 + (-0.011) + \cdots + (-0.046) = 0.5938.
\end{aligned}
$$

Suppose next that Y_i and N_i are the GDP and population of region i, respectively. Then, overall income inequality, as measured by Eq. (3.26), is decomposed into the within-region and between-region inequality components as follows.

$$
T = \sum_i \sum_j \sum_k \frac{Y_{ijk}}{Y} \ln\left(\frac{Y_{ijk}/Y}{N_{ijk}/N}\right) = \sum_i \left(\frac{Y_i}{Y}\right) T_{di} + T_{BR} \tag{3.29}
$$

where $T_{di} = \sum_j \sum_k \frac{Y_{ijk}}{Y_i} \ln\left(\frac{Y_{ijk}/Y_i}{N_{ijk}/N_i}\right)$ is income inequality within region i, while $T_{BR} = \sum_i \frac{Y_i}{Y} \ln\left(\frac{Y_i/Y}{N_i/N}\right)$ is income inequality between regions (between-region inequality component). Appendix 6 presents the derivation of Eq. (3.29).

Using the GDP and population shares of each district within region i, we can obtain T_{di} as follows. For region 1,

$$
\begin{aligned}
T_{d1} &= (0.119)\ln\left(\frac{0.119}{0.098}\right) + (0.149)\ln\left(\frac{0.149}{0.073}\right) + \cdots + (0.045)\ln\left(\frac{0.045}{0.110}\right) \\
&= 0.1214.
\end{aligned}
$$

For region 2,

$$
\begin{aligned}
T_{d2} &= (0.003)\ln\left(\frac{0.003}{0.026}\right) + (0.020)\ln\left(\frac{0.020}{0.077}\right) + \cdots + (0.067)\ln\left(\frac{0.067}{0.256}\right) \\
&= 0.5624.
\end{aligned}
$$

Using these values, the first term of Eq. (3.29) is given by

$$\sum_i \left(\frac{Y_i}{Y}\right) T_{di} = \left(\frac{10,050}{40,000}\right)(0.1214) + \left(\frac{29,950}{40,000}\right)(0.5624) = 0.4516,$$

while the second term of Eq. (3.29) is given by

$$T_{BR} = \left(\frac{10,050}{40,000}\right) \ln\left(\frac{10,050/40,000}{410/800}\right) + \left(\frac{29,950}{40,000}\right) \ln\left(\frac{29,950/40,000}{390/800}\right) = 0.1422.$$

We now have the following inequality decomposition result (decomposition of overall income inequality by region).

$$T = \sum_i \left(\frac{Y_i}{Y}\right) T_{di} + T_{BR}$$

$$\Rightarrow 0.5938 = 0.4516 + 0.1422.$$

Suppose next that Y_{ij} and N_{ij} are the GDP and population of province j in region i, respectively. Then, income inequality within region i can be further decomposed into the within-province and between-province inequality components as follows.

$$T_{di} = \sum_j \sum_k \frac{Y_{ijk}}{Y_i} \ln\left(\frac{Y_{ijk}/Y_i}{N_{ijk}/N_i}\right) = \sum_j \left(\frac{Y_{ij}}{Y_i}\right) T_{ij} + T_{pi}, \tag{3.30}$$

where $T_{ij} = \sum_k \frac{Y_{ijk}}{Y_{ij}} \ln\left(\frac{Y_{ijk}/Y_{ij}}{N_{ijk}/N_{ij}}\right)$ is income inequality within province j in region i (within-province income inequality of province j in region i), while $T_{pi} = \sum_j \frac{Y_{ij}}{Y_i} \ln\left(\frac{Y_{ij}/Y_i}{N_{ij}/N_i}\right)$ is income inequality between provinces in region i. Appendix 6 presents the derivation of Eq. (3.30). Substituting Eq. (3.30) into Eq. (3.29) results in the following two-stage nested Theil decomposition equation.

$$T = \sum_i \left(\frac{Y_i}{Y}\right) T_{di} + T_{BR} = \sum_i \left(\frac{Y_i}{Y}\right) \left(\sum_j \left(\frac{Y_{ij}}{Y_i}\right) T_{ij} + T_{pi}\right) + T_{BR}$$

$$= \sum_i \sum_j \left(\frac{Y_{ij}}{Y}\right) T_{ij} + \sum_i \left(\frac{Y_i}{Y}\right) T_{pi} + T_{BR} = T_{WP} + T_{BP} + T_{BR}. \tag{3.31}$$

$T_{WP} = \sum_i \sum_j \left(\frac{Y_{ij}}{Y}\right) T_{ij}$ is the within-province inequality component, which is a weighted average of within-province income inequalities. On the other hand,

$T_{BP} = \sum_i \left(\frac{Y_i}{Y}\right) T_{pi}$ is the between-province inequality component, which is a weighted average of between-province income inequalities.

To obtain T_{WP}, T_{ij} needs to be calculated for all provinces. For example, T_{11} is calculated as follows.

$$T_{11} = \sum_k \frac{Y_{11k}}{Y_{11}} \ln\left(\frac{Y_{11k}/Y_{11}}{N_{11k}/N_{11}}\right)$$

$$= (0.293)\ln\left(\frac{0.293}{0.333}\right) + (0.366)\ln\left(\frac{0.366}{0.250}\right) + (0.219)\ln\left(\frac{0.219}{0.250}\right)$$

$$+ (0.122)\ln\left(\frac{0.122}{0.167}\right)$$

$$= (-0.0381) + 0.1393 + (-0.0285) + (-0.0381) = 0.0346.$$

Using the values of all T_{ij}, we can obtain T_{WP} as follows.

$$T_{WP} = \sum_i \sum_j \left(\frac{Y_{ij}}{Y}\right) T_{ij}$$

$$= (0.1025)(0.0346) + (0.0625)(0.0978) + (0.0863)(0.1537) + (0.2938) \times (0.4976) + (0.4550)(0.5336)$$

$$= 0.4119.$$

To obtain T_{BP}, T_{pi} needs to be calculated for all regions. Using data in Table 3.10, T_{p1} and T_{p2} are calculated as follows.

$$T_{p1} = (0.408)\ln\left(\frac{0.408}{0.293}\right) + (0.249)\ln\left(\frac{0.249}{0.293}\right) + (0.343)\ln\left(\frac{0.343}{0.415}\right)$$

$$= 0.1355 + (-0.0405) + (-0.0648) = 0.0302.$$

$$T_{p2} = (0.392)\ln\left(\frac{0.392}{0.538}\right) + (0.608)\ln\left(\frac{0.608}{0.462}\right) = (-0.1242) + 0.1672$$

$$= 0.0429.$$

Using the values of all T_{pi}, we can obtain T_{BP} as follows.

$$T_{BP} = \sum_i \left(\frac{Y_i}{Y}\right) T_{pi} = (0.2512)(0.0302) + (0.7488)(0.0429) = 0.0397.$$

We can now present the decomposition result as follows.

Table 3.11 Two-stage nested Theil decomposition analysis: Theil *T*

Component	Theil *T*	Income share (%)	Contribution (%)
Within-province component (1)	0.4119	100.0	69.4
Province 1	0.0346	10.3	0.6
Province 2	0.0978	6.3	1.0
Province 3	0.1537	8.6	2.2
Province 4	0.4976	29.4	24.6
Province 5	0.5336	45.5	40.9
Between-province component (2)	0.0397	100.0	6.7
Region 1	0.0302	25.1	1.3
Region 2	0.0429	74.9	5.4
Between-region component (3)	0.1422		23.9
Total = (1) + (2) + (3)	0.5938		100.0

$$T = T_{WP} + T_{BP} + T_{BR} \Rightarrow 0.5938 = 0.4119 + 0.0397 + 0.1422.$$

By dividing both sides of this equation by overall income inequality, we can obtain the contribution of each inequality component as follows.

$$100\% = 69.4\% + 6.7\% + 23.9\%.$$

Table 3.11 summarizes the result of this two-stage nested Theil decomposition analysis by the Theil *T* index. The within-province inequality component accounts for 69.4% of overall income inequality. But, this is due mainly to a large inequality within province 5, which constitutes 40.9% of overall inequality.

(Note) Contribution is the contribution to overall income inequality

While Eq. (3.31) is the two-stage nested Theil decomposition equation by the Theil *T* index, we can obtain the decomposition equation using the following Theil *L* index.

$$L = \sum_i \sum_j \sum_k \frac{N_{ijk}}{N} \ln \left(\frac{N_{ijk}/N}{Y_{ijk}/Y} \right). \tag{3.32}$$

We should note that Eq. (3.32) is the population-weighted Theil *L* index since it can be modified to

$$L = \sum_i \sum_j \sum_k \frac{N_{ijk}}{N} \ln \left(\frac{y}{y_{ijk}} \right).$$

Therefore, the index measures interpersonal income inequality rather than regional income inequality. The unweighted counterpart is given by

Table 3.12 Two-stage nested Theil decomposition analysis: Theil *L*

Component	Theil *L*	Population share (%)	Contribution (%)
Within-province component (1)	0.3385	100.0	63.8
Province 1	0.0327	15.0	0.9
Province 2	0.0986	15.0	2.8
Province 3	0.1538	21.3	6.2
Province 4	0.5272	26.3	26.1
Province 5	0.6565	22.5	27.8
Between-province component (2)	0.0359	100.0	6.8
Region 1	0.0287	51.2	2.8
Region 2	0.0435	48.8	4.0
Between-region component (3)	0.1561		29.4
Total = (1) + (2) + (3)	0.5306		100.0

Note: Contribution is the contribution to overall income inequality

$$UWL = \frac{1}{K}\sum_i\sum_j\sum_k \ln\left(\frac{y}{y_{ijk}}\right),$$

where K is the total number of districts in the country.

The two-stage nested Theil decomposition equation for the Theil L index is given by

$$L = \sum_i\left(\frac{N_i}{N}\right)L_{di} + L_{BR} = \sum_i\left(\frac{N_i}{N}\right)\left(\sum_j\left(\frac{N_{ij}}{N_i}\right)L_{ij} + L_{pi}\right) + L_{BR}$$
$$= \sum_i\sum_j\left(\frac{N_{ij}}{N}\right)L_{ij} + \sum_i\left(\frac{N_i}{N}\right)L_{pi} + L_{BR} = L_{WP} + L_{BP} + L_{BR}. \quad (3.33)$$

Table 3.12 summarizes the decomposition result by the Theil L index. This result is similar to the one for the Theil T index. But, inequalities within provinces 4 and 5 contribute equally to overall income inequality; the combined contribution amounts to 53.9%. The difference in the decomposition result between the Theil T and L indices is attributable to the fact that the decomposition of the Theil L index uses population shares as weights, while that of the Theil T index uses income shares as weights.

Table 3.13 GDP, population, and labor for 10 regions

Region	GDP	Population	Labor	GDP per capita	Labor productivity	Labor participation rate
1	300	20	16	15.00	18.75	0.80
2	200	12	8	16.67	25.00	0.67
3	300	15	12	20.00	25.00	0.80
4	100	8	6	12.50	16.67	0.75
5	500	20	14	25.00	35.71	0.70
6	300	15	12	20.00	25.00	0.80
7	400	10	6	40.00	66.67	0.60
8	600	30	20	20.00	30.00	0.67
9	2000	40	20	50.00	100.00	0.50
10	300	10	6	30.00	50.00	0.60
Total or simple average	5000	180	120	24.92	39.28	0.69

5 Factor Decomposition Analysis of Regional Income Inequality

This section presents a factor decomposition method for regional income inequality developed by Cheng and Li (2006), which rectifies some of the shortcomings associated with the factor decomposition method advanced by Duro and Esteban (1998). Unlike conventional Theil's inequality decomposition methods introduced in the previous sections, their method provides additive inequality decomposition in the multiplicatively expressed variable to measure each individual factor's contribution to overall inequality. For example, per capita GDP is expressed as the product of labor productivity and labor participation rate. After linearizing this product by the natural logarithm, it additively decomposes regional inequality in per capita GDP into three components: regional inequality in labor productivity, regional inequality in labor participation rate, and an interpretive residual component.[4] The first two components in the decomposition equation are regional inequalities measured by the Theil index, which take nonnegative values. The last residual component represents the interaction between labor productivity and labor participation rate, which can be positive, negative, or zero if the two element variables are positively, negatively, or not correlated, respectively.

To illustrate Cheng and Li's method, suppose that a country consists of ten regions. Table 3.13 presents the GDP, population, and labor for these 10 regions. Before illustrating the method, we first show that per capita GDP is the product of labor productivity and labor participation rate. Let Y_i, N_i, and L_i be GDP, population, and labor for region i, respectively. Then, GDP per capita $\left(y_i = {}^{Y_i}\!/_{N_i}\right)$ is given by

[4]Cheng and Li's method has been employed in some studies on income inequality across regions or across countries. Kataoka (2018, 2019) provided a summary of these studies.

$$y_i = \left(\frac{Y_i}{L_i}\right)\left(\frac{L_i}{N_i}\right) = x_i l_i \tag{3.34}$$

where $x_i = \frac{Y_i}{L_i}$ and $l_i = \frac{L_i}{N_i}$ are labor productivity and labor participation rate, respectively. Thus, for each region, we have

$$(\text{per capita GDP})_i = (\text{labor productivity})_i \times (\text{labor participation rate})_i.$$

Next, let n and μ_y be the total number of regions in a country and the simple average of GDP per capita, respectively, where $\mu_y = \frac{1}{n}\sum_{i=1}^{n} y_i$. Using the data in Table 3.13, regional inequality in per capita GDP is measured by the Theil L index (Theil's second measure) as follows:

$$\begin{aligned} L_y &= \sum_{i=1}^{n} \frac{1}{n} \ln\left(\frac{\mu_y}{y_i}\right) = \frac{1}{n}\sum_{i=1}^{n} \ln\left(\frac{\mu_y}{y_i}\right) \\ &= \left(\frac{1}{10}\right)\ln\left(\frac{24.92}{15.00}\right) + \left(\frac{1}{10}\right)\ln\left(\frac{24.92}{16.67}\right) + \cdots + \left(\frac{1}{10}\right)\ln\left(\frac{24.92}{30.00}\right) \\ &= \left(\frac{1}{10}\right)(0.507 + 0.402 + \cdots + 0.186) = 0.090. \end{aligned} \tag{3.35}$$

On the other hand, using the Theil L index, regional inequality in labor productivity is given by

$$\begin{aligned} L_x &= \sum_{i=1}^{n} \frac{1}{n} \ln\left(\frac{\mu_x}{x_i}\right) = \frac{1}{n}\sum_{i=1}^{n} \ln\left(\frac{\mu_x}{x_i}\right) \\ &= \left(\frac{1}{10}\right)\ln\left(\frac{39.28}{18.75}\right) + \left(\frac{1}{10}\right)\ln\left(\frac{39.28}{25.00}\right) + \cdots + \left(\frac{1}{10}\right)\ln\left(\frac{39.28}{50.00}\right) \\ &= \left(\frac{1}{10}\right)(0.740 + 0.452 + \cdots - 0.241) = 0.161 \end{aligned} \tag{3.36}$$

while regional inequality in labor participation rate is given by

$$\begin{aligned} L_l &= \sum_{i=1}^{n} \frac{1}{n} \ln\left(\frac{\mu_l}{l_i}\right) = \frac{1}{n}\sum_{i=1}^{n} \ln\left(\frac{\mu_l}{l_i}\right) \\ &= \left(\frac{1}{10}\right)\ln\left(\frac{0.69}{0.80}\right) + \left(\frac{1}{10}\right)\ln\left(\frac{0.69}{0.67}\right) + \cdots + \left(\frac{1}{10}\right)\ln\left(\frac{0.69}{0.60}\right) \\ &= \left(\frac{1}{10}\right)(-0.150 + 0.032 + \cdots + 0.137) = 0.010, \end{aligned} \tag{3.37}$$

where $\mu_x = \frac{1}{n}\sum_{i=1}^{n} x_i$ and $\mu_l = \frac{1}{n}\sum_{i=1}^{n} l_i$. Evidently, regional inequality in per capita GDP is not equal to the sum of regional inequalities in labor productivity and labor participation rate since we have $0.090 \neq 0.161 + 0.010$ (=0.171). Therefore, an additional component is required.

Now, using $y_i = x_i l_i$ (Eq. 3.34), we can modify Eq. (3.35) as follows:

$$L_y = \frac{1}{n}\sum_{i=1}^{n} \ln\left(\frac{\mu_y}{x_i l_i}\right) = \frac{1}{n}\sum_{i=1}^{n} \ln\left(\frac{\mu_x \mu_l}{x_i l_i} \cdot \frac{\mu_y}{\mu_x \mu_l}\right)$$
$$= \frac{1}{n}\sum_{i=1}^{n} \ln\left(\frac{\mu_x}{x_i}\right) + \frac{1}{n}\sum_{i=1}^{n} \ln\left(\frac{\mu_l}{l_i}\right) + \ln\left(\frac{\mu_y}{\mu_x \mu_l}\right).$$

Since $L_x = \frac{1}{n}\sum_{i=1}^{n} \ln\left(\frac{\mu_x}{x_i}\right)$ (Eq. 3.36) and $L_l = \frac{1}{n}\sum_{i=1}^{n} \ln\left(\frac{\mu_l}{l_i}\right)$ (Eq. 3.37), we obtain

$$L_y = L_x + L_l + \ln\left(\frac{\mu_y}{\mu_x \mu_l}\right). \tag{3.38}$$

The first two terms in Eq. (3.38) are the Theil L indices for labor productivity and labor participation rate, respectively. However, the last residual term is not a Theil index.

To interpret this residual term, we consider the following covariance between labor productivity and labor participation rate.

$$\mathrm{cov}(\boldsymbol{x}, \boldsymbol{l}) = \frac{1}{n}\sum_{i=1}^{n} (x_i - \mu_x)(l_i - \mu_l)$$
$$= \frac{1}{n}\sum_{i=1}^{n} x_i l_i - \mu_l \frac{1}{n}\sum_{i=1}^{n} x_i - \mu_x \frac{1}{n}\sum_{i=1}^{n} l_i + \mu_x \mu_l. \tag{3.39}$$

Because $y_i = x_i l_i$ (Eq. 3.34), $\mu_y = \frac{1}{n}\sum_{i=1}^{n} y_i$, $\mu_x = \frac{1}{n}\sum_{i=1}^{n} x_i$, and $\mu_l = \frac{1}{n}\sum_{i=1}^{n} l_i$, Eq. (3.39) is modified as follows:

$$\mathrm{cov}(\boldsymbol{x}, \boldsymbol{l}) = \mu_y - \mu_x \mu_l \text{ or } \mu_y = \mathrm{cov}(\boldsymbol{x}, \boldsymbol{l}) + \mu_x \mu_l.$$

Dividing both sides of this equation by $\mu_x \mu_l$, we obtain

$$\frac{\mu_y}{\mu_x \mu_l} = \frac{\mathrm{cov}(\boldsymbol{x}, \boldsymbol{l})}{\mu_x \mu_l} + 1 > 0. \tag{3.40}$$

Using this equation, the last term of Eq. (3.38) is rewritten as follows.

$$\lambda(\boldsymbol{x}, \boldsymbol{l}) = \ln\left(\frac{\mu_y}{\mu_x \mu_l}\right) = \ln\left(\frac{\mathrm{cov}(\boldsymbol{x}, \boldsymbol{l})}{\mu_x \mu_l} + 1\right). \tag{3.41}$$

where $\lambda(\boldsymbol{x}, \boldsymbol{l})$ is the interpretive residual term representing the interaction between labor productivity and labor participation rate. It can be positive, negative, or zero depending on the value of $\frac{\mathrm{cov}(\boldsymbol{x}, \boldsymbol{l})}{\mu_x \mu_l}$ if the two element variables ($\boldsymbol{x}$ and $\boldsymbol{l}$) are positively, negatively, or not correlated, respectively. Using the data in Table 3.13, we obtain

$$\lambda(\boldsymbol{x},\boldsymbol{l}) = \ln\left(\frac{-24.92}{39.28\times 0.69}\right) = \ln\left(\frac{-2.12}{39.28\times 0.69}+1\right) = -0.081.$$

Substituting Eq. (3.41) into Eq. (3.38), we obtain the following inequality decomposition equation developed by Cheng and Li (2006).

$$L_y = L_x + L_l + \lambda(\boldsymbol{x},\boldsymbol{l}). \tag{3.42}$$

Based on the data in Table 3.13, the decomposition equation is given by

$$0.090 = 0.161 + 0.010 - 0.081.$$

Or in percentage terms,

$$100\% = 179\% + 11\% - 90\%.$$

This result shows that regional inequality in per capita GDP is attributable mainly to regional inequality in labor productivity. This result is reasonable because labor participation rate ranges between 0 and 1 and thus regional inequality in labor participation rate should be much smaller than regional inequality in labor productivity. On the other hand, a negative value of the residual term indicates that we have $-1 < \frac{\mathrm{cov}(\boldsymbol{l},\boldsymbol{x})}{\mu_x\mu_l} < 0$. There is a negative relationship between labor productivity and labor participation rate, meaning that a region with higher labor productivity tends to have a smaller labor participation rate.

We should note that Cheng and Li (2006) rectified Duro and Esteban's (1998) method, which employed the population-weighted Theil L index to measure regional inequality in per capita GDP.

$$L_y^* = \sum_{i=1}^{n}\frac{N_i}{N}\ln\left(\frac{\mu_y^*}{y_i}\right) = \sum_{i=1}^{n}\frac{N_i}{N}\ln\left(\frac{Y/N}{Y_i/N_i}\right). \tag{3.43}$$

where Y and N are GDP and population in a country, respectively. In Eq. (3.43), $\mu_y^* = Y/N$ is the population-weighted average of per capita GDP (or per capita GDP for the country), since we have

$$\mu_y^* = \frac{Y}{N} = \sum_{i=1}^{n}\frac{Y_i}{N} = \sum_{i=1}^{n}\left(\frac{N_i}{N}\right)\left(\frac{Y_i}{N_i}\right) = \sum_{i=1}^{n}\left(\frac{N_i}{N}\right)y_i.$$

This differs from the simple average per capita GDP defined by $\mu_y = \frac{1}{n}\sum_{i=1}^{n} y_i$. We have, in general, $\mu_y^* \neq \mu_y$. Using the data in Table 3.13, we obtain $\mu_y^* = 5{,}000/180 = 27.78$, which is larger than $\mu_y = 24.92$.

Now, we let $p_i = \frac{N_i}{N}$ be the population share of region i. Equation (3.43) is rewritten as

$$L_y^* = \sum_{i=1}^{n} p_i \ln\left(\frac{\mu_y^*}{y_i}\right). \tag{3.44}$$

If we let $\mu_x^* = Y/_L$ and $\mu_l^* = L/_N$ be labor productivity and labor participation rate for the country, respectively, Eq. (3.44) is modified as

$$L_y^* = \sum_{i=1}^{n} p_i \ln\left(\frac{\mu_x^*}{x_i}\frac{\mu_l^*}{l_i}\right) = \sum_{i=1}^{n} p_i \ln\left(\frac{\mu_x^*}{x_i}\right) + \sum_{i=1}^{n} p_i \ln\left(\frac{\mu_l^*}{l_i}\right) \tag{3.45}$$

since $y_i = x_i l_i$ and $\mu_y^* = \mu_x^* \mu_l^*$. In Eq. (3.45), there is no residual term. However, the first term on the right-hand side of Eq. (3.45) is not the Theil L index because we have

$$\sum_{i=1}^{n} p_i \ln\left(\frac{\mu_x^*}{x_i}\right) = \sum_{i=1}^{n} \frac{N_i}{N} \ln\left(\frac{Y/_L}{Y_i/_{L_i}}\right) = \sum_{i=1}^{n} \frac{N_i}{N} \ln\left(\frac{L_i/_L}{Y_i/_Y}\right). \tag{3.46}$$

In Eq. (3.46), the weight given in front of the natural logarithm is not the labor share of region i but the population share of region i. For Eq. (3.46) to be the Theil L index for regional inequality in labor productivity, the weight (population share) must be replaced by the numerator inside the natural logarithm (labor share) (Gisbert, 2001). On the other hand, the second term of Eq. (3.45) is the Theil L index for regional inequality in labor participation rate, because we have

$$\sum_{i=1}^{n} p_i \ln\left(\frac{\mu_l^*}{l_i}\right) = \sum_{i=1}^{n} \frac{N_i}{N} \ln\left(\frac{L/_N}{L_i/_{N_i}}\right) = \sum_{i=1}^{n} \frac{N_i}{N} \ln\left(\frac{N_i/_N}{L_i/_L}\right). \tag{3.47}$$

In this equation, the weight given before the natural logarithm (population share) is the same as the numerator inside the natural logarithm.

Appendix 1: Decomposition of the Squared Coefficient of Variation by Regions (Eq. 3.2)

Suppose that a country is divided into m regions and region i contains p_i provinces. Let y_{ij} and μ be, respectively, GDP per capita of province j in region i and the simple average of GDP per capita for all provinces. Then, the squared coefficient of variation can be decomposed into the within-region and between-region inequality components as follows.

$$\begin{aligned}CV^2 &= \frac{1}{\mu^2}\frac{1}{p}\sum_{i=1}^{m}\sum_{j=1}^{p_i}\left(y_{ij}-\mu\right)^2\\&= \frac{1}{\mu^2}\frac{1}{p}\sum_{i=1}^{m}\sum_{j=1}^{p_i}\left[\left(y_{ij}-\mu_i\right)+\left(\mu_i-\mu\right)\right]^2\\&= \frac{1}{\mu^2}\frac{1}{p}\sum_{i=1}^{m}\sum_{j=1}^{p_i}\left[\left(y_{ij}-\mu_i\right)^2+2\left(\mu_i-\mu\right)\left(y_{ij}-\mu_i\right)+\left(\mu_i-\mu\right)^2\right]\\&= \frac{1}{\mu^2}\frac{1}{p}\sum_{i=1}^{m}\sum_{j=1}^{p_i}\left(y_{ij}-\mu_i\right)^2+\frac{1}{\mu^2}\frac{1}{p}\sum_{i=1}^{m}\sum_{j=1}^{p_i}2\left(\mu_i-\mu\right)\left(y_{ij}-\mu_i\right)\\&\quad+\frac{1}{\mu^2}\frac{1}{p}\sum_{i=1}^{m}\sum_{j=1}^{p_i}\left(\mu_i-\mu\right)^2.\end{aligned}$$

Now, the second term of this equation is modified as follows.

$$\begin{aligned}\frac{1}{\mu^2}\frac{1}{p}\sum_{i=1}^{m}\sum_{j=1}^{p_i}2\left(\mu_i-\mu\right)\left(y_{ij}-\mu_i\right) &= \frac{1}{\mu^2}\frac{1}{p}\sum_{i=1}^{m}2\left(\mu_i-\mu\right)\sum_{j=1}^{p_i}\left(y_{ij}-\mu_i\right)\\&= \frac{1}{\mu^2}\frac{1}{p}\sum_{i=1}^{m}2\left(\mu_i-\mu\right)\left(\sum_{j=1}^{p_i}y_{ij}-p_i\mu_i\right).\end{aligned}$$

Since, by definition, $\mu_i=\frac{1}{p_i}\sum_{j=1}^{p_i}y_{ij}$ or $p_i\mu_i=\sum_{j=1}^{p_i}y_{ij}$, we have $\sum_{j=1}^{p_i}y_{ij}-p_i\mu_i=0$. Therefore, the second term vanishes. We now have the following decomposition equation.

$$\begin{aligned}CV^2 &= \frac{1}{\mu^2}\frac{1}{p}\sum_{i=1}^{m}\sum_{j=1}^{p_i}\left(y_{ij}-\mu_i\right)^2+\frac{1}{\mu^2}\frac{1}{p}\sum_{i=1}^{m}\sum_{j=1}^{p_i}\left(\mu_i-\mu\right)^2\\&= \sum_{i=1}^{m}\frac{p_i}{p}\left(\frac{\mu_i}{\mu}\right)^2CV_i^2+\frac{1}{\mu^2}\sum_{i=1}^{m}\frac{p_i}{p}\left(\mu_i-\mu\right)^2=CV_W^2+CV_B^2, \qquad (3.48)\end{aligned}$$

where $CV_i^2=\frac{1}{p_i}\frac{1}{(\mu_i)^2}\sum_{j=1}^{p_i}\left(y_{ij}-\mu_i\right)^2$.

$CV_W^2=\sum_{i=1}^{m}\frac{p_i}{p}\left(\frac{\mu_i}{\mu}\right)^2CV_i^2$ is the within-region inequality component, while $CV_B^2=\frac{1}{\mu^2}\sum_{i=1}^{m}\frac{p_i}{p}\left(\mu_i-\mu\right)^2$ is the between-region inequality component.

Appendix 2: Decomposition of the Squared Coefficient of Variation by GDP Components (Eqs. 3.9 and 3.10)

Suppose that total GDP consists of K components. Let y_{ijk} and μ_{ik} be, respectively, GDP per capita for sector k of province j in region i and the simple average of GDP per capita for sector k in region i where $y_{ij}=\sum_{k=1}^{K}y_{ijk}$ and $\mu_i=\sum_{k=1}^{K}\mu_{ik}$. Then, the squared coefficient of variation for region i can be decomposed by GDP components as follows.

$$\begin{aligned} CV_i^2 &= \frac{1}{(\mu_i)^2}\frac{1}{p_i}\sum\nolimits_{j=1}^{p_i}(y_{ij}-\mu_i)^2 \\ &= \frac{1}{(\mu_i)^2}\frac{1}{p_i}\sum\nolimits_{j=1}^{p_i}\sum\nolimits_{k=1}^{K}(y_{ijk}-\mu_{ik})(y_{ij}-\mu_i) \\ &= \sum\nolimits_{k=1}^{K}\left(\frac{\mu_{ik}}{\mu_i}\right)\left(\frac{1}{\mu_{ik}\mu_i}\right)\left[\frac{1}{p_i}\sum\nolimits_{j=1}^{p_i}(y_{ijk}-\mu_{ik})(y_{ij}-\mu_i)\right] \\ &= \sum\nolimits_{k=1}^{K}v_{ik}\left(\frac{\text{cov}_{ik}}{\mu_{ik}\mu_i}\right), \end{aligned} \tag{3.49}$$

where $\mu_{ik} = \frac{1}{p_i}\sum_{j=1}^{p_i} y_{ijk}$. In Eq. (3.49), $v_{ik} = \frac{\mu_{ik}}{\mu_i}$ is the share of industrial sector k in region i in terms of GDP per capita and $\text{cov}_{ik} = \frac{1}{p_i}\sum_{j=1}^{p_i}(y_{ijk}-\mu_{ik})(y_{ij}-\mu_i)$ is the covariance between GDP component k and total GDP in region i.

Similarly, the squared coefficient of variation for the between-region inequality can be decomposed by GDP components as follows.

$$CV_B^2 = \frac{1}{\mu^2}\sum\nolimits_{i=1}^{m}\frac{p_i}{p}(\mu_i-\mu)^2 = \sum\nolimits_{k=1}^{K}v_k\left(\frac{\text{cov}_k}{\mu_{\cdot k}\mu}\right), \tag{3.50}$$

where $\mu_{\cdot k} = \frac{1}{p}\sum_{i=1}^{m}\sum_{j=1}^{p_i} y_{ijk} = \sum_{i=1}^{m}\frac{p_i}{p}\mu_{ik}$ is the simple average of sector k's GDP per capita for all provinces. In Eq. (3.50), $v_k = \frac{\mu_{\cdot k}}{\mu}$ is the share of industrial sector k in the country in terms of GDP per capita while $\text{cov}_k = \sum_{i=1}^{m}\frac{p_i}{p}(\mu_{ik}-\mu_{\cdot k})(\mu_i-\mu)$ is the covariance between GDP component k and total GDP in the country. We should note that we have $\mu = \sum_{k=1}^{K}\mu_{\cdot k} = \sum_{k=1}^{K}\sum_{i=1}^{m}\frac{p_i}{p}\mu_{ik} = \sum_{i=1}^{m}\frac{p_i}{p}\mu_i$ since $\mu_i = \sum_{k=1}^{K}\mu_{ik}$.

Appendix 3: Bidimensional Inequality Decomposition Equation based on the Squared Coefficient of Variation (Eq. 3.13)

Substituting Eqs. (3.49) and (3.50) into Eq. (3.48), we can obtain the following bidimensional inequality decomposition equation based on the squared coefficient of variation.

$$CV^2 = \sum\nolimits_{i=1}^{m}\frac{p_i}{p}\left(\frac{\mu_i}{\mu}\right)^2\left[\sum\nolimits_{k=1}^{K}v_{ik}\left(\frac{\text{cov}_{ik}}{\mu_{ik}\mu_i}\right)\right] + \sum\nolimits_{k=1}^{K}v_k\left(\frac{\text{cov}_k}{\mu_{\cdot k}\mu}\right). \tag{3.51}$$

Dividing Eq. (3.51) by CV^2 yields

$$1 = \sum_{i=1}^{m} \sum_{k=1}^{K} c_{ik} + \sum_{k=1}^{K} c_{k}. \tag{3.52}$$

In Eq. (3.52),

$$c_{ik} = v_{ik} \frac{p_i}{p} \left(\frac{\mu_i}{\mu} \right)^2 \left(\frac{\mathrm{cov}_{ik}}{\mu_{ik} \mu_i} \right) / CV^2 \text{ and } c_k = v_k \left(\frac{\mathrm{cov}_k}{\mu_{\cdot k} \mu} \right) / CV^2$$

c_{ik} is the contribution of region i's inter-provincial inequality for sector k to overall inter-provincial inequality and c_k is the contribution of between-region inequality for sector k to overall inter-provincial inequality. Since the country consists of m regions and K industrial sectors, there are $(m + 1) \times k$ components in Eq. (3.52).

Appendix 4: Bidimensional Inequality Decomposition Equation based on the Population-weighted Coefficient of Variation (Eq. 3.16)

Let N, N_{ij}, y, and y_{ij} be, respectively, population of the whole country, population of province j in region i, GDP per capita of the whole country, and GDP per capita of province j in region i. Then, by the squared population-weighted coefficient of variation, overall income inequality can be measured by

$$WCV^2 = \frac{1}{y^2} \sum_{i=1}^{m} \sum_{j=1}^{p_i} \frac{N_{ij}}{N} \left(y_{ij} - y \right)^2, \tag{3.53}$$

where $y = \frac{1}{N} \sum_{i=1}^{m} \sum_{j=1}^{p_i} N_{ij} y_{ij}$.

Next, let y_i be GDP per capita of region i where $y_i = \frac{1}{N_i} \sum_{j=1}^{p_i} N_{ij} y_{ij}$. Then, WCV^2 in Eq. (3.53) can be modified as follows.

$$\begin{aligned} WCV^2 &= \frac{1}{y^2} \sum_{i=1}^{m} \sum_{j=1}^{p_i} \frac{N_{ij}}{N} \left[\left(y_{ij} - y_i \right) + \left(y_i - y \right) \right]^2 \\ &= \frac{1}{y^2} \sum_{i=1}^{m} \sum_{j=1}^{p_i} \frac{N_{ij}}{N} \\ &\quad \times \left[\left(y_{ij} - y_i \right)^2 + 2 \left(y_i - y \right) \left(y_{ij} - y_i \right) + \left(y_i - y \right)^2 \right] \\ &= \frac{1}{y^2} \sum_{i=1}^{m} \sum_{j=1}^{p_i} \frac{N_{ij}}{N} \left(y_{ij} - y_i \right)^2 + \frac{1}{y^2} \sum_{i=1}^{m} \sum_{j=1}^{p_i} 2 \frac{N_{ij}}{N} \left(y_i - y \right) \\ &\quad \times \left(y_{ij} - y_i \right) + \frac{1}{y^2} \sum_{i=1}^{m} \sum_{j=1}^{p_i} \frac{N_{ij}}{N} \left(y_i - y \right)^2. \end{aligned} \tag{3.54}$$

If we let N_i be population of region i, then the second term of Eq. (3.54) will be

$$\frac{1}{.y^2}\sum_{i=1}^{m}\sum_{j=1}^{p_i}2\frac{N_{ij}}{N}(y_i-y)(y_{ij}-y_i)=\frac{1}{y^2}\sum_{i=1}^{m}\frac{2}{N}(y_i-y)\sum_{j=1}^{p_i}N_{ij}(y_{ij}-y_i)$$
$$=\frac{1}{y^2}\sum_{i=1}^{m}\frac{2}{N}(y_i-y)$$
$$\times\left(\sum_{j=1}^{p_i}N_{ij}y_{ij}-y_i\sum_{j=1}^{p_i}N_{ij}\right)$$
$$=\frac{1}{y^2}\sum_{i=1}^{m}2(y_i-y)\frac{1}{N}$$
$$\times\left(\sum_{j=1}^{p_i}N_{ij}y_{ij}-N_iy_i\right).$$

Since $y_i=\frac{1}{N_i}\sum_{j=1}^{p_i}N_{ij}y_{ij}$ or $N_iy_i=\sum_{j=1}^{p_i}N_{ij}y_{ij}$, we have $\sum_{j=1}^{p_i}N_{ij}y_{ij}-N_iy_i=0$. Thus, the second term vanishes and Eq. (3.54) can be modified as follows.

$$WCV^2=\frac{1}{y^2}\sum_{i=1}^{m}\sum_{j=1}^{p_i}\frac{N_{ij}}{N}(y_{ij}-y_i)^2+\frac{1}{y^2}\sum_{i=1}^{m}\sum_{j=1}^{p_i}\frac{N_{ij}}{N}(y_i-y)^2$$
$$=\sum_{i=1}^{m}\frac{N_i}{N}\left(\frac{y_i}{y}\right)^2\left[\frac{1}{y_i^2}\sum_{j=1}^{p_i}\frac{N_{ij}}{N_i}(y_{ij}-y_i)^2\right]$$
$$+\frac{1}{y^2}\sum_{i=1}^{m}\frac{1}{N}(y_i-y)^2\sum_{j=1}^{p_i}N_{ij}$$
$$=\sum_{i=1}^{m}\frac{N_i}{N}\left(\frac{y_i}{y}\right)^2WCV_i^2+\frac{1}{y^2}\sum_{i=1}^{m}\frac{N_i}{N}(y_i-y)^2$$
$$=WCV_W^2+WCV_B^2, \tag{3.55}$$

where $WCV_i^2=\frac{1}{y_i^2}\sum_{j=1}^{p_i}\frac{N_{ij}}{N_i}(y_{ij}-y_i)^2$ is the squared population-weighted coefficient of variation for region i. In Eq. (3.55), $WCV_W^2=\sum_{i=1}^{m}\frac{N_i}{N}\left(\frac{y_i}{y}\right)^2WCV_i^2$ is the within-region inequality component, while $WCV_B^2=\frac{1}{y^2}\sum_{i=1}^{m}\frac{N_i}{N}(y_i-y)^2$ is the between-region inequality component.

Suppose next that total GDP consists of K GDP components. Let y_{ijk} and y_{ik} be, respectively, GDP per capita for sector k of province j in region i and GDP per capita for sector k of region i, where $y_{ik}=\sum_{j=1}^{p_i}\frac{N_{ij}}{N_i}y_{ijk}$. Since we have $y_{ij}=\sum_{k=1}^{K}y_{ijk}$ and $y_i=\sum_{k=1}^{K}y_{ik}$, WCV_i^2 can be decomposed by GDP components as follows.

$$\begin{aligned} WCV_i^2 &= \frac{1}{y_i^2}\sum\nolimits_{j=1}^{p_i}\frac{N_{ij}}{N_i}\left(y_{ij}-y_i\right)^2 \\ &= \frac{1}{y_i^2}\sum\nolimits_{j=1}^{p_i}\frac{N_{ij}}{N_i}\sum\nolimits_{k=1}^{K}\left(y_{ijk}-y_{ik}\right)\left(y_{ij}-y_i\right) \\ &= \sum\nolimits_{k=1}^{K}\left(\frac{y_{ik}}{y_i}\right)\left(\frac{1}{y_{ik}y_i}\right)\left[\sum\nolimits_{j=1}^{p_i}\frac{N_{ij}}{N_i}\left(y_{ijk}-y_{ik}\right)\left(y_{ij}-y_i\right)\right] \\ &= \sum\nolimits_{k=1}^{K}w_{ik}\left(\frac{\text{wcov}_{ik}}{y_{ik}y_i}\right). \end{aligned} \tag{3.56}$$

In Eq. (3.56), $w_{ik} = \frac{y_{ik}}{y_i}$ is the GDP share of industrial sector k in region i and $\text{wcov}_{ik} = \sum\nolimits_{j=1}^{p_i}\frac{N_{ij}}{N_i}\left(y_{ijk}-y_{ik}\right)\left(y_{ij}-y_i\right)$ is the population-weighted covariance between GDP component k and total GDP in region i.

Similarly, the squared population-weighted coefficient of variation for the between-region inequality can be decomposed by GDP components as follows.

$$WCV_B^2 = \frac{1}{y^2}\sum\nolimits_{i=1}^{m}\frac{N_i}{N}(y_i-y)^2 = \sum\nolimits_{k=1}^{K}w_k\left(\frac{\text{wcov}_k}{y_{\cdot k}y}\right), \tag{3.57}$$

where $y_{\cdot k} = \sum\nolimits_{i=1}^{m}\sum\nolimits_{j=1}^{p_i}\frac{N_{ij}}{N}y_{ijk} = \sum\nolimits_{i=1}^{m}\frac{N_i}{N}y_{ik}$ is GDP per capita for sector k of the country. In Eq. (3.57), $w_k = \frac{y_{\cdot k}}{y}$ is the GDP share of industrial sector k in the country while $\text{wcov}_k = \sum\nolimits_{i=1}^{m}\frac{N_i}{N}(y_{ik}-y_{\cdot k})(y_i-y)$ is the population-weighted covariance between GDP component k and total GDP in the country.

Substituting Eqs. (3.56) and (3.57) into Eq. (3.55), we can obtain the following bidimensional inequality decomposition equation based on the population-weighted coefficient of variation.

$$WCV^2 = \sum\nolimits_{i=1}^{m}\frac{N_i}{N}\left(\frac{y_i}{y}\right)^2\left[\sum\nolimits_{k=1}^{K}w_{ik}\left(\frac{\text{wcov}_{ik}}{y_{ik}y_i}\right)\right] + \sum\nolimits_{k=1}^{K}w_k\left(\frac{\text{wcov}_k}{y_{\cdot k}y}\right). \tag{3.58}$$

Since the country consists of m regions and K industrial sectors, there are $(m + 1) \times k$ components in Eq. (3.58).

Appendix 5: Sectoral Inequality Decomposition Equation (Eqs. 3.22 and 3.25)

Suppose that a country comprises p provinces. Let y_i and μ be, respectively, GDP per capita of province i and the simple average of GDP per capita for all provinces. Then, by the squared coefficient of variation, overall inter-provincial inequality in GDP per capita can be measured by

$$CV^2 = \frac{1}{\mu^2}\frac{1}{p}\sum\nolimits_{i=1}^{p}(y_i - \mu)^2. \tag{3.59}$$

Suppose next that total GDP consists of K GDP components. Let y_{ik} and μ_k be, respectively, GDP per capita for sector k of province i and the simple average of GDP per capita for sector k in the country, where $y_i = \sum_{k=1}^{K} y_{ik}$ and $\mu = \sum_{k=1}^{K} \mu_k$. Then, the squared coefficient of variation can be decomposed by GDP components as follows.

$$\begin{aligned}
CV^2 &= \frac{1}{\mu^2}\frac{1}{p}\sum\nolimits_{i=1}^{p}(y_i - \mu)^2 \\
&= \frac{1}{\mu^2}\frac{1}{p}\sum\nolimits_{i=1}^{p}[(y_{i1} - \mu_1) + (y_{i2} - \mu_2) + \cdots + (y_{iK} - \mu_K)]^2 \\
&= \frac{1}{\mu^2}\frac{1}{p}\sum\nolimits_{i=1}^{p}\sum\nolimits_{k=1}^{K}\left[(y_{ik} - \mu_k)^2 + \sum_{j\neq k}(y_{ik} - \mu_k)(y_{ij} - \mu_j)\right] \\
&= \sum\nolimits_{k=1}^{K}\left(\frac{\mu_k^2}{\mu^2}\right)\left(\frac{1}{\mu_k^2}\frac{1}{p}\sum\nolimits_{i=1}^{p}(y_{ik} - \mu_k)^2\right) + \sum\nolimits_{k=1}^{K}\sum_{j\neq k}\left(\frac{\mu_k}{\mu}\right)\left(\frac{\mu_j}{\mu}\right) \\
&\quad \times \left(\frac{1}{\mu_k\mu_j}\frac{1}{p}\sum\nolimits_{i=1}^{p}(y_{ik} - \mu_k)(y_{ij} - \mu_j)\right) \\
&= \sum\nolimits_{k=1}^{K} v_k^2 CV_k^2 + \sum\nolimits_{k=1}^{K}\sum_{j\neq k} v_k v_j COV_{kj}.
\end{aligned} \tag{3.60}$$

In this equation, $v_k = \frac{\mu_k}{\mu}$ and $v_j = \frac{\mu_j}{\mu}$ are, respectively, the shares of components k and j in terms of GDP per capita. On the other hand, $CV_k^2 = \frac{1}{\mu_k^2}\frac{1}{p}\sum_{i=1}^{p}(y_{ik} - \mu_k)^2$ is the squared coefficient of variation for GDP component k, while $COV_{kj} = \frac{1}{\mu_k\mu_j}\frac{1}{p}\sum_{i=1}^{p}(y_{ik} - \mu_k)(y_{ij} - \mu_j)$ is the coefficient of covariation between GDP components k and j.

When total GDP consists of three components, then Eq. (3.60) is written as

$$\begin{aligned}
CV^2 = v_1^2 CV_1^2 + v_2^2 CV_2^2 + v_3^2 CV_3^2 + 2v_1v_2COV_{12} + 2v_1v_3COV_{13} \\
+ 2v_2v_3COV_{23}.
\end{aligned} \tag{3.61}$$

In the decomposition equation given by Eq. (3.60), the squared coefficient of variation is used. We now develop a similar decomposition equation by the squared population-weighted coefficient of variation. Let N, N_i, y, and y_i be, respectively, population of the whole country, population of province i, GDP per capita of the country, and GDP per capita of province i. Then, by the squared population-weighted coefficient of variation, overall income inequality can be measured by

$$WCV^2 = \frac{1}{y^2}\sum_{i=1}^{p}\frac{N_i}{N}(y_i - y)^2, \tag{3.62}$$

where $y = \frac{1}{N}\sum_{i=1}^{p} N_i y_i$.

Suppose next that total GDP consists of K GDP components. Let y_{ik} and $y_{\cdot k}$ be, respectively, GDP per capita for sector k of province i and GDP per capita for sector k in the country, where $y_{\cdot k} = \frac{1}{N}\sum_{i=1}^{p} N_i y_{ik}$. Since we have $y_i = \sum_{k=1}^{K} y_{ik}$ and $y = \sum_{k=1}^{K} y_{\cdot k}$, WCV^2 in Eq. (3.62) can be decomposed by GDP components as follows.

$$\begin{aligned}
WCV^2 &= \frac{1}{y^2}\sum_{i=1}^{p}\frac{N_i}{N}(y_i - y)^2 \\
&= \frac{1}{y^2}\sum_{i=1}^{p}\frac{N_i}{N}\left[(y_{i1} - y_{\cdot 1}) + (y_{i2} - y_{\cdot 2}) + \cdots + (y_{iK} - y_{\cdot K})\right]^2 \\
&= \frac{1}{y^2}\sum_{i=1}^{p}\frac{N_i}{N}\sum_{k=1}^{K}\left[(y_{ik} - y_{\cdot k})^2 + \sum_{j \neq k}(y_{ik} - y_{\cdot k})(y_{ij} - y_{\cdot j})\right] \\
&= \sum_{k=1}^{K}\left(\frac{y_{\cdot k}^2}{y^2}\right)\left(\frac{1}{y_{\cdot k}^2}\sum_{i=1}^{p}\frac{N_i}{N}(y_{ik} - y_{\cdot k})^2\right) \\
&\quad + \sum_{k=1}^{K}\sum_{j \neq k}\left(\frac{y_{\cdot k}}{y}\right)\left(\frac{y_{\cdot j}}{y}\right) \\
&\quad \times \left(\frac{1}{y_{\cdot k} y_{\cdot j}}\sum_{i=1}^{p}\frac{N_i}{N}(y_{ik} - y_{\cdot k})(y_{ij} - y_{\cdot j})\right) \\
&= \sum_{k=1}^{K} w_k^2 WCV_k^2 + \sum_{k=1}^{K}\sum_{j \neq k} w_k w_j WCOV_{kj}
\end{aligned} \tag{3.63}$$

In this equation, $w_k = \frac{y_{\cdot k}}{y}$ and $w_j = \frac{y_{\cdot j}}{y}$ are, respectively, the GDP shares of components k and j. On the other hand, $WCV_k^2 = \frac{1}{y_{\cdot k}^2}\sum_{i=1}^{p}\frac{N_i}{N}(y_{ik} - y_{\cdot k})^2$ is the squared population-weighted coefficient of variation for GDP component k, while $WCOV_{kj} = \frac{1}{y_{\cdot k} y_{\cdot j}}\sum_{i=1}^{p}\frac{N_i}{N}(y_{ik} - y_{\cdot k})(y_{ij} - y_{\cdot j})$ is the population-weighted coefficient of covariation between GDP components k and j.

When total GDP consists of three components, then Eq. (3.63) is written as

$$\begin{aligned}
WCV^2 = {} & w_1^2 WCV_1^2 + w_2^2 WCV_2^2 + w_3^2 WCV_3^2 + 2w_1 w_2 WCOV_{12} \\
& + 2w_1 w_3 WCOV_{13} + 2w_2 w_3 \mathrm{WCOV}_{23}.
\end{aligned} \tag{3.64}$$

Appendix 6: Decomposition of Theil T by Region (Eqs. 3.29, 3.30, and 3.31)

Let N and Y be, respectively, the population and GDP of the country and let N_{ijk} and Y_{ijk} be, respectively, the population and GDP of district k in province j of region i. Then, using the Theil T index, overall income inequality is measured by

$$T = \sum_i \sum_j \sum_k \frac{Y_{ijk}}{Y} \ln\left(\frac{Y_{ijk}/Y}{N_{ijk}/N}\right). \tag{3.65}$$

Suppose next that Y_i and N_i are the GDP and population of region i, respectively. Then, overall income inequality, as measured by Eq. (3.65), is decomposed into the within-region and between-region inequality components as follows.

$$\begin{aligned}
T &= \sum_i \sum_j \sum_k \left(\frac{Y_i}{Y}\right)\left(\frac{Y_{ijk}}{Y_i}\right)\left[\ln\left(\frac{Y_{ijk}/Y_i}{N_{ijk}/N_i}\right) + \ln\left(\frac{Y_i/Y}{N_i/N}\right)\right] \\
&= \sum_i \sum_j \sum_k \left(\frac{Y_i}{Y}\right)\left(\frac{Y_{ijk}}{Y_i}\right) \ln\left(\frac{Y_{ijk}/Y_i}{N_{ijk}/N_i}\right) + \sum_i \sum_j \sum_k \left(\frac{Y_i}{Y}\right) \\
&\quad \times \left(\frac{Y_{ijk}}{Y_i}\right) \ln\left(\frac{Y_i/Y}{N_i/N}\right) \\
&= \sum_i \left(\frac{Y_i}{Y}\right)\left[\sum_j \sum_k \left(\frac{Y_{ijk}}{Y_i}\right) \ln\left(\frac{Y_{ijk}/Y_i}{N_{ijk}/N_i}\right)\right] \\
&\quad + \left[\sum_i \left(\frac{Y_i}{Y}\right) \ln\left(\frac{Y_i/Y}{N_i/N}\right)\right] \sum_j \sum_k \left(\frac{Y_{ijk}}{Y_i}\right) \\
&= \sum_i \left(\frac{Y_i}{Y}\right)\left[\sum_j \sum_k \left(\frac{Y_{ijk}}{Y_i}\right) \ln\left(\frac{Y_{ijk}/Y_i}{N_{ijk}/N_i}\right)\right] + \sum_i \left(\frac{Y_i}{Y}\right) \ln\left(\frac{Y_i/Y}{N_i/N}\right) \\
&= \sum_i \left(\frac{Y_i}{Y}\right) T_{di} + T_{BR}
\end{aligned} \tag{3.66}$$

since $\sum_j \sum_k Y_{ijk} = Y_i$ and thus $\sum_j \sum_k \left(\frac{Y_{ijk}}{Y_i}\right) = 1$. $T_{di} = \sum_j \sum_k \frac{Y_{ijk}}{Y_i} \ln\left(\frac{Y_{ijk}/Y_i}{N_{ijk}/N_i}\right)$ is income inequality within region i, while $T_{BR} = \sum_i \frac{Y_i}{Y} \ln\left(\frac{Y_i/Y}{N_i/N}\right)$ is income inequality between regions (between-region inequality component).

Suppose next that Y_{ij} and N_{ij} are the GDP and population of province j in region i, respectively. Then, income inequality within region i can be further decomposed into the within-province and between-province inequality components as follows.

$$
\begin{aligned}
T_{di} &= \sum_j \sum_k \left(\frac{Y_{ij}}{Y_i}\right)\left(\frac{Y_{ijk}}{Y_{ij}}\right)\left[\ln\left(\frac{Y_{ijk}/Y_{ij}}{N_{ijk}/N_{ij}}\right) + \ln\left(\frac{Y_{ij}/Y_i}{N_{ij}/N_i}\right)\right] \\
&= \sum_j \sum_k \left(\frac{Y_{ij}}{Y_i}\right)\left(\frac{Y_{ijk}}{Y_{ij}}\right)\ln\left(\frac{Y_{ijk}/Y_{ij}}{N_{ijk}/N_{ij}}\right) + \sum_j \sum_k \left(\frac{Y_{ij}}{Y_i}\right)\left(\frac{Y_{ijk}}{Y_{ij}}\right)\ln\left(\frac{Y_{ij}/Y_i}{N_{ij}/N_i}\right) \\
&= \sum_j \left(\frac{Y_{ij}}{Y_i}\right)\left[\sum_k \left(\frac{Y_{ijk}}{Y_{ij}}\right)\ln\left(\frac{Y_{ijk}/Y_{ij}}{N_{ijk}/N_{ij}}\right)\right] \\
&\quad + \left[\sum_j \left(\frac{Y_{ij}}{Y_i}\right)\ln\left(\frac{Y_{ij}/Y_i}{N_{ij}/N_i}\right)\right]\sum_k \left(\frac{Y_{ijk}}{Y_{ij}}\right) \\
&= \sum_j \left(\frac{Y_{ij}}{Y_i}\right)\left[\sum_k \left(\frac{Y_{ijk}}{Y_{ij}}\right)\ln\left(\frac{Y_{ijk}/Y_{ij}}{N_{ijk}/N_{ij}}\right)\right] + \left[\sum_j \left(\frac{Y_{ij}}{Y_i}\right)\ln\left(\frac{Y_{ij}/Y_i}{N_{ij}/N_i}\right)\right] \\
&= \sum_j \left(\frac{Y_{ij}}{Y_i}\right) T_{ij} + T_{pi},
\end{aligned} \tag{3.67}
$$

since $\sum_k Y_{ijk} = Y_{ij}$ and thus $\sum_k \left(\frac{Y_{ijk}}{Y_{ij}}\right) = 1$. $T_{ij} = \sum_k \frac{Y_{ijk}}{Y_{ij}} \ln\left(\frac{Y_{ijk}/Y_{ij}}{N_{ijk}/N_{ij}}\right)$ is income inequality within province j in region i (within-province income inequality of province j in region i), while $T_{pi} = \sum_j \frac{Y_{ij}}{Y_i} \ln\left(\frac{Y_{ij}/Y_i}{N_{ij}/N_i}\right)$ is income inequality between provinces in region i.

By substituting Eq. (3.67) into Eq. (3.66), we obtain the following two-stage nested Theil decomposition equation.

$$
\begin{aligned}
T &= \sum_i \left(\frac{Y_i}{Y}\right) T_{di} + T_{BR} = \sum_i \left(\frac{Y_i}{Y}\right)\left(\sum_j \left(\frac{Y_{ij}}{Y_i}\right) T_{ij} + T_{pi}\right) + T_{BR} \\
&= \sum_i \sum_j \left(\frac{Y_{ij}}{Y}\right) T_{ij} + \sum_i \left(\frac{Y_i}{Y}\right) T_{pi} + T_{BR} = T_{WP} + T_{BP} + T_{BR}.
\end{aligned} \tag{3.68}
$$

$T_{WP} = \sum_i \sum_j \left(\frac{Y_{ij}}{Y}\right) T_{ij}$ is the within-province inequality component, which is a weighted-average of within-province income inequalities. On the other hand, $T_{BP} = \sum_i \left(\frac{Y_i}{Y}\right) T_{pi}$ is the between-province inequality component, which is a weighted average of between-province income inequalities, while T_{BR} is the between-region inequality component.

References

Akita, T. (2003). Decomposing regional income inequality in China and Indonesia using two-stage nested Theil decomposition method. *The Annals of Regional Science, 37*(1), 55–77.

Akita, T., & Alisjahbana, A. S. (2002). Regional income inequality in Indonesia and the initial impact of the economic crisis. *Bulletin of Indonesian Economic Studies, 38*(2), 201–222.

Akita, T., Kurniawan, P. A., & Miyata, S. (2011). Structural changes and regional income inequality in Indonesia: A bi-dimensional decomposition analysis. *Asian Economic Journal, 25*(1), 55–77.81.

Akita, T., & Lukman, R. A. (1995). Interregional inequalities in Indonesia: A sectoral decomposition analysis for 1975–92. *Bulletin of Indonesian Economic Studies, 31*, 61.

Akita, T., & Miyata, S. (2010). The bi-dimensional decomposition of regional inequality based on the weighted coefficient of variation. *Letters in Spatial and Resource Sciences, 3*(3), 91–100.

Akita, T., & Miyata, S. (2018). Spatial inequalities in Indonesia. 1996-2010: A hierarchical decomposition analysis. *Social Indicators Research, 138*(3), 829–852.

Alisjahbana, A., & Akita, T. (2020). Economic tertiarization and regional income inequality in a decentralized Indonesia: A bi-dimensional inequality decomposition analysis. *Social Indicators Research, 151*, 51–80.

Cheng, Y. S., & Li, S. K. (2006). Income inequality and efficiency: A decomposition approach and applications to China. *Economics Letters, 91*(1), 8–14.

Duro, J. A., & Esteban, J. (1998). Factor decomposition of cross-country income inequality, 1960-1990. *Economics Letters, 60*(3), 269–275.

Gisbert, F. J. G. (2001). On factor decomposition of cross-country income inequality: some extensions and qualifications. *Economics Letters, 70*(3), 303–309.

Kataoka, M. (2018). Inequality convergence in inefficiency and interprovincial income inequality in Indonesia for 1990–2010. *Asia-Pacific Journal of Regional Science, 2*(2), 297–313.

Kataoka, M. (2019). Interprovincial differences in labor force distribution and utilization based on educational attainment in Indonesia, 2002–2015. *Regional Science Policy & Practice, 11*(1), 39–54.

Paredes, D., Iturra, V., & Lufin, M. (2014). A spatial decomposition of income inequality in Chile. *Regional Studies, 50*(5), 771–789.

Wu, D., Yuan, L., Li, R., & Li, J. (2018). Decomposing inequality in research funding by university-institute sub-group: A three-stage nested Theil index. *Journal of Informetrics, 12*, 1312–1326.

Part II
Analysis of Regional Inequality: Applications

Chapter 4
Economic Tertialization, Output Deindustrialization, and Income Inequality in Indonesia: A Bidimensional Inequality Decomposition Analysis

Abstract Over the last four decades, Indonesia has undergone substantial structural changes. While agriculture and mining lowered their GDP shares, the services sector raised its share. Meanwhile, the GDP share of manufacturing exhibited an inverted U-shaped pattern. In the 1980s and 1990s, it has increased gradually; but after reaching the peak in the early 2000s, it has been declining. Economic tertialization seems to have been associated with output deindustrialization since the financial crisis. Changes in the industrial structure are accompanied by changes in the spatial distribution of economic activities. While Sumatra and Kalimantan lowered their GDP shares due to the declining share of oil and gas production, Java-Bali raised its share. Sulawesi also increased its GDP share, but Eastern Indonesia did not exhibit a significant change. This chapter attempts to explore the determinants of inequality in per capita GDP across provinces in Indonesia over the period 2010–2019 by using the bidimensional inequality decomposition method. In particular, it tries to analyze how economic tertialization and concurrent output deindustrialization affected inequality in per capita GDP.

Keywords Structural changes · Economic tertialization · Output deindustrialization · Bidimensional inequality decomposition analysis · Indonesia

1 Introduction

As the world's largest island country with more than 13 thousand islands and 300 ethnic groups, Indonesia has undergone substantial structural changes over the last four decades (Fig. 4.1). While agriculture and mining lowered their GDP shares, the services sector raised its GDP share, particularly after the 1997/98 Asian financial crisis; in 2019, it accounted for 46.0% of total GDP. Meanwhile, the GDP share of manufacturing exhibited an inverted U-shaped pattern. In the 1980s

This chapter is written by Takahiro Akita based partly on Alisjahbana and Akita (2020).

T. Akita, M. Kataoka, *Regional Inequality and Development*, New Frontiers in Regional Science: Asian Perspectives 63,
https://doi.org/10.1007/978-981-19-2968-7_4

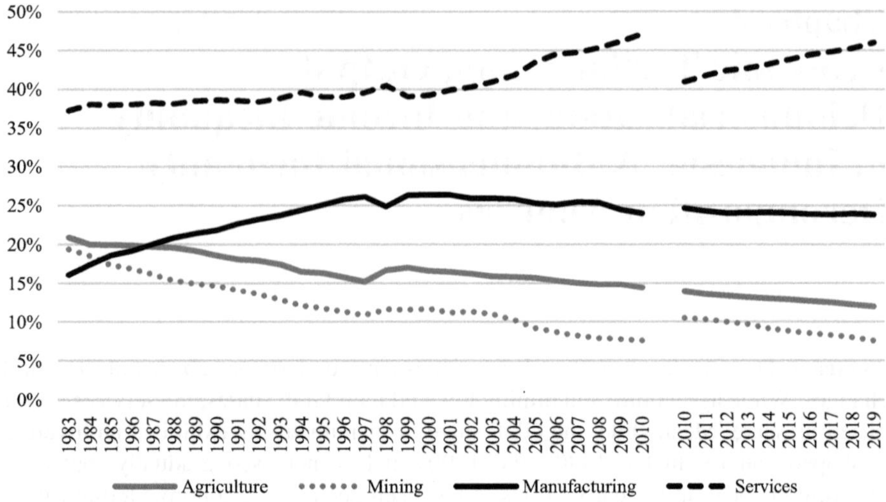

Fig. 4.1 Change in industrial structure in GDP. Note: GDP at 2000 constant prices for 1983–2010; GDP at 2010 constant prices for 2010–2019. Sources: Calculated based on Central Bureau of Statistics (various issues)

and 1990s under the Suharto's New Order Regime, it has increased gradually; but, after reaching the peak at 26.4% in the early 2000s, it has been declining. In 2019, the sector accounted for 23.8% of the total GDP. Economic tertialization seems to have been associated with output deindustrialization since the Asian financial crisis.[1]

Changes in the industrial structure are accompanied by changes in the spatial distribution of economic activities. Figure 4.2 presents the map of Indonesia, where the country is divided into 5 regions: Sumatra, Kalimantan, Java-Bali, Sulawesi, and Eastern Indonesia. In the period from 1983 to 2019, Sumatra and Kalimantan regions lowered their GDP shares due primarily to the declining share of oil and gas production in the provinces of Aceh, Riau, and East Kalimantan (from 26.9% to 21.1% in Sumatra and from 9.2% to 8.3% in Kalimantan). On the other hand, Java-Bali region raised its GDP share from 57.5% to 60.5%, where the three adjacent provinces of Jakarta, West Java, and Banten seem to have contributed to the rise. Sulawesi region also increased its GDP share from 3.3% to 6.4%. Meanwhile, Eastern Indonesia did not exhibit a significant change in its GDP share.

Despite these structural changes, large disparities in socioeconomic indicators persist among its regions and provinces due largely to unequal distributions of resource endowments, public infrastructure, and economic activities. At the provincial level, the ratio of the largest to smallest per capita GDP is very high at around 14–15. The largest per capita GDP is registered by the capital province of Jakarta,

[1]Economic tertialization refers to the expansion of the services sector. Indonesia's output deindustrialization appears to be premature in the sense that it started at a much lower development level than most developed countries (Rodrik, 2016).

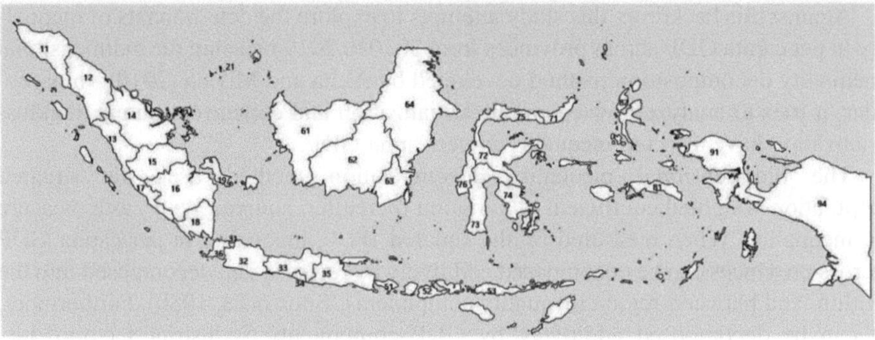

Region	Provincial code	Province
Sumatra	11	Aceh
	12	North Sumatera
	13	West Sumatera
	14	Riau
	15	Jambi
	16	South Sumatera
	17	Bengkulu
	21	Riau Islands
Kalimantan	61	West Kalimantan
	62	Central Kalimantan
	63	South Kalimantan
	64	East Kalimantan
Java-Bali	31	Jakarta
	32	West Java
	33	Central Java
	34	Yogyakarta
	35	East Java
	36	Banten
	51	Bali
Sulawesi	71	North Sulawesi
	72	Central Sulawesi
	73	South Sulawesi
	74	S.E. Sulawesi
	75	Gorontalo
	76	West Sulawesi
Eastern Indonesia	52	West Nusa Tenggara
	53	East Nusa Tenggara
	81	Maluku
	82	North Maluku
	91	West Papua
	94	Papua

Fig. 4.2 Map of Indonesia. Note: Five regions

which is followed by East Kalimantan, Riau Islands, West Papua, and Riau. On the other hand, East Nusa Tenggara registered the smallest, which is followed by the provinces of Maluku and North Maluku. These poor provinces are all in Eastern Indonesia.

Against this backdrop, this study attempts to explore the determinants of inequality in per capita GDP across provinces from 2010 to 2019 by using the bidimensional inequality decomposition method developed by Akita and Miyata (2010). In particular, it tries to analyze how economic tertialization and concurrent output deindustrialization have affected inequality in per capita GDP.

The bidimensional inequality decomposition method uses the squared population-weighted coefficient of variation (hereafter, squared *WCV*) as a measure of inequality. When measured by the squared *WCV*, inequality in per capita GDP across provinces can be decomposed additively by regions, i.e., decomposed into the within- and between-region inequality components (Shorrocks, 1980). Furthermore, it can be decomposed additively by GDP components (industrial sectors), i.e., expressed as the sum of contributions from GDP components (industrial sectors) (Shorrocks, 1982). The bidimensional inequality decomposition method combines these two decomposition properties. It can thus examine the contribution of each GDP component (industrial sector) to overall inequality in per capita GDP through within-region and between-region inequalities in a coherent framework.

2 Literature Review

Numerous studies have been conducted to investigate income inequality in Indonesia using provincial GDP and population data. They include Akita and Lukman (1995), Garcia and Soelistianingsih (1998), Hill et al. (2008), Akita and Miyata (2010), Akita et al. (2011), Vidyattama (2013), Hill and Vidyattama (2016), and Alisjahbana and Akita (2020).

Based on provincial GDP data from 1975 to 1992, Akita and Lukman (1995) conducted an inequality decomposition analysis by GDP components (i.e., industrial sectors) using the *WCV* to explore the determinants of inequality in per capita GDP across provinces. They found that if the mining sector is excluded, inequality in per capita GDP remained fairly stable over the period 1975–1992, but it has undergone a significant change in structure. While the contribution of the tertiary sector to inequality, though still dominant, has gradually declined, the secondary sector has been playing an increasingly important role, reflecting its growing share in GDP. Hill and Vidyattama (2016) calculated inequality in per capita GDP across provinces over the period 1975–2010 using provincial GDP. They found that if the mining sector is excluded, inequality, as measured by the *WCV*, has been remarkably stable since the late 1970s and argued that decentralization does not appear to have led to an increase in inequality, at least as measured at the provincial level.

Garcia and Soelistianingsih (1998) examined absolute and conditional β-convergence across Indonesian provinces using provincial GDP from 1975 to 1993.[2] They

[2] Barro and Sala-i-Martin (1991) introduced the concepts of σ-convergence and β-convergence. Section 6 of Chap. 2 provides a detailed account of the concept of absolute and conditional β-convergence.

found that if mining is included, the provinces exhibited absolute β-convergence, meaning that poorer provinces grew faster than richer provinces over the period 1975–1993. However, the inclusion of variables other than the initial per capita GDP, such as education, fertility, and natural resource endowment, increased the speed of convergence. Hill et al. (2008) investigated absolute β-convergence using provincial GDP from 1975 to 2002 and found that when the mining sector is included, there was absolute β-convergence over the period 1975–2002. But, they found also that the speed of convergence varies significantly across subperiods. While the speed was quite high during the period 1975–1986 thanks to the falling share of oil and gas in the economy, it has declined gradually since the export-oriented policies were implemented in the mid-1980s. During the crisis and post-crisis period 1997–2002, no significant absolute β-convergence was observed.

Vidyattama (2013) examined whether the spatial neighborhood effect is significant in β-convergence using provincial as well as district-level GDP from 1999 to 2008. In the period 1999–2008, there was no significant β-convergence whether provincial or district-level GDP is used. However, β-convergence occurred at the district level for the period 2005–2008 due partly to the impact of the spatial neighborhood effect. The article also investigated whether there is a significant difference between the Sumatra and Java regions in terms of the speed of convergence over the period 1999–2008 using district-level GDP and found that while Sumatra districts exhibited β-convergence, there is an indication that Java districts diverged in per capita GDP, though not statistically significant.

Akita et al. (2011) conducted a bidimensional inequality decomposition analysis using provincial GDP by industrial sectors from 1983 to 2004 and examined the changes in the determinants of inequality in per capita GDP associated with structural changes. They found that with a falling share of mining in GDP, the manufacturing sector has played an increasingly important role in determining inequality in the Sumatra and Kalimantan regions. They found also that with strong urbanization economies, facilitated by globalization and economic liberalization, the primacy of Jakarta has determined much of Java-Bali region's inequality, and thus overall inequality in Indonesia.

Based on an updated dataset of provincial GDP by industrial sectors from 2005 to 2013, Alisjahbana and Akita (2020) also performed a bidimensional inequality decomposition analysis and investigated how economic tertialization has affected the determinants of inequality in per capita GDP. The main finding of their study is that economic tertiarization has raised the importance of service activities in determining overall inequality, particularly within the Java region. They argued that with the advancement of IC and financial technologies, further development of the IC and financial sectors is likely to increase inequality unless policies that could facilitate spatial dispersion of these service activities are implemented. Our study is similar to their studies in terms of the method. But it updates their studies by using provincial GDP from 2010 to 2019 and analyzes inequality in per capita GDP from the viewpoint of economic tertialization and concurrent output deindustrialization.

3 Data and Method

3.1 Data

Inequality in per capita GDP is measured by using provincial GDP at constant 2010 prices. The dataset is constructed based on various issues of *Gross Regional Domestic Product of Provinces in Indonesia by Industrial Origin* published by the Central Bureau of Statistics (CBS, various issues, n.d.). It contains provincial GDP for 33 provinces.

To conduct a bidimensional decomposition analysis, the 9-sector classification is used. These 9 sectors are (1) agriculture; (2) mining; (3) manufacturing; (4) electricity, gas, and water; (5) construction; (6) trade, hotel, and restaurant; (7) transportation, information, and communication (transportation and IC); (8) financial and business services, and (9) other services. On the other hand, 33 provinces are grouped into three regions; region 1 includes Sumatra and Kalimantan provinces; region 2 includes Java provinces and Bali; and region 3 consists of Sulawesi provinces and provinces in Eastern Indonesia (see Fig. 4.2).

3.2 Bidimensional Inequality Decomposition Method

To obtain the bidimensional inequality decomposition method, consider a country consisting of 33 provinces.[3] These provinces are divided into three regions where region i contains p_i provinces. Let N, N_{ij}, y, and y_{ij} be, respectively, population of the whole country, population of province j in region i, GDP per capita of the whole country, and GDP per capita of province j in region i. Then, by the squared population-weighted coefficient of variation (squared *WCV*), overall inequality in per capita GDP can be measured by

$$WCV^2 = \frac{1}{y^2}\sum_{i=1}^{3}\sum_{j=1}^{p_i}\frac{N_{ij}}{N}\left(y_{ij}-y\right)^2, \tag{4.1}$$

where $y = \frac{1}{N}\sum_{i=1}^{3}\sum_{j=1}^{p_i} N_{ij}y_{ij}$.

Let N_i and y_i be, respectively, population and GDP per capita of region i where $N_i = \sum_{j=1}^{p_i} N_{ij}$ and $y_i = \sum_{j=1}^{p_i}\frac{N_{ij}}{N_i}y_{ij}$. Then, WCV^2 can be decomposed into the within-region and between-region inequality components as follows.

[3]Section 2 of Chap. 3 provides a detailed account of the method.

$$\begin{aligned} WCV^2 &= \sum\nolimits_{i=1}^{3} \frac{N_i}{N}\left(\frac{y_i}{y}\right)^2 WCV_i^2 + \frac{1}{y^2}\sum\nolimits_{i=1}^{3} \frac{N_i}{N}(y_i - y)^2 \\ &= WCV_W^2 + WCV_B^2 \end{aligned} \tag{4.2}$$

where $WCV_i^2 = \frac{1}{y_i^2}\sum_{j=1}^{p_i} \frac{N_{ij}}{N_i}\left(y_{ij} - y_i\right)^2$ is the squared population-weighted coefficient of variation for region i. In Eq. (4.2), $WCV_W^2 = \sum_{i=1}^{m} \frac{N_i}{N}\left(\frac{y_i}{y}\right)^2 WCV_i^2$ is the within-region inequality component, while $WCV_B^2 = \frac{1}{y^2}\sum_{i=1}^{m} \frac{N_i}{N}(y_i - y)^2$ is the between-region inequality component.

Suppose next that total GDP consists of 9 GDP components (i.e., GDP from 9 industrial sectors). Then, WCV_i^2 can be decomposed by GDP components (industrial sectors) as follows.

$$WCV_i^2 = \sum\nolimits_{k=1}^{9} w_{ik}\left(\frac{\text{wcov}_{ik}}{y_{ik}y_i}\right), \tag{4.3}$$

where $y_{ik} = \sum_{j=1}^{p_i} \frac{N_{ij}}{N_i} y_{ijk}$ is GDP per capita for sector k of region i. In Eq. (4.3), $w_{ik} = \frac{y_{ik}}{y_i}$ is the GDP share of industrial sector k in region i and $\text{wcov}_{ik} = \sum_{j=1}^{p_i} \frac{N_{ij}}{N_i}\left(y_{ijk} - y_{ik}\right)\left(y_{ij} - y_i\right)$ is the population-weighted covariance between GDP component k and total GDP in region i.

Similarly, WCV_B^2 can be decomposed by GDP components (industrial sectors) as follows.

$$WCV_B^2 = \sum\nolimits_{k=1}^{9} w_k\left(\frac{\text{wcov}_k}{y_{\cdot k}y}\right), \tag{4.4}$$

where $y_{\cdot k} = \sum_{i=1}^{3} \frac{N_i}{N} y_{ik}$ is GDP per capita for sector k of the country. In Eq. (4.4), $w_k = \frac{y_{\cdot k}}{y}$ is the GDP share of sector k in the country, while $\text{wcov}_k = \sum_{i=1}^{3} \frac{N_i}{N} \times (y_{ik} - y_{\cdot k})(y_i - y)$ is the population-weighted covariance between GDP component k and total GDP in the country.

Substituting Eqs. (4.3) and (4.4) into Eq. (4.2), we obtain the following bidimensional inequality decomposition equation based on the squared population-weighted coefficient of variation.

$$WCV^2 = \sum\nolimits_{i=1}^{3} \frac{N_i}{N}\left(\frac{y_i}{y}\right)^2 \left[\sum\nolimits_{k=1}^{9} w_{ik}\left(\frac{\text{wcov}_{ik}}{y_{ik}y_i}\right)\right] + \sum\nolimits_{k=1}^{9} w_k\left(\frac{\text{wcov}_k}{y_{\cdot k}y}\right). \tag{4.5}$$

Since the country consists of three regions and 9 industrial sectors, there are (3 + 1) × 9 = 36 components in Eq. (4.5).

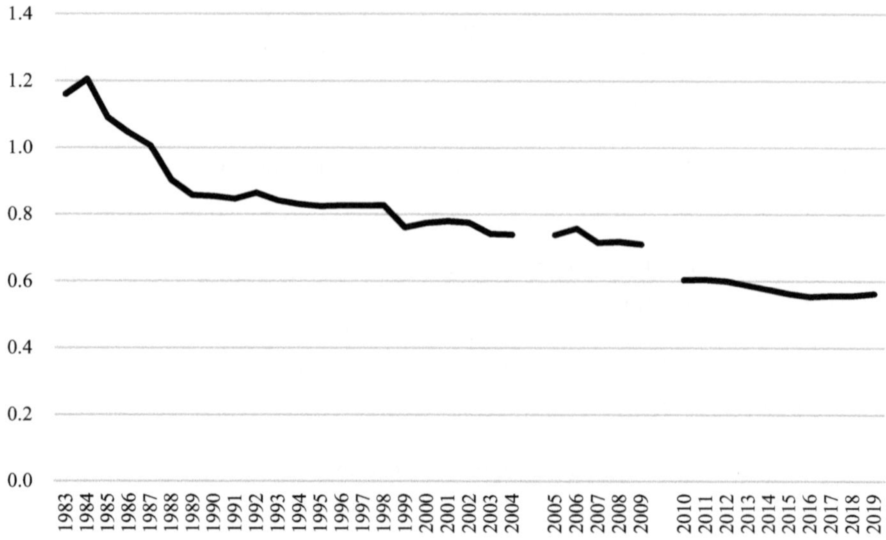

Fig. 4.3 Inequality in per capita GDP by squared *WCV*. Note: Inequality for 1983–2009 at constant 2000 prices; inequality for 2010–2019 at constant 2010 prices. (Sources) Calculated based on Central Bureau of Statistics (various issues)

4 Empirical Results

4.1 Level and Trend of Inequality in Per Capita GDP

Figure 4.3 presents inequality in per capita GDP for the period 1983–2019 by the squared *WCV*, where inequality for 1983–2004 is obtained from Akita et al. (2011) and inequality for 2005–2009 is obtained from Alisjahbana and Akita (2020).[4] There is a clear downward trend over the period. But, the declining speed has been getting smaller. The squared *WCV* was very high at 1.16 in 1983; however, it declined prominently to 0.86 in 1989. Between 1989 and 1997, inequality became stable at around 0.83–0.85. The country faced a severe financial crisis for the period 1997–99, during which inequality fell sharply to 0.76. After the financial crisis, inequality became stable again; the squared *WCV* was around 0.75 between 1999 and 2004. For the period 2005–2019, inequality exhibited a slight downward trend; between 2005 and 2009, the squared *WCV* declined from 0.74 to 0.71 and between 2010 and 2019, from 0.61 to 0.56.[5]

[4]Inequality for 1983–2004 is measured across 26 provinces, while for 2005–2019, across 33 provinces.

[5]For 1983–2009, GDP at 2000 constant prices is used, while for 2010–2019, GDP at 2010 constant prices is used.

4.2 Regional Convergence in Per Capita GDP

It is found in the previous section that overall inequality in per capita GDP across provinces had a slight downward trend over the period 2010–2019 (σ-convergence). To examine whether poorer provinces tend to grow faster than richer provinces, we conduct a β-convergence analysis. Figure 4.4 presents per capita GDP in 2010 and annual average growth rate of per capita GDP between 2010 and 2019. In 2010, East Kalimantan had the largest per capita GDP, followed by Jakarta, Riau, and Riau Islands. Among poor provinces, East Nusa Tenggara registered the smallest per capita GDP, followed by Maluku, North Maluku and West Sulawesi. Over the period 2010–2019, Sulawesi provinces performed relatively well in terms of per capita GDP growth. Central Sulawesi recorded the highest growth rate, which was followed by West Sulawesi, Southeast Sulawesi, and Gorontalo. Meanwhile, resource-rich provinces, such as Aceh, Riau, East Kalimantan, and Papua, grew less rapidly. Papua had the smallest per capita GDP growth, followed by Riau and East Kalimantan.

Figure 4.5 provides a scatterplot of per capita GDP growth against log of per capita GDP in 2010. There appears to be a negative relationship between these two variables, i.e., poorer provinces tend to grow faster than richer provinces. To formerly test the existence of absolute β-convergence for the period 2010–2019, we estimate the following equation.

$$\frac{1}{T}\ln\left(\frac{y_{iT}}{y_{i0}}\right) = \alpha + \beta \ln\left(y_{i0}\right) + u_i,$$

where y_{i0}, y_{iT}, and u_i are, respectively, per capita GDP in the initial year, per capita GDP in the terminal year, and error term, while $\frac{1}{T}\ln\left(\frac{y_{iT}}{y_{i0}}\right)$ is the annual average growth rate of GDP per capita.

The result is given in column 1 of Table 4.1. The coefficient associated with log of per capita GDP in 2010 is significant at the 5% level and negative, indicating the existence of absolute β-convergence. According to the Ramsey RESET test for omitted variables however the model may suffer from omitted variable bias. The R-squared is also small at 0.194. According to Alisjahbana and Akita (2020), the financial sector has played an important role in the economic growth. We thus add the GDP share of the financial sector as an independent variable. The result of multiple regression analysis is presented in column 2 of Table 4.1. The coefficient associated with log of per capita GDP in 2010 is significant at the 1% significance level and negative. The coefficient of the GDP share of the financial sector is also significant at the 1% level and has an expected sign.

The model explains 33.4% of the variation in the dependent variable. The result shows that there is conditional β-convergence among provinces for the 2010–2019 period. In other words, after controlling for the additional variable, poorer provinces tend to grow faster than richer provinces. It reveals also that provinces with a larger GDP share of the financial sector tend to grow faster, confirming the importance of the financial sector in per capita GDP growth.

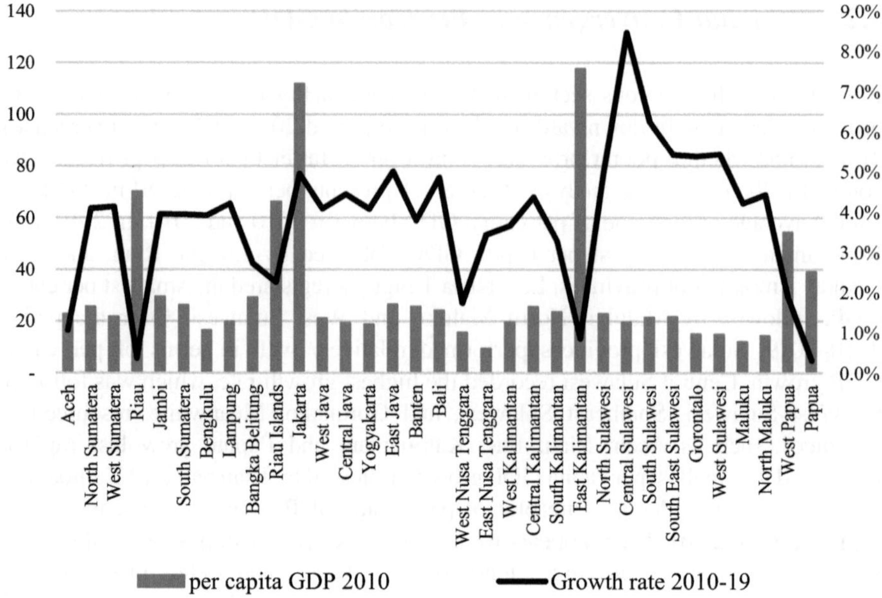

Fig. 4.4 Per capita GDP in 2010 and growth rate of per capita GDP 2010–2019. Sources: Calculated based on Central Bureau of Statistics (various issues)

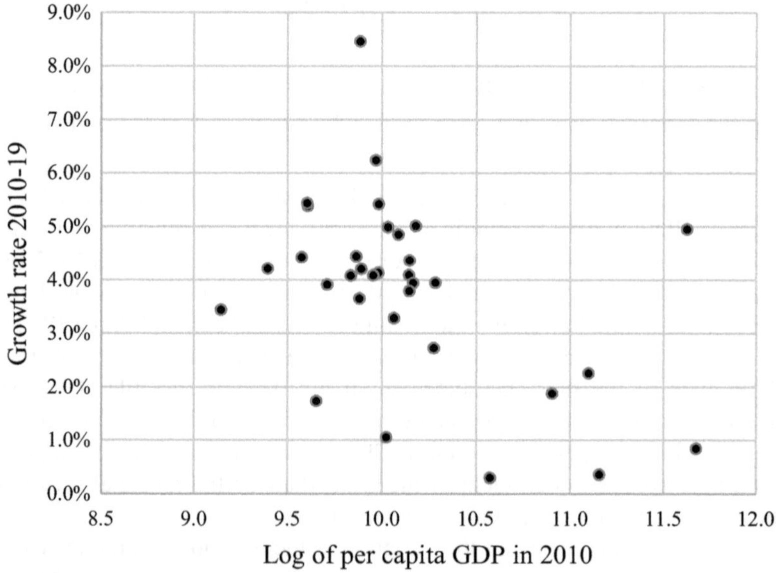

Fig. 4.5 Scatter Plot: Growth rate 2010–2019 against log of per capita GDP in 2010. Sources: Calculated based on Central Bureau of Statistics (various issues)

Table 4.1 Regression analysis: β-convergence across provinces for 2010–2019. Dependent variable = growth rate of per capita GDP from 2010 to 2019

	(1)		(2)	
Variables	Coefficient	Robust STD error	Coefficient	Robust STD error
Log of per capita GDP 2010	−0.0131**	0.0059	−0.0151***	0.0033
GDP share of financial sector 2010			0.1644***	0.0340
Constant	0.1711***	0.0589	0.1811***	0.0343
R-squared	0.1940		0.3338	
Number of observations	33		33	
Ramsey test for omitted variables	F(3, 28) = 1.96	Prob. > F: 0.1429	F(3, 27) = 1.79	Prob. > F: 0.1726

Note: Null hypothesis H_0 for Ramsey RESET test: model has no omitted variables.
*** significant at 1% level; ** significant at 5% level; * significant at 10% level
Source: Authors' calculation based on Central Bureau of Statistics (various issues).

4.3 Inequalities in Per Capita GDP by Industrial Sectors

As discussed above, inequality in per capita GDP across provinces has declined gradually. But, it is still very high. In 2019, the ratio of the largest to smallest per capita GDP (Jakarta/East Nusa Tenggara) was very high at 13.7, and Jakarta's per capita GDP was 4.2 times the national average and 1.3 times the second largest (East Kalimantan). To explore the determinants of inequality in per capita GDP for the period from 2010 to 2019, inequality is calculated by the industrial sector for each region using the *WCV*. The result is presented in Table 4.2, while the change in industrial structure is shown in Table 4.3. By the *WCV*, region 2 (Java-Bali) had the largest inequality in per capita GDP since its services sectors, such as financial and business services, had high inequalities. Region 1 (Sumatra and Kalimantan) follows next, since it includes two major resource-rich provinces of Riau and East Kalimantan. But, as the GDP share of mining has declined, region 1's inequality has been getting smaller. As compared to regions 1 and 2, region 3 (Sulawesi and Eastern Indonesia) had a relatively small inequality in per capita GDP.

Each region exhibits a distinct pattern of inequalities. In region 1, mining had the largest inequality in 2019, reflecting a very uneven spatial distribution of natural resources within the region, and it was followed by the electricity, gas, and water sector though its GDP share was very small. Despite a declining trend, the manufacturing sector had a relatively high inequality in the region, indicating that manufacturing activities, mainly resource-based activities, have been developed very unevenly across provinces.

In region 2, financial and business services had the largest inequality in the study period, which was followed by the other services sector and the transportation and IC sector. Particularly, the financial and business services sector had a very large inequality. However, if Jakarta is hypothetically merged with the adjacent province of West Java the sector's inequality drops substantially. This implies that there is a

Table 4.2 Inequality in per capita GDP by industrial sectors by *WCV*

	1	2	3	4	5	6	7	8	9	Total
Region 1										
2010	0.46	1.75	1.02	1.41	0.69	0.33	0.45	0.32	0.30	0.74
2019	0.44	1.72	0.90	1.27	0.61	0.30	0.44	0.29	0.32	0.58
Region 2										
2010	0.38	0.61	0.32	0.73	1.21	0.90	1.07	2.21	1.36	0.79
2019	0.41	0.82	0.27	0.85	1.03	0.87	1.23	2.22	1.29	0.83
Region 3										
2010	0.29	1.56	1.47	0.50	0.42	0.32	0.30	0.39	0.23	0.46
2019	0.34	1.04	1.14	0.46	0.49	0.40	0.38	0.44	0.27	0.40

Note: 1 agriculture, 2 mining, 3 manufacturing, 4 electricity/gas/water, 5 construction, 6 trade/hotel/restaurant, 7 transportation/IC, 8 financial and business services, and 9 other services.
Sources: Calculated based on Central Bureau of Statistics (various issues).

Table 4.3 Industrial structure (in %)

	1	2	3	4	5	6	7	8	9	Tertiary sector = 6+7+8+9	Total
Region 1											
2010	20.1	22.6	20.4	0.2	8.7	11.4	5.6	4.3	6.7	28.0	100
2019	19.7	17.6	19.5	0.2	10.2	13.2	7.1	4.9	7.5	32.8	100
Region 2											
2010	9.0	2.6	29.5	0.5	10.0	20.0	8.3	10.3	9.7	48.3	100
2019	6.7	2.1	28.0	0.4	10.1	20.5	11.1	11.2	9.9	52.7	100
Region 3											
2010	23.3	18.7	9.0	0.2	9.6	11.6	8.1	5.1	14.3	39.1	100
2019	20.9	11.7	11.1	0.2	11.9	13.7	9.6	5.8	15.1	44.2	100

Note: 1 agriculture, 2 mining, 3 manufacturing, 4 electricity/gas/water, 5 construction, 6 trade/hotel/restaurant, 7 transportation/IC, 8 financial and business services, and 9 other services.
Sources: Calculated based on Central Bureau of Statistics (various issues).

very large disparity between Jakarta and the other Java-Bali provinces in financial and business activities. The other services sector and the transportation and IC sector also lower their inequalities if Jakarta is hypothetically merged with West Java. These observations suggest that region 2's very high inequality is due mainly to a very high disparity in tertiary activities between Jakarta and the other Java-Bali provinces. We should note here that in Jakarta, the tertiary sector accounted for three-quarters of its total GDP in 2019, which is much larger than the tertiary sector's GDP share in the other Java-Bali provinces.[6] If Jakarta is merged with West Java, region 2's within-region inequality drops conspicuously.

In region 3, the mining sector had the largest inequality in 2010, which is followed by manufacturing and construction. But, it lowered its inequality

[6]Tertiary sector includes sectors 6, 7, 8, and 9.

substantially between 2010 and 2019. On the other hand, due mainly to the rapid development of liquid natural gas (LNG) in West Papua, the manufacturing sector raised its inequality and surpassed mining. In 2019, it had the largest inequality.

4.4 Bidimensional Decomposition Analysis

To explore the determinants of inequality in a unified region-industry framework, a bidimensional inequality decomposition analysis is conducted using the squared *WCV* (see Eq. 4.5). Table 4.4 presents the result. Much of inequality in per capita GDP across provinces is accounted for by the within-region inequality component, contributing more than 95% of overall inequality. Region 2 dominated the within-region component and raised its contribution to overall inequality from 60.6% to 77.3% between 2010 and 2019. Much of this increase was attributable to the rise in the contribution of the tertiary sector. Meanwhile, region 1 reduced its contribution from 33.6% to 18.4%, and much of this decrease was due to the declining contributions of mining and manufacturing. With its small GDP share and low inequality, region 3 had a very small contribution.

We can now identify several important determinants of inequality in per capita GDP across Indonesian provinces. First, mining's inequality is still the main determinant of region 1's within-region inequality, though its contribution has been declining substantially. When mining is excluded however the manufacturing sector dominated region 1's inequality. Non-oil and gas manufacturing has played an increasingly important role in determining manufacturing's within-region inequality. They are concentrated in two Sumatra provinces, that is, North Sumatra and Riau Islands.[7] Meanwhile, no significant non-oil and gas manufacturing activities exist in the provinces of Bengkulu, Central Kalimantan, and Aceh.

Second, the tertiary sector has played an important role in determining region 2's within-region inequality. Among four tertiary sectors, the financial and business services sector and the trade, hotel, and restaurant sector contributed a lot to region 2's inequality. Even if Jakarta is merged with West Java hypothetically, these two sectors played an important role. Though the contribution is not large as compared to these two sectors, the transportation and IC sector raised their contribution.

In the tertiary sector, five subsectors can be identified as major contributors. They are wholesale and retail trade, IC, banking, business services, and private services. Among these five subsectors, wholesale and retail trade is an inequality-reducing subsector. On the other hand, IC, banking, business services, and private services are inequality-raising subsectors in the tertiary sector, implying that if these four subsectors raise their GDP shares, region 2's within-region inequality will be even

[7]North Sumatra includes the Medan metropolitan area, which consists of Medan city, Binjai city, Deli Serdang regency, and Karo regency. This area is the biggest metropolitan area outside Java and serves as a hub for western Indonesia.

Table 4.4 Bidimensional inequality decomposition analysis. % contribution to overall inequality

	1	2	3	4	5	6	7	8	9	Tertiary =6+7+8+9	Total
2010											
Total (B + W)	1.2	19.5	16.2	0.2	12.0	15.4	7.3	17.7	10.4	50.8	100.0
Between-region (B)	0.6	1.1	1.2	0.0	0.2	0.3	0.1	0.1	−0.2	0.3	3.5
Within-region (W)	0.5	18.4	15.0	0.2	11.8	15.1	7.3	17.6	10.6	50.6	96.5
Region 1 (W1)	2.1	17.4	9.1	0.0	2.3	1.3	0.5	0.3	0.5	2.6	33.6
Region 2 (W2)	−1.7	−0.2	5.4	0.2	9.3	13.7	6.7	17.2	10.0	47.6	60.6
Region 3 (W3)	0.1	1.2	0.4	0.0	0.2	0.1	0.1	0.1	0.1	0.4	2.3
2019											
Total (B + W)	−0.2	9.0	11.8	0.3	11.7	18.2	13.3	23.7	12.1	67.3	100.0
Between-region (B)	−0.2	0.0	1.3	0.0	0.1	0.6	0.2	0.4	−0.1	1.1	2.3
Within-region (W)	0.0	9.1	10.6	0.3	11.6	17.6	13.1	23.4	12.2	66.2	97.7
Region 1 (W1)	1.2	8.8	5.0	0.0	1.6	0.9	0.4	0.2	0.4	1.8	18.4
Region 2 (W2)	−1.4	−0.2	5.1	0.3	9.7	16.5	12.6	23.1	11.7	63.9	77.3
Region 3 (W3)	0.2	0.4	0.5	0.0	0.3	0.2	0.1	0.1	0.2	0.6	2.1

Note: 1 agriculture, 2 mining, 3 manufacturing, 4 electricity/gas/water, 5 construction, 6 trade/hotel/restaurant, 7 transportation/IC, 8 financial and business services, and 9 other services

Sources: Calculated based on Central Bureau of Statistics (various issues)

higher. Particularly, the IC sector should be paid attention to, as its GDP share has been rising rapidly over the study period. We should note that the IC, banking, and business services sectors are concentrated in Jakarta.

Third, the contribution of manufacturing to region 2's within-region inequality has been declining, though slightly, as its GDP share and inequality have both decreased (see Tables 4.1 and 4.2). West Java accounted for 34% of region 2's GDP from manufacturing, while Jakarta 12%. This is in contrast with the tertiary sector, where West Java and Jakarta constituted, respectively, 17% and 39% of region 2's GDP from the tertiary sector. The manufacturing sector contributed 43% of West Java's total GDP, much larger than the national figure of 24%. Manufacturing activities appear to have been shifting from Jakarta to the two adjacent provinces of West Java and Banten, particularly to Jakarta's neighboring districts, such as Bogor, Depok, and Bekasi in West Java and Tangerang in Banten.[8]

Fourth, the construction sector had a relatively high inequality and its contribution to overall inequality was 11.7% in 2019. Particularly, it had a very large within-region inequality in region 2. Construction activities are concentrated in major cities. Particularly, Jakarta generated one-third of region 2's GDP from construction, which is much larger than its population share of 6.2% in region 2.

Fifth, the contribution of the between-region inequality was not large. The major contributor to the between-region inequality is the manufacturing sector, as the sector accounted for more than half of the total contribution of the between-region inequality. Region 2 dominated as it constituted three-quarters of total GDP from manufacturing in 2019; its manufacturing activities are mostly non-oil and gas activities. According to Table 4.2, the manufacturing sector contributed 28% of region 2's total GDP in 2019, which is compared to 20% in region 1 and 11% in region 3.

5 Conclusion

This study explored the determinants of inequality in per capita GDP across provinces in Indonesia from 2010 to 2019 using the bidimensional inequality decomposition method. The following provides a summary of the findings.

First, despite a declining trend, inequality was still very high at around 0.6 by the squared population-weighted coefficient of variation; the largest per capita GDP registered by Jakarta was more than 14 times the smallest. Second, according to the bidimensional inequality decomposition analysis, much of inequality is accounted for by the within-region inequality component. While region 2 (Java-Bali) dominated the within-region inequality component and raised its contribution to overall

[8]It should be noted that besides the Jakarta metropolitan area, region 2 contains three large metropolitan areas in Indonesia, namely, the Surabaya, Bandung, and Semarang metropolitan areas. They accommodate a variety of manufacturing activities.

inequality due to the rising contribution of the tertiary sector, region 1 (Sumatra and Kalimantan) lowered its contribution due to the declining contributions of mining and manufacturing. With its small GDP share and low inequality, the contribution of region 3 (Sulawesi and Eastern Indonesia) was very small.

Third, although mining has reduced its contribution, it is still the main contributor to region 1's within-region inequality. If mining is excluded however the manufacturing sector dominated region 1's inequality, where non-oil and gas manufacturing played an increasingly important role. Fourth, the tertiary sector played a pivotal role in region 2's within-region inequality. Among tertiary subsectors, wholesale and retail trade, information and communication (IC), banking, business services, and private services contributed a lot to region 2's inequality. Of these five subsectors, IC, banking, business services, and private services are mostly concentrated in Jakarta and served to increase region 2's within-region inequality. Particularly, the IC sector raised its GDP share rapidly and its contribution to region 2's inequality has increased substantially.

Fifth, the manufacturing sector reduced its contribution to region 2's within-region inequality as its GDP share and inequality both declined. Manufacturing activities appear to have been shifting from Jakarta to West Java and Banten, particularly to Jakarta's neighboring districts, such as Bogor, Depok, Tangerang, and Bekasi. In West Java, the manufacturing sector contributed more than 40% of its total GDP, which is much larger than the national figure of 24%. Sixth, the construction sector had a relatively high inequality in per capita GDP. In region 2, construction activities are concentrated in Jakarta, generating one-third of region 2's GDP from construction. Finally, the contribution of the between-region inequality was not large. The major contributor is the manufacturing sector. Region 2 dominated the sector as it accommodated three-quarters of total GDP from manufacturing.

While deindustrialization lowered the relative importance of manufacturing in determining overall inequality, manufacturing activities are still very unevenly distributed among regions and provinces. Non-oil and gas manufacturing activities are mostly located in Java-Bali. But they are expected to play an increasingly important role outside Java-Bali. With the development of economic infrastructures throughout Java-Bali, inequality in manufacturing activities is likely to decrease in the region. But many provinces outside Java-Bali lack economic infrastructures and human resources. Further development of non-oil and gas manufacturing activities is likely to increase inequalities outside Java-Bali since these activities tend to be located where economic infrastructures and human resources are relatively abundant. The government needs to implement policies that are conducive to the balanced development of non-oil and gas manufacturing based on regional comparative advantages and disadvantages, where further development of economic infrastructures and human resources, particularly outside Java-Bali, is essential.

In contrast, economic tertialization raised the importance of service activities in determining overall inequality, particularly inequality within Java-Bali. The tertiary sector accounts for more than half of the total GDP in Java-Bali, and many service activities, such as IC, banking, business services, and private services, are concentrated in Jakarta and neighboring districts. Particularly, with the advancement of IC technologies, the IC sector expanded rapidly. Together with banking, business services, and private services, further development of the IC sector is likely to increase within-region inequality in Java-Bali unless policies that could facilitate spatial dispersion of these service activities are implemented.

References

Akita, T., Kurniawan, P. A., & Miyata, S. (2011). Structural changes and regional income inequality in Indonesia: A bi-dimensional decomposition analysis. *Asian Economic Journal, 25*(1), 55–77.

Akita, T., & Lukman, R. A. (1995). Interregional inequalities in Indonesia: A sectoral decomposition analysis for 1975-92. *Bulletin of Indonesian Economic Studies, 31*(2), 61–81.

Akita, T., & Miyata, S. (2010). The bi-dimensional decomposition of regional inequality based on the weighted coefficient of variation. *Letters in Spatial and Resource Sciences, 3*(3), 91–100.

Alisjahbana, A., & Akita, T. (2020). Economic tertialization and regional income inequality in a decentralized Indonesia: A bi-dimensional inequality decomposition analysis. *Social Indicators Research, 151*, 51–80.

Barro, R. J., & Sala-i-Martin, X. (1991). Convergence across states and regions. *Brookings Papers on Economic Activity, 1*, 107–182.

Central Bureau of Statistics (CBS). (n.d.) (various issues). *Gross Regional Domestic Product of Provinces in Indonesia by Industrial Origin*. Central Bureau of Statistics.

Garcia, J. G., & Soelistianingsih, L. (1998). Why do differences in provincial incomes persists in Indonesia? *Bulletin of Indonesian Economic Studies, 34*(1), 95–120.

Hill, H., Resosudarmo, B. P., & Vidyattama, Y. (2008). Indonesia's changing economic geography. *Bulletin of Indonesian Economic Studies, 44*, 407–435.

Hill, H., & Vidyattama, Y. (2016). Regional development dynamics In Indonesia before and after the 'Big Bang' decentralization. *The Singapore Economic Review, 61*(2), 1–26.

Rodrik, D. (2016). Premature deindustrialization. *Journal of Economic Growth, 21*(1), 1–33.

Shorrocks, A. (1980). The class of additively decomposable inequality measures. *Econometrica, 48*(3), 613–625.

Shorrocks, A. (1982). Inequality decomposition by factor components. *Econometrica, 50*(1), 193–211.

Vidyattama, Y. (2013). Regional convergence and the role of the neighborhood effect in decentralized Indonesia. *Bulletin of Indonesian Economic Studies, 49*(2), 193–211.

Chapter 5
Structural Changes and Regional Income Inequality in the Indonesian Manufacturing Industry: An Inequality Decomposition Analysis

Abstract Over the last two decades, the manufacturing industry has grown at an annual average rate of 4.5% in Indonesia. However, its share in total GDP has fallen gradually. This output deindustrialization appears to be premature in the sense that it started at a much lower development level than in most developed countries. But, if we look at manufacturing subsectors, their growth performances are quite heterogeneous. While labor-intensive industries such as food processing and textile grew relatively rapidly, industries tied to coal, oil, and natural gas were stagnant. This chapter attempts to examine how structural changes in the manufacturing industry affected regional income inequality in Indonesia over the period 2010–2019. By using provincial GDP by manufacturing subsectors, this chapter first conducts a shift and share analysis to explore the determinants of provincial growth in the manufacturing industry. It then performs an inequality decomposition analysis to investigate the extent to which each manufacturing subsector contributes to inter-provincial inequality in manufacturing GDP.

Keywords Structural changes · Inter-provincial inequality · Manufacturing industry · Inequality decomposition analysis · Indonesia

1 Introduction

Over the last two decades, the manufacturing industry has grown at an annual average rate of 4.5% in Indonesia. However, its share in total GDP has fallen gradually. This output deindustrialization appears to be premature in the sense that it started at a much lower development level than in most developed countries (Rodrik, 2016). But, if we look at manufacturing subsectors, their growth performances are quite heterogeneous. While labor-intensive industries such as food processing and textile industries grew relatively rapidly, industries tied to coal, oil,

This chapter is written by Takahiro Akita.

T. Akita, M. Kataoka, *Regional Inequality and Development*, New Frontiers in Regional Science: Asian Perspectives 63,
https://doi.org/10.1007/978-981-19-2968-7_5

and natural gas were stagnant. Over the period 2010–2019, the share of the coal and refined petroleum products sector in manufacturing GDP fell from 11.0% to 7.3%. On the other hand, the food products and beverages sector raised its share notably from 23.7% to 29.6%.

Changes in the structure of the manufacturing industry were associated with the changes in the spatial distribution of manufacturing activities. At the provincial level, Aceh's manufacturing experienced a large negative growth in GDP over the period 2010–2019 due to its high dependence on such natural resources as natural gas and oil. For the same reason, East Kalimantan's manufacturing sector was stagnant and its share in total manufacturing GDP fell from 5.8% to 3.9%. On the other hand, the manufacturing sector grew very rapidly in most Sulawesi provinces thanks to relatively rapid expansion of food processing, nonmetallic mineral products, and basic metals industries. The Sulawesi region raised its share in manufacturing GDP from 2.3% to 3.5%.

How have these structural changes affected regional income inequality in the Indonesian manufacturing industry over the period 2010–2019? This study attempts to answer the question by using provincial GDP by industrial sectors. It first conducts a shift and share analysis to explore the determinants of provincial growth in the manufacturing industry. It then performs an inequality decomposition analysis to investigate the extent to which each industrial sector contributes to inter-provincial inequality in manufacturing GDP.

The inequality decomposition analysis employs the coefficient of variation (*CV*) and the Gini coefficient (Gini) as a measure of inequality. The *CV* and the Gini satisfy several desirable properties, such as anonymity, income homogeneity, population homogeneity, and the Pigou-Dalton principle of transfers (Anand, 1983). They are also additively decomposable by factor components (Pyatt et al., 1980; Shorrocks, 1982). With provincial GDP by industrial sectors, overall inter-provincial inequality, as measured by the *CV* and the Gini, can thus be expressed as the sum of contributions from industrial sectors.

There has been a spate of studies on regional income inequality in Indonesia. Most of these studies used provincial GDP and population to estimate regional income inequality owing to the availability of longer term provincial time series data. They include Esmara (1975), Uppal and Handoko (1986), Akita (1988), Hill (1992), Akita and Lukman (1995), Garcia and Soelistianingsih (1998), Hill et al. (2008), Vidyattama (2013), and Hill and Vidyattama (2016).

To the best of our knowledge, only a few studies used provincial GDP by industrial sectors to examine regional inequalities by industrial sectors. Among them, Akita and Lukman (1995) performed a sectoral inequality decomposition analysis to explore the determinants of inequality in per capita GDP across provinces from 1975 to 1992 based on provincial GDP by industrial sectors. Our study updates their study by using provincial GDP from 2010 to 2019. But, it focuses on the manufacturing sector and investigates the determinants of inter-provincial inequality in manufacturing GDP. Unlike their study, which used the *population-weighted* coefficient of variation

Table 5.1 Sector classification

	9 sectors		16 sectors
M1	Coal, gas, and refined petroleum products	1	Coal, gas, and refined petroleum products
M2	Food, tobacco, and beverages	2	Food products and beverages
		3	Tobacco products
M3	Textile, wearing apparel, and leather products	4	Textiles; and wearing Apparel
		5	Leather and related products and footwear
M4	Wood and paper products	6	Wood products and cork
		7	Paper products and printing
		8	Furniture
M5	Chemical, rubber, and nonmetallic mineral products	9	Chemical and pharmaceutical products
		10	Rubber and plastic products
		11	Nonmetallic mineral products
M6	Basic metals and fabricated metal products	12	Basic metals
		13	Fabricated metal and optical products and computer
M7	Machinery and equipment	14	Machinery and equipment
M8	Transport equipment	15	Transport equipment
M9	Other manufacturing	16	Other manufacturing products

Source: Central Bureau of Statistics (various issues)

(*WCV*), our study employs the *CV* to measure inequality.[1] As discussed below, the *CV* and the Gini measure inter-provincial inequality in per capita GDP, while the *WCV* attempts to measure interpersonal income inequality by assuming that individuals in each province receive the per capita GDP of the province.

2 Data and Methods

2.1 Data

Inter-provincial inequalities in per capita GDP are measured over the period 2010–2019 by using provincial GDP by industrial sectors at constant 2010 prices. The dataset is constructed based on various issues of *Gross Regional Domestic Product of Provinces in Indonesia by Industrial Origin* compiled by the Central Bureau of Statistics (CBS, various issues, n.d.). While it contains provincial GDP for 52 industrial sectors, this study focuses on 16 manufacturing sectors (see Table 5.1). In a shift and share analysis, these 16 sectors are used. However, in an inequality decomposition analysis, they are aggregated into 9 sectors based on the characteristics of the 16 manufacturing sectors.

[1] Williamson (1965) popularized the *WCV* in his seminal article on regional income inequality and national economic development.

2.2 Methods

2.2.1 Shift and Share Analysis

Shift and share analysis is a method that has been widely used to examine the determinants of regional economic growth (Armstrong & Taylor, 1985). It divides a region's growth into three components. The first component is the region's share of national growth (*RS*). If a region grows at the national growth rate, it will maintain its share of national output. Let x_i, X_N, and ΔX_N be, respectively, regional output of sector i in the initial year, national output in the initial year, and the change in national output. Then, *RS* for sector i can be expressed as follows.

$$RS_i = x_i\left(\frac{\Delta X_N}{X_N}\right). \tag{5.1}$$

The second component, industry-mix shift component (*IMS*), is based on the premise that a region that has a relatively larger share of output in fast-growing industries should grow faster than the nation as a whole. Let X_i and ΔX_i be, respectively, national output of sector i in the initial year and the change in national output of sector i. Then, *IMS* for sector i is defined as follows.

$$IMS_i = x_i\left(\frac{\Delta X_i}{X_i} - \frac{\Delta X_N}{X_N}\right). \tag{5.2}$$

The third component is the competitive shift component (*CS*). A region may have a competitive advantage in some industries relative to other regions because its environment is conducive to the growth of these industries. Let Δx_i be the change in regional output of sector i. Then, *CS* for sector i is defined as follows.

$$CS_i = x_i\left(\frac{\Delta x_i}{x_i} - \frac{\Delta X_i}{X_i}\right). \tag{5.3}$$

The actual output growth of sector i of a region, Δx_i, is given as the sum of these three components (Eqs. 5.1, 5.2, and 5.3).

$$\begin{aligned}\Delta x_i &= RS_i + IMS_i + CS_i \\ &= x_i\left(\frac{\Delta X_N}{X_N}\right) + x_i\left(\frac{\Delta X_i}{X_i} - \frac{\Delta X_N}{X_N}\right) + x_i\left(\frac{\Delta x_i}{x_i} - \frac{\Delta X_i}{X_i}\right). \end{aligned} \tag{5.4}$$

Equation (5.4) is a shift and share equation for sector i. On the other hand, total output growth of a region is given by

$$\sum_{i=1}^{n} \Delta x_i = \sum_{i=1}^{n} (RS_i + IMS_i + CS_i),$$

where n is the total number of industrial sectors. Moving the RS_i term to the left-hand side, we obtain the following equation.

$$\sum_{i=1}^{n} \Delta x_i - \sum_{i=1}^{n} RS_i = \sum_{i=1}^{n} IMS_i + \sum_{i=1}^{n} CS_i. \tag{5.5}$$

The difference between the actual growth $\left(\sum_{i=1}^{n} \Delta x_i\right)$ and the hypothetical growth that a region could achieve if it grew at the national growth rate $\left(\sum_{i=1}^{n} RS_i\right)$ should be the sum of the industry-mix shift and competitive shift components. This study calculates Eq. (5.5) for each province.

2.2.2 Inequality Decomposition by Factor Components: Coefficient of Variation (CV)

Consider a country consisting of p provinces. Let y_i and μ be, respectively, per capita GDP of province i and the simple average of per capita GDP, where $\mu = \frac{1}{p}\sum_{i=1}^{p} y_i$. Then, by the squared coefficient of variation (squared CV), overall inter-provincial inequality in per capita GDP is measured by

$$CV^2 = \frac{1}{\mu^2} \frac{1}{p} \sum_{i=1}^{p} (y_i - \mu)^2 \tag{5.6}$$

Suppose next that total manufacturing GDP is composed of K GDP components (GDP from K manufacturing subsectors). Then, per capita GDP of province i can be written as

$$y_i = \sum_{k=1}^{K} y_{ik}, \tag{5.7}$$

where y_{ik} is per capita GDP for component k of province i. Let μ_k be the simple average of per capita GDP for component k. Then, we have

$$\mu = \sum_{k=1}^{K} \mu_k. \tag{5.8}$$

Using Eqs. (5.7) and (5.8), the squared CV given by Eq. (5.6) can be decomposed by GDP components as follows.

$$CV^2 = \sum_{k=1}^{K} v_k \left(\frac{cov_k}{\mu_k \mu} \right), \tag{5.9}$$

where $v_k = \frac{\mu_k}{\mu}$ is the share of component k in terms of per capita GDP and $cov_k = \frac{1}{p}\sum_{i=1}^{p}(y_{ik} - \mu_k)(y_i - \mu)$ is the covariance between GDP component k and total GDP.[2] Since the coefficient of correlation between the distribution of per capita GDP from component k and the distribution of total per capita GDP is defined by $\rho_k = \frac{cov_k}{\sigma_k \sigma}$, where σ and σ_k are, respectively, the standard deviation of total per capita GDP and the standard deviation of per capita GDP from component k, we can modify Eq. (5.9) as follows.

$$CV^2 = \sum_{k=1}^{K} v_k \rho_k \left(\frac{\sigma_k}{\mu_k}\right)\left(\frac{\sigma}{\mu}\right) = \sum_{k=1}^{K} v_k \rho_k (CV_k)(CV).$$

where CV_k is the coefficient of variation for component k. By dividing both sides by CV, we obtain the following inequality decomposition equation.[3]

$$CV = \sum_{k=1}^{K} v_k \rho_k CV_k \,. \tag{5.10}$$

If we let $s_k = \frac{\rho_k CV_k}{CV}$, then Eq. (5.10) can be modified to

$$1 = \sum_{k=1}^{K} v_k s_k \,. \tag{5.11}$$

s_k is called the relative concentration coefficient ($k = 1, 2, \ldots, K$). If $s_k > 1$ ($s_k < 1$), then GDP component k is an inequality-raising component (an inequality-reducing component). In other words, if $s_k > 1$ ($s_k < 1$), then GDP component k serves to raise (reduce) overall inequality; if GDP component k did not exist, then overall inequality would have been smaller (larger). In this study, the relative concentration coefficient is used to determine whether a manufacturing subsector is an inequality-raising or inequality-reducing sector.

2.2.3 Inequality Decomposition by Factor Components: Gini Coefficient

By the Gini coefficient (Gini), overall inter-provincial inequality in per capita GDP can be measured by

$$G = \frac{2}{p\mu} cov(\mathbf{y}, i(\mathbf{y})), \tag{5.12}$$

[2]We should note that v_k is not the share of component k in GDP, since μ is the simple average of *per capita* GDP.

[3]See Sect. 3 of Chap. 2 for the derivation of Eq. (5.10).

where $\boldsymbol{y} = (y_1, y_2, \ldots, y_p)$ and $i(\boldsymbol{y})$ is the ranking of provinces with respect to per capita GDP. Suppose that total manufacturing GDP is made up of K GDP components (GDP from K manufacturing subsectors). Then, the Gini given by Eq. (5.12) can be decomposed by K GDP components as follows.[4]

$$G = \sum\nolimits_{k=1}^{K} v_k R_k G_k, \tag{5.13}$$

where $R_k = \frac{cov(\boldsymbol{y}_k, i(\boldsymbol{y}))}{cov(\boldsymbol{y}_k, i(\boldsymbol{y}_k))}$ is the rank correlation ratio and $G_k = \frac{2}{p\mu_k} cov(\boldsymbol{y}_k, i(\boldsymbol{y}_k))$ is the Gini for component k.

If we let $g_k = \frac{R_k G_k}{G}$, then Eq. (5.13) can be modified to

$$1 = \sum\nolimits_{k=1}^{K} v_k g_k \,. \tag{5.14}$$

g_k is called the relative concentration ratio ($k = 1, 2, \ldots, K$). If $g_k > 1$ ($g_k < 1$) then GDP component k is an inequality-raising component (an inequality-reducing component). In other words, if $g_k > 1$ ($g_k < 1$), then GDP component k serves to raise (reduce) overall inequality; if GDP component k did not exist, then overall inequality would have been smaller (larger). In this study, the relative concentration ratio is also used to determine whether a manufacturing subsector is an inequality-raising or inequality-reducing sector.

3 Results

3.1 *Provincial Growth in Manufacturing GDP Between 2010 and 2019: A Shift and Share Analysis*

Before analyzing inter-provincial inequality in manufacturing GDP, we conduct a shift and share analysis to explore the determinants of provincial growth in manufacturing GDP over the period from 2010 to 2019. The result is presented in Tables 5.2 and 5.3, where Table 5.3 classifies provinces in terms of the values of the industry-mix shift component (*IMS*) and the competitive shift component (*CS*). Seven provinces have positive *IMS* and positive *CS*, of which 5 are Sulawesi provinces. These Sulawesi provinces grew rapidly in manufacturing GDP; their growth rates were all exceeding the national growth rate of 4.9%. Particularly, Central Sulawesi grew very rapidly at an annual rate of 23.9%; but this is due wholly to the rapid development of the nonmetallic mineral products sector in the mid-2010s.

[4] See Sect. 3 of Chap. 2 for the derivation of Eq. (5.13).

Table 5.2 Shift and share analysis

Code	Province	Growth (A)	RS (B)	Growth - RS (C) = (A) - (B) = (D) + (E)	IMS (D)	CS (E)	Average growth rate
11	Aceh	−2642	5003	−7645	−1902	−5742	−3.9
12	North Sumatera	26,820	39,290	−12,470	17,116	−29,587	3.6
13	West Sumatera	3842	6839	−2997	1549	−4545	3.0
14	Riau	59,620	52,096	7524	14,083	−6559	5.5
15	Jambi	5170	5769	−599	−1629	1030	4.5
16	South Sumatera	22,218	20,386	1832	−5890	7722	5.3
17	Bengkulu	1058	959	99	518	−419	5.3
18	Lampung	20,915	14,404	6511	5228	1283	6.6
19	Bangka Belitung	2755	5110	−2355	2365	−4720	2.9
21	Riau Islands	26,888	23,500	3388	−1341	4729	5.5
31	Jakarta	64,393	85,024	−20,631	4710	−25,341	3.9
32	West Java	237,779	224,780	12,999	−1840	14,839	5.1
33	Central Java	123,665	119,837	3828	−8835	12,664	5.0
34	Yogyakarta	3987	5133	−1146	1380	−2526	4.0
35	East Java	206,166	163,031	43,135	3640	39,495	5.9
36	Banten	47,043	60,045	−13,002	2686	−15,688	4.0
51	Bali	3801	3655	146	−126	272	5.1
52	West Nusa Tenggara	1247	1788	−541	345	−885	3.6
53	East Nusa Tenggara	364	309	55	73	−18	5.6
61	West Kalimantan	7410	8213	−803	2681	−3483	4.5
62	Central Kalimantan	6679	4838	1841	2135	−294	6.3
63	South Kalimantan	5168	6517	−1349	1614	−2963	4.1
64	East Kalimantan	4359	54,637	−50,278	−37,371	−12,907	0.5
71	North Sulawesi	2671	3181	−510	1732	−2242	4.3
72	Central Sulawesi	26,061	1906	24,155	248	23,907	23.9
73	South Sulawesi	21,226	13,147	8079	2385	5694	7.1

(continued)

Table 5.2 (continued)

Code	Province	Growth (A)	RS (B)	Growth - RS (C) = (A) - (B) = (D) + (E)	IMS (D)	CS (E)	Average growth rate
74	South East Sulawesi	2862	1797	1065	848	217	7.1
75	Gorontalo	526	353	173	95	78	6.7
76	West Sulawesi	2035	833	1202	487	714	9.5
81	Maluku	640	563	77	−159	237	5.5
82	North Maluku	1152	473	679	−190	869	9.5
91	West Papua	5321	7531	−2210	−6521	4311	3.7
94	Papua	915	1168	−253	−113	−140	4.0
	Indonesia	942,114	942,114	0	0	0	4.9

Source: Calculated based on Central Bureau of Statistics (various issues)

South Sulawesi, Southeast Sulawesi, West Sulawesi, and Gorontalo also grew very rapidly in manufacturing GDP, respectively, at 7.1%, 7.1%, 9.5%, and 6.7% per annum. In West Sulawesi, the food products and beverages sector is the dominant sector as it accounted for 91% of the province's manufacturing GDP. On the other hand, in addition to the food products and beverages sector, the rubber and plastics products, and nonmetallic mineral products sectors played an important role in the growth of South Sulawesi and Southeast Sulawesi, respectively. In Gorontalo, one of the smallest provinces established in 2000, the food products and beverages sector is the main sector by accounting for 67% of the province's manufacturing GDP; but, the wood products, transport equipment, and rubber and plastics sectors contributed equally to the manufacturing sector.

Lampung, one of the Sumatra provinces, grew rapidly in manufacturing GDP. Main contributor to this rapid growth was the food products and beverages sector as the sector accounted for 80% of the province's total manufacturing GDP and grew at 8.3% per annum. East Java also grew relatively rapidly. Like Lampung, the main contributor was the food products and beverages sector as the sector grew at 9.3% per annum, much larger than the sector's growth rate of 7.4% in the nation. Though the growth rate was not high, the tobacco products sector (e.g., clove cigarettes) also contributed to the province's rapid growth due to its large GDP share (24% of the province's manufacturing GDP).

Fourteen provinces are in the category of positive *IMS* and negative *CS*, of which five are Sumatra provinces, three are Java provinces, and three are Kalimantan provinces. These 14 provinces have a relatively large share of fast-growing manufacturing sectors, though some of these sectors are less competitive than in the nation. Riau, one of the Sumatra provinces, grew relatively rapidly in manufacturing GDP at 5.5% per annum. The food products and beverages sector,

Table 5.3 Shift and share analysis: classification of provinces in terms of the values of IMS and CS PI

Code	Province	IMS (−)	CS (+)	GR	Code	Province	IMS (+)	CS (+)	GR
15	Jambi	−1629	1030	4.5	18	Lampung	5228	1283	6.6
16	South Sumatera	−5890	7722	5.3	35	East Java	3640	39,495	5.9
21	Riau Islands	−1341	4729	5.5	72	Central Sulawesi	248	23,907	23.9
32	West Java	−1840	14,839	5.1	73	South Sulawesi	2385	5694	7.1
33	Central Java	−8835	12,664	5.0	74	South East Sulawesi	848	217	7.1
51	Bali	−126	272	5.1	75	Gorontalo	95	78	6.7
81	Maluku	−159	237	5.5	76	West Sulawesi	487	714	9.5
82	North Maluku	−190	869	9.5					
91	West Papua	−6521	4311	3.7					
Code	Province	IMS (−)	CS (−)	GR	Code	Province	IMS (+)	CS (−)	GR
11	Aceh	−1902	−5742	−3.9	12	North Sumatera	17,116	−29,587	3.6
64	East Kalimantan	−37,371	−12,907	0.5	13	West Sumatera	1549	−4545	3.0
94	Papua	−113	−140	4.0	14	Riau	14,083	−6559	5.5
					17	Bengkulu	518	−419	5.3
					19	Bangka Belitung	2365	−4720	2.9
					31	Jakarta	4710	−25,341	3.9
					34	Yogyakarta	1380	−2526	4.0
					36	Banten	2686	−15,688	4.0
					52	West Nusa Tenggara	345	−885	3.6
					53	East Nusa Tenggara	73	−18	5.6
					61	West Kalimantan	2681	−3483	4.5
					62	Central Kalimantan	2135	−294	6.3
					63	South Kalimantan	1614	−2963	4.1
					71	North Sulawesi	1732	−2242	4.3

Source: Calculated based on Central Bureau of Statistics (various issues)

one of the fast-growing industries, dominates the province by accounting for 72% of the province's manufacturing GDP and grew relatively rapidly at 6.6% per annum. Though the growth rate was smaller than the national average (7.4%), this made the sum of *IMS* and *CS* positive. On the other hand, North Sumatra grew less rapidly than the nation as a whole. Like Riau, the food products and beverages sector dominates the province by accounting for 72% of the province's manufacturing GDP. However, it was less competitive and its growth rate was 4.4%. This made the sum of *IMS* and *CS* negative.

In West Sumatra, manufacturing activities are more diversified than in Riau and North Sumatra. While the food products and beverages sector accounted for 47% of the province's manufacturing GDP, the textiles and wearing apparel, rubber and plastics products, and chemical and pharmaceutical products sectors contributed 21%, 17%, and 13%, respectively. However, they were all less competitive; thus, the province grew less rapidly than the nation as a whole. In Bangka Belitung, the nonmetallic mineral products sector is the main sector by accounting for 55% of the province's manufacturing GDP. But, it was less competitive than the nation with a growth rate of 1% per annum, making the sum of *IMS* and *CS* negative. The province thus grew less rapidly than the nation as a whole.

In Jakarta, the machinery and equipment sector is the main sector by accounting for 52% of the province's manufacturing GDP. The furniture sector contributed another 14%. However, these sectors were much less competitive than in the nation, making the sum of *IMS* and *CS* negative. Banten, Jakarta's neighboring province established in 2000, has a more diversified manufacturing structure. Furniture is its main sector but accounted for 22% of the province's manufacturing GDP. The basic metals, food products and beverages, and textiles and wearing apparel sectors contributed 18%, 11%, and 11%, respectively. Except furniture, these sectors were less competitive, making the sum of *IMS* and *CS* negative. In Yogyakarta, the food products and beverages sector is the main sector by accounting for 57% of the province's manufacturing GDP. The textiles and wearing apparel sector followed next with 11%. But, these sectors were less competitive, making the sum of *IMS* and *CS* negative.

Among the Kalimantan provinces, Central Kalimantan grew relatively rapidly in manufacturing GDP at 6.3% per annum. The food products and beverages sector dominates the province by constituting 84% of the province's manufacturing GDP. It grew very rapidly at 7.5% per annum, making the sum of *IMS* and *CS* positive. Like in Central Kalimantan, the food products and beverages sector is the main sector in West and South Kalimantan accounting for 77% and 67%, respectively. However, it was less competitive than in the nation, making the sum of *IMS* and *CS* negative. We should note that in South Kalimantan, the chemical and pharmaceutical products sector contributed 12% of the province's manufacturing GDP. Though it grew at 2.2% per annum, the growth rate exceeded its national average.

Among the Nusa Tenggara provinces, East Nusa Tenggara grew relatively rapidly in manufacturing GDP at 5.6% per annum. While the food products and beverages sector is its main sector accounting for 45% of the province's manufacturing GDP, the textile and wearing apparel and rubber and plastics products sectors contributed 16% and 13%, respectively. Among these sectors, the rubber and plastics products sector grew very rapidly at 6.1%, making the sum of *IMS* and *CS* positive. In West Nusa Tenggara, the food products and beverages and tobacco sectors are the main sectors by accounting, respectively, for 51% and 24%. But, these sectors were less competitive than in the nation and grew, respectively, at 5.1% and 1.3% per annum, making the sum of *IMS* and *CS* negative. Among the Sulawesi provinces, only North Sulawesi is in the category of positive *IMS* and negative *CS*. The food products and beverages sector dominates the province by accounting for 80% of the province's manufacturing GDP. But, it was less competitive, making the sum of *IMS* and *CS* negative.

Nine provinces are in the category of negative *IMS* and positive *CS*, of which three are Sumatra provinces and two are Java provinces. Riau Islands, one of the Sumatra provinces established in 2002, grew relatively rapidly in manufacturing GDP at 5.5% per annum. The basic metals sector is its main sector, accounting for 57% of the province's manufacturing GDP. Thanks to its geographical proximity to Singapore, it was very competitive and grew rapidly at 8.1% per annum. Together with the machinery and equipment sector, which contributed 9% of the province's manufacturing GDP, this made the sum of *IMS* and *CS* positive.

South Sumatra also grew relatively rapidly at 5.3% per annum. The food products and beverages sector is its main sector, accounting for 40% of the province's manufacturing GDP. It grew very rapidly at 9.9% per annum, much larger than the national average. The chemical and pharmaceutical products sector contributed another 16%. Though its growth rate was not high, it grew more rapidly than in the nation. These two sectors made the sum of *IMS* and *CS* positive. We should note that the coal and refined petroleum products sector is another main sector accounting for 20%. Though the sector is a declining industry nationally, its growth rate was positive in South Sumatra at 1.2%. Jambi has a similar manufacturing structure to South Sumatra, where the food products and beverages and coal and refined petroleum products sectors accounted, respectively, for 39% and 30% of the province's manufacturing GDP. However, these sectors were less competitive than in the nation, making the sum of *IMS* and *CS* negative.

West and Central Java grew relatively rapidly in manufacturing GDP. They have a diversified manufacturing structure. In West Java, the basic metals, machinery and equipment, and textiles and wearing apparel sectors are the main sectors, each of which accounted for around 20% of the province's manufacturing GDP. They were very competitive and grew more rapidly than in the nation. This made the sum of *IMS* and *CS* positive. On the other hand, in Central Java, the food products and beverages, tobacco products, and textiles and wearing apparel sectors are the main sectors accounting for 35%, 19%, and 9% of the province's manufacturing GDP, respectively. Among them, the food products and beverages and textiles and wearing apparel sectors grew more rapidly than in the nation, making the sum of *IMS* and *CS* positive. Owing to a large-scale oil refinery in the Cilacap district, the coal and refined petroleum products sector is another main sector accounting for 16%. Though the sector is a declining industry nationally, its growth rate was positive in Central Java at 1.7%.

As a tourist destination, Bali grew at 5.1% per annum. The food products and beverages and wood products sectors are the main sectors accounting for 41% and 30% of the province's manufacturing GDP, respectively. Though the GDP share was much smaller than these two sectors, the textiles and wearing apparel sector was very competitive and grew more rapidly than in the nation. This made the sum of *IMS* and *CS* positive. In West Papua, the coal and refined petroleum products sector dominates the manufacturing sector by accounting for 91% of the province's manufacturing GDP. Though the sector is a declining industry nationally, it achieved positive growth, enabling the province to grow at 3.7% per annum.

In North Maluku, one of the smallest provinces established in 1999, the nonmetallic mineral products and wood products sectors are the main sectors, accounting, respectively, for 45% and 35% of the province's manufacturing GDP. Thanks to the rapid development of the nonmetallic mineral products sector, North Maluku grew very rapidly in manufacturing GDP at 9.5%. In Maluku, the chemical products, food products and beverages, and wood products sectors are the main sectors, accounting for 42%, 31%, and 23% of the province's manufacturing GDP, respectively. Among them, the chemical products and wood products sectors were very competitive and grew more rapidly than in the nation, making the sum of *IMS* and *CS* positive.

Only three provinces, that is, Aceh, East Kalimantan, and Papua, are in the category of negative *IMS* and negative *CS*. Aceh is the only province that recorded negative growth. The coal and refined petroleum products sector was the main sector in 2010 accounting for more than half of the province's manufacturing GDP; but, it contracted substantially, and in 2019, it constituted less than 20%. Now, the food products and beverages and furniture sectors are the main sectors. In East Kalimantan, the second richest province next to Jakarta, the coal and refined petroleum products sector still dominates the manufacturing sector by accounting for 62% of the province's manufacturing GDP. But, since it registered negative growth, the province grew only at 0.5% per annum. In Papua, the food products and beverages and wood products sectors are the main sectors accounting for 47% and 36% of the province's manufacturing GDP, respectively. Though both *IMS* and *CS* are negative, the province grew at 4.0% per annum.

3.2 Levels and Trends of Inter-provincial Inequalities in GDP Between 2010 and 2019

Owing to the very uneven spatial distribution of mining activities, the mining sector has the highest inter-provincial inequality in per capita GDP (Fig. 5.1). However, its inequality exhibits a decreasing trend over the period 2010–2019; the Gini declined from 0.72 to 0.67. On the other hand, the agricultural sector has the lowest inter-provincial inequality since agricultural activities are closely tied to population distribution. But, its inequality shows a slight increasing trend; the Gini increased from 0.26 to 0.29. The services sector has the same level of inter-provincial

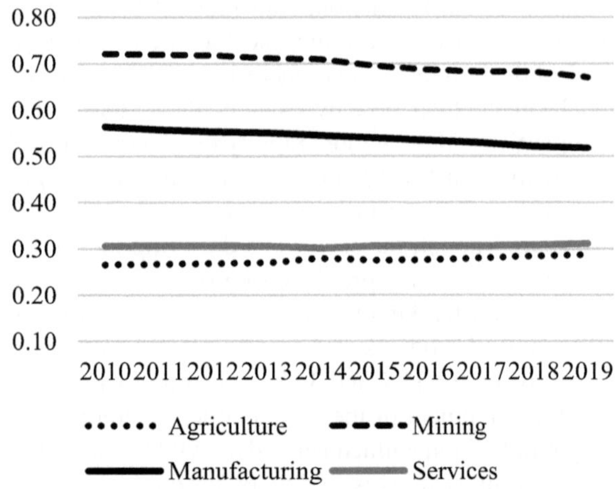

Fig. 5.1 Inter-provincial inequalities in GDP for agriculture, mining, manufacturing, and services by the Gini coefficient, 2010–2019. Source: Calculated based on Central Bureau of Statistics (various issues)

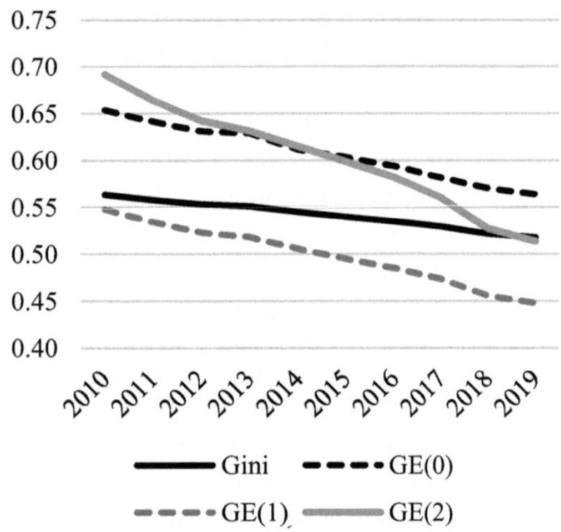

Fig. 5.2 Inter-provincial inequality in manufacturing GDP, 2010–2019. Source: Calculated based on Central Bureau of Statistics (various issues)

inequality as the agricultural sector. But, its Gini was quite stable. Since some manufacturing activities are concentrated in major cities and resource-rich regions, the manufacturing sector has a relatively high level of inter-provincial inequality, though not as high as the mining sector. Fig. 5.2 presents manufacturing sector's inter-provincial inequality by the generalized entropy class of inequality measures (*GE*(0), *GE*(1), and *GE*(2)) in addition to the Gini.[5] By all these inequality indices, it exhibits a clear downward trend; the Gini decreased from 0.56 to 0.52.

[5] *GE*(0), *GE*(1), and *GE*(2) are defined, respectively, as $GE(0) = \frac{1}{p}\sum_{i=1}^{p} \ln\left(\frac{\mu}{y_i}\right)$, $GE(1) = \frac{1}{p}\sum_{i=1}^{p} \frac{y_i}{\mu} \ln\left(\frac{y_i}{\mu}\right)$, and $GE(2) = \frac{1}{2}CV^2$. *GE*(0) and *GE*(1) are usually called the Theil *L* and

3.3 *Identifying Inequality-Reducing and Inequality-Raising Manufacturing Subsectors: An Inequality Decomposition Analysis by the* CV *and Gini Coefficient*

Which manufacturing subsectors helped to reduce overall inter-provincial inequality in manufacturing GDP? To answer this question, overall inter-provincial inequality is decomposed by manufacturing subsectors using Eqs. (5.10) and (5.13). The results are presented in Tables 5.4 and 5.5, where the manufacturing sector is disaggregated into 9 subsectors (see Table 5.1). Four manufacturing subsectors, that is, the food, tobacco and beverages, textile, wearing apparel and leather products, wood and paper products, and chemical, rubber and nonmetallic mineral products sectors, are identified as inequality-reducing sectors as their relative concentration coefficients (RCC) and relative concentration ratios (RCR) are smaller than one in the study period. Of these four subsectors, the first three are relatively labor-intensive, while the last subsector is capital-intensive.

If an inequality-reducing sector raises its GDP share, then overall inter-provincial inequality in manufacturing GDP will decrease with all other things being equal. Among the inequality-reducing sectors, the food, tobacco, and beverages sector raised its share in manufacturing GDP notably from 31.5% to 36.7% over the period 2010–2019; thus, it helped to reduce overall inter-provincial inequality in manufacturing GDP, though its inequality in per capita GDP remained unchanged (at 1.2 by the *CV* and 0.5 by the Gini). Spatially, its activities are concentrated in the Java region, particularly in the provinces of East and Central Java, which accounted for half of the GDP generated by the sector in 2019.

Another inequality-reducing sector, the textile, wearing apparel, and leather products sector, also raised its GDP share, but only slightly; thus, its effect on overall inter-provincial inequality in manufacturing GDP was small. Spatially, its activities are concentrated in the Java region. But, the province of West Java served as the center by accounting for more than half of the GDP generated by the sector. Combined with the neighboring provinces of Jakarta and Banten, almost three-quarters of its GDP was produced in 2019.

The wood and paper products and chemical, rubber, and nonmetallic mineral products sectors also served as inequality-reducing sectors. While their inter-provincial inequalities in per capita GDP are relatively small with the Gini of 0.56–0.57, they reduced their shares in manufacturing GDP (from 8.9% to 7.4% and from 14.4% to 13.4%, respectively). In the wood and paper products sector, the Java region accounted for 70% of the sector's GDP in 2019, about half of which was contributed by East Java. On the other hand, in the chemical, rubber, and nonmetallic mineral products sector, the Java region constituted three-quarters of the sector's

T indices, respectively. They all satisfy anonymity, income homogeneity, population homogeneity, and the Pigou-Dalton principle of transfers.

Table 5.4 Decomposition of inter-provincial inequality in manufacturing GDP by subsectors: coefficient of variation

	2010				2015				2019			
Sector	Share	CV	RCC	Contribution	Share	CV	RCC	Contribution	Share	CV	RCC	Contribution
M1	11.0	3.2	1.80	41.7	8.4	3.2	1.53	28.1	7.3	3.2	1.51	24.5
M2	31.5	1.2	0.31	8.4	34.2	1.2	0.36	11.5	36.7	1.2	0.42	13.9
M3	7.4	2.1	0.56	2.1	7.6	2.1	0.67	2.6	8.1	2.0	0.75	2.9
M4	8.9	1.3	0.80	7.1	7.7	1.2	0.78	6.2	7.4	1.2	0.86	6.4
M5	14.4	1.1	0.62	7.4	14.3	1.1	0.63	7.5	13.4	1.1	0.68	7.7
M6	13.6	3.0	1.33	20.5	14.1	3.1	1.72	28.7	14.2	2.7	1.54	28.4
M7	2.6	3.5	1.45	2.2	2.4	3.5	1.78	2.5	2.4	3.4	1.78	2.3
M8	9.7	3.8	1.25	8.4	10.4	3.8	1.48	10.8	9.7	3.8	1.67	11.5
M9	1.0	3.6	1.65	2.1	0.9	3.4	1.93	2.1	0.8	3.5	2.08	2.3
Total	100.0	1.2		100.0	100.0	1.1		100.0	100.0	1.0		100.0

Note: See Table 5.1 for the classification of manufacturing sectors (M1, M2, and so on). Share is % share in GDP, not % share in per capita GDP. RCC is the relative concentration coefficient. Contribution is % contribution to overall inter-provincial inequality in manufacturing GDP

Source: Calculated based on Central Bureau of Statistics (various issues)

Table 5.5 Decomposition of inter-provincial inequality in manufacturing GDP by subsectors: Gini coefficient

	2010				2015				2019			
Sector	Share	Gini	RCR	Contribution	Share	Gini	RCR	Contribution	Share	Gini	RCR	Contribution
M1	11.0	0.90	1.45	33.6	8.4	0.89	1.41	25.9	7.3	0.90	1.41	22.8
M2	31.5	0.50	0.56	15.2	34.2	0.50	0.60	18.9	36.7	0.50	0.61	20.2
M3	7.4	0.80	0.91	3.3	7.6	0.79	0.94	3.6	8.1	0.79	0.96	3.7
M4	8.9	0.57	0.79	7.0	7.7	0.56	0.78	6.2	7.4	0.55	0.85	6.3
M5	14.4	0.57	0.80	9.6	14.3	0.57	0.83	10.0	13.4	0.57	0.84	9.5
M6	13.6	0.86	1.23	19.0	14.1	0.86	1.34	22.3	14.2	0.84	1.27	23.5
M7	2.6	0.91	1.30	2.0	2.4	0.91	1.40	2.0	2.4	0.91	1.47	1.9
M8	9.7	0.91	1.28	8.6	10.4	0.92	1.35	9.8	9.7	0.92	1.50	10.3
M9	1.0	0.84	1.29	1.7	0.9	0.83	1.36	1.5	0.8	0.84	1.46	1.6
Total	100.0	0.56		100.0	100.0	0.54		100.0	100.0	0.52		100.0

Note: See Table 5.1 for the classification of manufacturing sectors (M1, M2, and so on). Share is % share in GDP, not % share in per capita GDP. RCR is the relative concentration ratio. Contribution is % contribution to overall inter-provincial inequality in manufacturing GDP

Source: Calculated based on Central Bureau of Statistics (various issues)

GDP; but, the activities were relatively evenly distributed among the provinces of Jakarta, West Java, Banten, and East Java.

The coal, gas, and refined petroleum products sector is an inequality-raising sector as its RCC and RCR are greater than one. However, it reduced its share in manufacturing GDP from 11.0% to 7.3% in the study period; thus, it helped to reduce overall inter-provincial inequality in manufacturing GDP. Its contribution to overall inter-provincial inequality decreased prominently from 33.6% to 22.8% by the Gini (from 41.7% to 24.5% by the *CV*). The sector has a very high inter-provincial inequality with a Gini of 0.9. With a large-scale LNG plant in Bontang and oil refineries in Balikpapan, East Kalimantan contributed one-third of the GDP generated by the sector. Another 40% of the sector's GDP was generated by the provinces of West and Central Java due to several large-scale oil refineries located in these provinces.

All other subsectors (the basic metals and fabricated metal products, machinery and equipment, transport equipment, and other manufacturing sectors) are identified as inequality-raising sectors with their RCC and RCR greater than one. They are capital-intensive and have very high inter-provincial inequalities. If an inequality-raising sector raises its GDP share, then overall inter-provincial inequality in manufacturing GDP will increase with all other things being equal. Among the inequality-raising sectors, the basic metals and fabricated metal products sector raised its GDP share slightly from 13.6% to 14.2% over the study period; thus, it served to increase overall inter-provincial inequality in manufacturing GDP though its inter-provincial inequality declined slightly (from 3.0 to 2.7 by the *CV* and from 0.86 to 0.84 by the Gini). Spatially, its activities are concentrated in the Java region, particularly in the province of West Java, which accounted for 43% of GDP generated by the sector. However, with three special economic zones in the Batam and Bintan islands, the province of Riau Islands, one of the Sumatra provinces close to Singapore, constituted 12% of the sector's GDP.

While the machinery and equipment sector is an inequality-raising sector, its share in manufacturing GDP was very small and remained constant. Its contribution to overall inter-provincial inequality in manufacturing GDP was only around 2%. The province of West Java dominated the sector by accounting for 85% of GDP generated by the sector. On the other hand, the transport equipment sector raised its contribution to overall inter-provincial inequality notably from 8.4% to 11.5% by the *CV* (from 8.6% to 10.3% by the Gini), though its share in manufacturing GDP remained constant at 9.7%. The Java region produced 97% of the sector's GDP; but the provinces of Jakarta and West Java dominated the sector, each accounting for 45%.

3.4 *Determinants of Inter-provincial Inequality in Manufacturing GDP*

Due to its very high inter-provincial inequality, the coal, gas, and refined petroleum products sector was the main determinant in 2010 accounting for 33.6% of overall inter-provincial inequality by the Gini.[6] While the basic metals and fabricated metal products sector had a slightly smaller inter-provincial inequality, it followed next with 19.6%. The food, tobacco, and beverages sector had the smallest inter-provincial inequality; but with its large GDP share (31.5%), it contributed 15.2% to overall inter-provincial inequality in manufacturing GDP.

Over the period 2010–2019, the coal, gas, and refined petroleum products sector reduced its GDP share from 11.0% to 7.3%. Though its inter-provincial inequality remained constant, it lowered its contribution to overall inter-provincial inequality substantially to 22.8% in 2019 by the Gini. On the other hand, the basic metals and fabricated metal products sector raised its GDP share slightly from 13.6% to 14.2%. But, with its high inter-provincial inequality, it surpassed the coal, gas, and refined petroleum products sector and became the largest contributor to overall inter-provincial inequality with 23.5%.

On the other hand, the food, tobacco, and beverages sector increased its GDP share substantially to 36.7%. Despite its small inter-provincial inequality, in 2019 it contributed 20.2% of overall inter-provincial inequality in manufacturing GDP. We should note that the transport equipment sector raised its contribution from 8.6% to 10.3% by the Gini and became the fourth largest contributor though its GDP share remained unchanged. This is due mainly to its very high inter-provincial inequality (0.92 by the Gini).

4 Concluding Remarks

This study examined the effects of structural changes on regional income inequality in the Indonesian manufacturing industry. Using provincial GDP and population data, it first conducted a shift and share analysis to explore the determinants of provincial growth in the manufacturing industry. It then performed an inequality decomposition analysis to investigate the extent to which each industrial sector contributes to overall inter-provincial inequality in manufacturing GDP. Major findings and their implications are summarized as follows.

It is not easy to reduce inter-provincial inequality in the coal, gas, and refined petroleum products sector since the sector is resource-oriented and most of its plants are located where natural resources are available. Over the period 2010–2019 however its share in manufacturing GDP declined; thus, it lowered its contribution

[6]This section discusses the determinants of overall inter-provincial inequality based on the Gini. But, the result is similar qualitatively even if the *CV* is used.

to overall inter-provincial inequality substantially. If this continues, the sector will further reduce its role in determining overall inter-provincial inequality.

With its high inter-provincial inequality, the basic metals and fabricated metal products sector became the largest contributor to overall inter-provincial inequality, though its GDP share increased only slightly. Most of its manufacturing plants are located in the three adjacent provinces of Jakarta, Banten, and West Java, which together accounted for three-quarters of its total GDP. The sector is an inequality-raising sector. Therefore, if its share in manufacturing GDP increases, it will raise overall inter-provincial inequality unless the dispersion of its activities to provinces outside Java is promoted.

While the transport equipment sector has a much smaller share in manufacturing GDP than the basic metals and fabricated metal products sector, it became the fourth largest contributor to overall inter-provincial inequality due to its very high inter-provincial inequality. The sector is capital-intensive, and most of its manufacturing plants are located in the Java region, where East Java serves as its center. It is an inequality-raising sector. Like the basic metals and fabricated metal products sector, if its share increases, it will raise overall inter-provincial inequality unless the dispersion of its activities to provinces outside Java is promoted.

On the other hand, the food, tobacco, and beverages sector is labor-intensive, and many of its factories are located close to their markets. They are evenly distributed across provinces relative to the population distribution. In 13 out of 33 provinces, the food, tobacco, and beverages sector is the main manufacturing sector constituting more than half of their manufacturing GDP. Thus, it had the smallest inter-provincial inequality. Over the period 2010–2019, its GDP share has increased prominently, and it raised its contribution to overall inter-provincial inequality significantly. The sector is likely to play an increasingly important role in determining overall inter-provincial inequality. Since it is an inequality-reducing sector, its further expansion will help to reduce overall inter-provincial inequality in manufacturing GDP.

Though the chemical, rubber, and nonmetallic mineral products sector has almost the same GDP share as the basic metals and fabricated metal products sector, its contribution to overall inter-provincial inequality is much smaller owing to its small inter-provincial inequality. More than half of its manufacturing plants are located in the Java region, but they are evenly distributed across Java provinces relative to the population distribution. The sector is an inequality-reducing sector. Thus, if its GDP share increases and its expansion is promoted not only in Java provinces but also in provinces outside Java, it will help to reduce overall inter-provincial inequality.

References

Akita, T. (1988). Regional development and income disparities in Indonesia. *Asian Economic Journal, 2*(2), 165–191.

Akita, T., & Lukman, R. A. (1995). Interregional inequalities in Indonesia: A sectoral decomposition analysis for 1975–92. *Bulletin of Indonesian Economic Studies, 31*(2), 61–81.

Anand, S. (1983). *Inequality and poverty in Malaysia: Measurement and decomposition*. World Bank Research Publication, Oxford University Press.

Armstrong, H. W., & Taylor, J. (1985). *Regional economics and policy*. Blackwell.

Central Bureau of Statistics. (n.d.). (CBS, various issues). *Gross Regional Domestic Product of Provinces in Indonesia by Industrial Origin,* Jakarta.

Esmara, H. (1975). Regional income disparities. *Bulletin of Indonesian Economic Studies, 11*(1), 41–57.

Garcia, J. G., & Soelistianingsih, L. (1998). Why do differences in provincial incomes persists in Indonesia? *Bulletin of Indonesian Economic Studies, 34*(1), 95–120.

Hill, H. (1992). Regional development in a boom and bust petroleum economy: Indonesia since 1970. *Economic Development and Cultural Change, 40*(2), 351–379.

Hill, H., Resosudarmo, B. P., & Vidyattama, Y. (2008). Indonesia's changing economic geography. *Bulletin of Indonesian Economic Studies, 44*(3), 407–435.

Hill, H., & Vidyattama, Y. (2016). Regional development dynamics In Indonesia before and after the 'Big Bang' decentralization. *The Singapore Economic Review, 61*(2), 1–26.

Pyatt, G., Chen, C., & Fei, J. (1980). The distribution of income by factor components. *Quarterly Journal of Economics, 95*(3), 451–473.

Rodrik, D. (2016). Premature deindustrialization. *Journal of Economic Growth, 21*(1), 1–33.

Shorrocks, A. (1982). Inequality decomposition by factor components. *Econometrica, 50*(1), 193–211.

Uppal, J. S., & Handoko, B. S. (1986). Regional income disparities in Indonesia. *Ekonomi dan Keuangan Indonesia, 34*(3), 286–304.

Vidyattama, Y. (2013). Regional convergence and the role of the neighborhood effect in decentralized Indonesia. *Bulletin of Indonesian Economic Studies, 49*(2), 193–211.

Williamson, J. G. (1965). Regional inequality and the process of national development: A description of the patterns. *Economic Development and Cultural Change, 13*(4), 3–45.

Chapter 6
The Impact of the 1997 Economic Crisis on Income Inequality in Indonesia: A Two-Stage Nested Theil Decomposition Analysis

Abstract During the 1990s, before the 1997 financial crisis, Indonesia achieved an annual average growth rate of more than 7% in real GDP, comparable to the rapid growth period of the 1970s. However, the crisis exerted an enormous impact on the Indonesian economy. It cast a shadow not only on the financial but also on the real sector of the economy; in 1998, the country contracted by 13%. The rapid economic growth before the financial crisis was accompanied by declining regional inequality. However, large disparities persisted in socioeconomic indicators between regions and provinces; in 1997, the per capita GDP of the richest province was almost ten times that of the poorest. How the 1997 financial crisis affected regional economies and income inequality remains one of the important policy questions in Indonesia. This chapter conducts a two-stage nested Theil decomposition analysis to examine the impact of the financial crisis on regional income inequality based on district-level population and GDP data.

Keywords 1997 financial crisis · Income inequality across districts · Two-stage nested Theil decomposition analysis · Indonesia

1 Introduction

During the 1990s, before the 1997 financial crisis, Indonesia achieved an annual average growth rate of more than 7% in real GDP. This was comparable to the rapid growth period of the 1970s, though it was achieved without the benefit of oil revenue windfalls. However, the 1997 financial crisis suddenly brought the economy to a standstill; in 1998, the economy contracted by 13%. The crisis cast a shadow not only on the financial but also on the real sector of the Indonesian economy.

The rapid economic growth before the financial crisis was accompanied by a relatively stable level of regional inequality if the oil and gas sectors are excluded;

This chapter is written by Takahiro Akita based partly on Akita (2003).

T. Akita, M. Kataoka, *Regional Inequality and Development*, New Frontiers in Regional Science: Asian Perspectives 63,
https://doi.org/10.1007/978-981-19-2968-7_6

from 1993 to 1997, the population-weighted coefficient of variation (*WCV*) in provincial GDP was in the range of 0.66–0.67 as measured at 1993 constant prices.[1] If the oil and gas sectors are included, the *WCV* was much larger due to these two sectors' very uneven spatial distribution; but, it has declined gradually as the GDP share of the oil and gas sectors has fallen.

As the world's largest archipelagic country including more than 13 thousand islands and 300 ethnic groups, Indonesia is spatially diverse in terms of its ecology, natural resource endowments, economy, ethnicity, and culture, and large differences still persisted in socioeconomic indicators between regions. In 1997 before the crisis, Java, representing slightly over 6% of total land area, accounted for 58.6% of the total population. If the oil and gas sectors are excluded, they constituted 64.1% of total GDP. Meanwhile, the resource-rich province of Irian Jaya (currently called Papua), representing 20% of the total land area, accounted for a mere 1.0% of the population and 1.6% of the total non-oil and gas GDP. The per capita GDP of the richest province (Jakarta) was almost ten times that of the poorest (East Nusa Tenggara). Thus, regional income inequality receives a great deal of public attention in Indonesia.

The 1997 financial crisis exerted an enormous impact on the Indonesian economy. How it has affected regional economies and income inequality is one of the important policy questions in Indonesia. The main objective of this study is to examine the impact of the 1997 crisis on income inequality in Indonesia by using the two-stage nested Theil decomposition method developed by Akita (2003). The method uses district-level GDP and population data to measure inequality in per capita GDP. Most previous studies, such as Esmara (1975), Uppal and Handoko (1986), and Akita and Lukman (1995), relied on provincial GDP and population data; thus, they were unable to measure inequality within provinces. Our use of district-level rather than provincial data enables us to measure not only between-province but also within-province inequalities.

The method employs the Theil indices as a measure of inequality. By the Theil indices, income inequality can be decomposed additively by population subgroups; that is, decomposed into the within- and between-group inequality components (Bourguignon, 1979; Shorrocks, 1980). In the three-level hierarchical structure of a country (region-province-district), the two-stage nested Theil decomposition method uses this decomposition property in two stages. In other words, it first decomposes inequality in per capita GDP across districts into the within- and between-region inequality components and then decomposes each within-region inequality into the within- and between-province inequality components.

---

[1] Williamson (1965) introduced the population-weighted coefficient of variation as a measure of income inequality.

2 Data and Methods

2.1 Data

Inequality in per capita GDP is measured by using district-level GDP and population data from the Central Bureau of Statistics (1997, 1998, 2000a), where GDP figures are reported in constant 1993 prices. The district-level income accounts provide data on total GDP and GDP excluding the oil and gas sectors. Regional GDP shows the amount of income generated within a region, rather than the income received by people in the region. Before the implementation of the fiscal decentralization law in 2001, much of value-added generated by a resource-rich region through extraction activities has not accrued to the people of the region, but has gone instead to other regions or abroad. Like previous studies on regional income inequality, this study excludes the oil and gas sectors in the estimation of inequality in per capita GDP across districts. It also uses provincial GDP data from the Central Bureau of Statistics (2000b) to analyze provincial differences in the growth rate of GDP in the crisis period by conducting a shift and share analysis.

2.2 Methods

2.2.1 Two-Stage Nested Theil Decomposition Method

To obtain the two-stage nested Theil decomposition method, consider the following hierarchical structure of a country: region-province-district.[2] In this study, 27 provinces are divided into five regions: Sumatra, Java-Bali, Kalimantan, Sulawesi, and Others. Let N and Y be, respectively, the population and GDP of the country and N_{ijk} and Y_{ijk} be, respectively, the population and GDP of district k in province j of region i. Then, by the Theil T index, overall income inequality is measured by

$$T = \sum_i \sum_j \sum_k \frac{Y_{ijk}}{Y} \ln\left(\frac{Y_{ijk}/Y}{N_{ijk}/N}\right). \tag{6.1}$$

If y and y_{ijk} denote, respectively, GDP per capita of the whole country and district k in province j of region i, then Eq. (6.1) can be rewritten as

$$T = \sum_i \sum_j \sum_k \left(\frac{N_{ijk}}{N}\right)\left(\frac{y_{ijk}}{y}\right) \ln\left(\frac{y_{ijk}}{y}\right), \tag{6.2}$$

[2] Section 4 of Chap. 3 provides a detailed account of the method.

since $Y = Ny$ and $Y_{ijk} = N_{ijk}y_{ijk}$. Equation (6.2) is the population-weighted Theil T index; thus, Eq. (6.1) measures interpersonal income inequality, where individuals in each district are assumed to receive the per capita GDP of their district.

Suppose now that Y_i and N_i are the GDP and population of region i, respectively. Then, overall income inequality, as measured by Eq. (6.1), is decomposed into the within-region and between-region inequality components as follows.

$$T = \sum_i \sum_j \sum_k \frac{Y_{ijk}}{Y} \ln\left(\frac{Y_{ijk}/Y}{N_{ijk}/N}\right) = \sum_i \left(\frac{Y_i}{Y}\right) T_{di} + T_{BR} = T_{WR} + T_{BR}, \tag{6.3}$$

where $T_{di} = \sum_j \sum_k \frac{Y_{ijk}}{Y_i} \ln\left(\frac{Y_{ijk}/Y_i}{N_{ijk}/N_i}\right)$ is income inequality within region i, while $T_{BR} = \sum_i \frac{Y_i}{Y} \ln\left(\frac{Y_i/Y}{N_i/N}\right)$ is income inequality between regions (between-region inequality component).

Next, let Y_{ij} and N_{ij} be the GDP and population of province j in region i, respectively. Then, income inequality within region i can be further decomposed into the within-province and between-province inequality components as follows.

$$T_{di} = \sum_j \sum_k \frac{Y_{ijk}}{Y_i} \ln\left(\frac{Y_{ijk}/Y_i}{N_{ijk}/N_i}\right) = \sum_j \left(\frac{Y_{ij}}{Y_i}\right) T_{ij} + T_{pi}, \tag{6.4}$$

where $T_{ij} = \sum_k \frac{Y_{ijk}}{Y_{ij}} \ln\left(\frac{Y_{ijk}/Y_{ij}}{N_{ijk}/N_{ij}}\right)$ is income inequality within province j in region i (within-province income inequality of province j in region i), while $T_{pi} = \sum_j \frac{Y_{ij}}{Y_i} \ln\left(\frac{Y_{ij}/Y_i}{N_{ij}/N_i}\right)$ is income inequality between provinces in region i (between-province income inequality in region i).

Substituting Eq. (6.4) into Eq. (6.3), we finally obtain the following two-stage nested Theil decomposition equation.

$$\begin{aligned} T &= \sum_i \left(\frac{Y_i}{Y}\right) T_{di} + T_{BR} = \sum_i \sum_j \left(\frac{Y_{ij}}{Y}\right) T_{ij} + \sum_i \left(\frac{Y_i}{Y}\right) T_{pi} + T_{BR} \\ &= T_{WP} + T_{BP} + T_{BR}. \end{aligned} \tag{6.5}$$

The method decomposes overall inequality in per capita GDP across districts into three components: within-province, between-province, and between-region inequality components. The within-province component (T_{WP}) is a weighted average of within-province income inequalities, while the between-province component (T_{BP}) is a weighted average of between-province income inequalities. On the other hand, the between-region component (T_{BR}) measures inequality in per capita GDP between regions. The two-stage nested Theil decomposition method can therefore examine, in a coherent framework, the contribution of within-province as well as between-province and between-region inequalities.

2.2.2 Shift and Share Analysis

Shift and share analysis is a method that has been widely used to examine the determinants of regional economic growth (Armstrong & Taylor, 1985). It divides a region's growth into three components. The first component is the region's share of national growth (*RS*). If a region grows at the national growth rate, it will maintain its share of national output. Let x_i, X_N, and ΔX_N be, respectively, regional output of sector i in the initial year, national output in the initial year, and the change in national output. Then, *RS* for sector i can be expressed as follows.

$$RS_i = x_i\left(\frac{\Delta X_N}{X_N}\right). \tag{6.6}$$

The second component, the industry-mix shift component (*IMS*), is based on the premise that a region that has a relatively larger share of output in fast growing industries should grow faster than the nation as a whole. Let X_i and ΔX_i be, respectively, national output of sector i in the initial year and the change in national output of sector i. Then, *IMS* for sector i is defined as follows.

$$IMS_i = x_i\left(\frac{\Delta X_i}{X_i} - \frac{\Delta X_N}{X_N}\right). \tag{6.7}$$

The third component is the competitive shift component (*CS*). A region may have a competitive advantage in some industries relative to other regions because its environment is conducive to the growth of these industries. Let Δx_i be the change in regional output of sector i. Then, *CS* for sector i is defined as follows.

$$CS_i = x_i\left(\frac{\Delta x_i}{x_i} - \frac{\Delta X_i}{X_i}\right). \tag{6.8}$$

The output growth of sector i of a region, Δx_i, is now given as the sum of these three components (Eqs. 6.6, 6.7, and 6.8).

$$\begin{aligned}\Delta x_i &= RS_i + IMS_i + CS_i \\ &= x_i\left(\frac{\Delta X_N}{X_N}\right) + x_i\left(\frac{\Delta X_i}{X_i} - \frac{\Delta X_N}{X_N}\right) + x_i\left(\frac{\Delta x_i}{x_i} - \frac{\Delta X_i}{X_i}\right).\end{aligned} \tag{6.9}$$

Equation (6.9) is a shift and share equation for sector i. On the other hand, total output growth of a region is given by

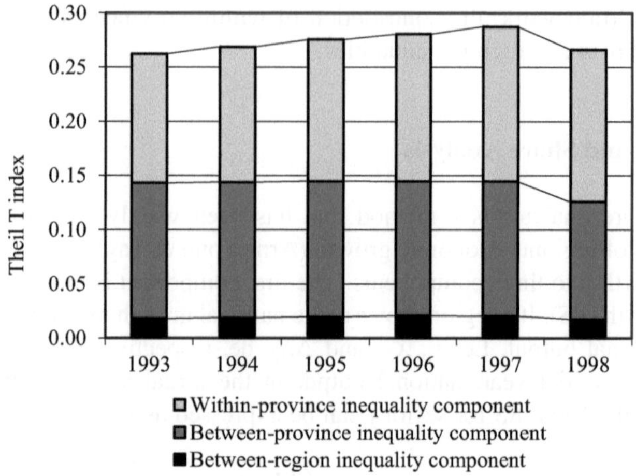

Fig. 6.1 Two-stage nested inequality decomposition, 1993–1998 (excluding the Oil and Gas Sectors). Sources: Central Bureau of Statistics (2000a)

$$\sum\nolimits_{i=1}^{n} \Delta x_i = \sum\nolimits_{i=1}^{n} (RS_i + IMS_i + CS_i),$$

where n is the total number of industrial sectors. Moving the RS_i term to the left-hand side, we obtain the following equation.

$$\sum\nolimits_{i=1}^{n} \Delta x_i - \sum\nolimits_{i=1}^{n} RS_i = \sum\nolimits_{i=1}^{n} IMS_i + \sum\nolimits_{i=1}^{n} CS_i. \tag{6.10}$$

This study calculates Eq. (6.10) for each province.

3 Results

3.1 Income Inequality before the Economic Crisis

Figure 6.1 and Table 6.1 present the results of the two-stage nested Theil decomposition analysis. Before the economic crisis, overall income inequality in per capita GDP increased significantly, from 0.262 in 1993 to 0.287 in 1997. Decomposition of overall inequality into the within-province, between-province, and between-region components reveals that this increase was due primary to the rise in the within-province inequality component; its contribution to overall inequality rose notably from 45.5% to 49.7%. The between-region component also contributed to the increase, but only slightly. On the other hand, the between-province component was very stable at around 0.125; thus, its contribution fell from 47.7% to 43.1%.

Table 6.1 Two-stage nested inequality decomposition, 1993–1998 (excluding the oil and gas sectors)

			1993		1997		1998	
Region		Province	Theil	Contrib.	Theil	Contrib.	Theil	Contrib.
Sumatra (73)			0.024	1.7	0.031	2.0	0.032	2.3
	1	DI Aceh (10)	0.019	0.1	0.020	0.1	0.018	0.1
	2	North Sumatra (17)	0.043	1.0	0.038	0.8	0.034	0.8
	3	West Sumatra (14)	0.082	0.7	0.088	0.6	0.111	0.9
	4	Riau (7)	0.225	1.8	0.299	2.3	0.303	2.8
	5	Jambi (6)	0.033	0.1	0.037	0.1	0.036	0.1
	6	South Sumatra (10)	0.032	0.4	0.036	0.4	0.031	0.4
	7	Bengkulu (4)	0.016	0.0	0.019	0.0	0.016	0.0
	8	Lampung (5)	0.066	0.5	0.065	0.4	0.048	0.3
Java-Bali (116)			0.172	43.4	0.167	38.6	0.146	35.1
	9	DKI Jakarta (5)	0.074	5.0	0.090	5.5	0.118	7.1
	10	West Java (25)	0.083	5.7	0.115	7.7	0.101	6.8
	11	Central Java (35)	0.161	6.7	0.187	6.7	0.166	6.6
	12	D I Yogyakarta (5)	0.059	0.3	0.069	0.3	0.068	0.3
	13	East Java (37)	0.311	19.3	0.377	20.9	0.365	22.0
	14	Bali (9)	0.097	0.7	0.097	0.7	0.090	0.7
Kalimantan (29)			0.066	1.8	0.069	1.8	0.076	2.3
	15	West Kalimantan (7)	0.110	0.8	0.105	0.7	0.103	0.8
	16	Central Kalimantan (6)	0.033	0.1	0.039	0.2	0.039	0.2
	17	South Kalimantan (10)	0.066	0.4	0.058	0.3	0.069	0.4
	18	East Kalimantan (6)	0.025	0.3	0.024	0.2	0.027	0.3
Sulawesi (38)			0.002	0.0	0.006	0.1	0.008	0.2
	19	North Sulawesi (7)	0.038	0.1	0.041	0.1	0.046	0.2
	20	Central Sulawesi (4)	0.002	0.0	0.001	0.0	0.002	0.0
	21	South Sulawesi (23)	0.068	0.7	0.077	0.7	0.070	0.7
	22	Southeast Sulawesi (4)	0.011	0.0	0.013	0.0	0.017	0.0
Others (47)			0.059	0.8	0.059	0.7	0.056	0.8
	23	West Nusa Tenggara (7)	0.022	0.1	0.024	0.1	0.025	0.1
	24	East Nusa Tenggara (12)	0.047	0.1	0.060	0.2	0.056	0.2
	25	East Timor (13)	0.079	0.1	0.083	0.1	0.073	0.1
	26	Maluku (5)	0.041	0.1	0.063	0.2	0.062	0.2
	27	Irian Jaya (10)	0.112	0.4	0.141	0.5	0.136	0.5
Within-Province			0.119	45.5	0.143	49.7	0.141	52.8
Between-Province			0.125	47.7	0.124	43.1	0.108	40.6
Between-Region			0.018	6.9	0.021	7.2	0.018	6.6

(continued)

Table 6.1 (continued)

			1993		1997		1998	
Region		Province	Theil	Contrib.	Theil	Contrib.	Theil	Contrib.
Total			0.262	100.0	0.287	100.0	0.266	100.0

Notes: "Contrib" is the % contribution to overall inequality in per capita GDP. The number in the parentheses are the number of districts
Sources: Central Bureau of Statistics (2000a)

3.1.1 Between-Region and Between-Province Inequalities

Among the five regions, the Kalimantan region had the highest per capita GDP over the 1993–1997 period, which was followed by Java-Bali, Sumatra, Sulawesi, and Others (Table 6.2). The modest increase in the between-region inequality in the precrisis period seems to have been due to an increasing disparity between Sumatra/ Java-Bali/Kalimantan and Sulawesi/Others.

Though the between-province inequality component remained almost constant, each region exhibited a distinct movement in between-province inequality (see Table 6.1 and Fig. 6.2). Due primary to the dominance of the capital province of Jakarta, Java-Bali's between-province inequality was the highest. However, it exhibited a slight declining trend, mainly because per capita GDP grew much faster in the province of West Java than in the other Java-Bali provinces. Accordingly, by 1997 West Java's per capita GDP had become the third highest after Jakarta and Bali, though it was the second lowest among the Java-Bali provinces in 1993. It should be noted that in the precrisis period, West Java's non-oil and gas manufacturing grew rapidly at an annual average rate of 12.5%, larger than the national rate of 10.4%. In 1997, it accounted for 37.5% of the province's non-oil and gas GDP, much larger than the comparable figure for Indonesia (24.5%).

East Java had a growth pattern similar to that of West Java in the precrisis period. Again, non-oil and gas manufacturing was the engine of growth, recording an annual average growth rate of 12.0%; in 1997, it accounted for 30.2% of the province's total GDP. Unlike West and East Java, Jakarta's GDP growth was led by the construction sector, which grew at an annual average growth rate of 12.6%. In 1997, the construction sector accounted for 15.4% of the province's total GDP.

In contrast with the Java-Bali region, the regions of Sumatra, Kalimantan, and Sulawesi recorded rising levels of between-province inequality in the precrisis period (see Table 6.1 and Fig. 6.2). Kalimantan had the second highest between-province inequality after Java-Bali and registered a very slight increase. In Kalimantan, there are very large differences in per capita GDP between the resource-rich province (East Kalimantan) and the other three provinces, and these differences seem to have increased in relative terms. In 1997, the ratio of the per capita GDP of East Kalimantan to that of the poorest province was 2.4.

On the other hand, Sumatra's GDP was more evenly distributed among its provinces and population; but, the between-province inequality increased in the precrisis period. The disparities between its richest province (North Sumatra) and

Table 6.2 Per capita GDP, excluding the oil and gas sectors

Region		Province	Per Capita GDP (thousand Rupiah)			Growth Rate (%)	
			1993	1997	1998	93–97	97–98
Sumatra			1342.1	1717.5	1583.8	6.4	−7.8
	1	DI Aceh	1308.3	1644.3	1521.6	5.9	−7.5
	2	North Sumatra	1648.5	2186.6	1981.1	7.3	−9.4
	3	West Sumatra	1448.7	1815.5	1678.7	5.8	−7.5
	4	Riau	1635.1	2162.9	2119.1	7.2	−2.0
	5	Jambi	1077.9	1296.7	1180.1	4.7	−9.0
	6	South Sumatra	1245.9	1573.3	1442.4	6.0	−8.3
	7	Bengkulu	1100.1	1225.7	1171.2	2.7	−4.4
	8	Lampung	853.4	1059.8	959.1	5.6	−9.5
Java-Bali			1661.6	2173.8	1852.5	6.9	−14.8
	9	DKI Jakarta	5801.7	7424.2	5979.2	6.4	−19.5
	10	West Java	1377.3	1882.3	1546.5	8.1	−17.8
	11	Central Java	1069.8	1338.9	1211.1	5.8	−9.5
	12	D I Yogyakarta	1390.5	1760.1	1562.5	6.1	−11.2
	13	East Java	1405.4	1827.8	1632.1	6.8	−10.7
	14	Bali	2009.6	2579.3	2447.2	6.4	−5.1
Kalimantan			2043.5	2681.6	2585.0	7.0	−3.6
	15	West Kalimantan	1506.3	1963.1	1888.8	6.8	−3.8
	16	Central Kalimantan	1968.4	2538.5	2372.9	6.6	−6.5
	17	South Kalimantan	1624.0	2092.3	1965.0	6.5	−6.1
	18	East Kalimantan	3516.0	4619.3	4558.8	7.1	−1.3
Sulawesi			1007.5	1264.1	1200.8	5.8	−5.0
	19	North Sulawesi	1091.3	1465.4	1443.4	7.6	−1.5
	20	Central Sulawesi	948.5	1138.3	1070.4	4.7	−6.0
	21	South Sulawesi	1022.9	1283.7	1211.1	5.8	−5.7
	22	Southeast Sulawesi	860.8	995.1	917.1	3.7	−7.8
Others			872.6	1096.2	1030.1	5.9	−6.0
	23	West Nusa Tenggara	719.0	897.3	859.1	5.7	−4.3
	24	East Nusa Tenggara	610.1	771.4	718.3	6.0	−6.9
	25	East Timor	623.6	825.6	813.4	7.3	−1.5
	26	Maluku	1219.8	1441.5	1342.6	4.3	−6.9
	27	Irian Jaya	1398.2	1828.8	1694.3	6.9	−7.4
Total			1520.9	1973.8	1738.1	6.7	−11.9

Sources: Central Bureau of Statistics (2000a)

the other seven provinces seem to have been increasing. While GDP was more evenly distributed among provinces and population in Sulawesi than in Sumatra, Sulawesi exhibited a growth pattern similar to those of Sumatra and Kalimantan, with per capita GDP growing faster in the richest province (North Sulawesi) than in the other provinces. Thus, Sulawesi's between-province inequality rose in the precrisis period.

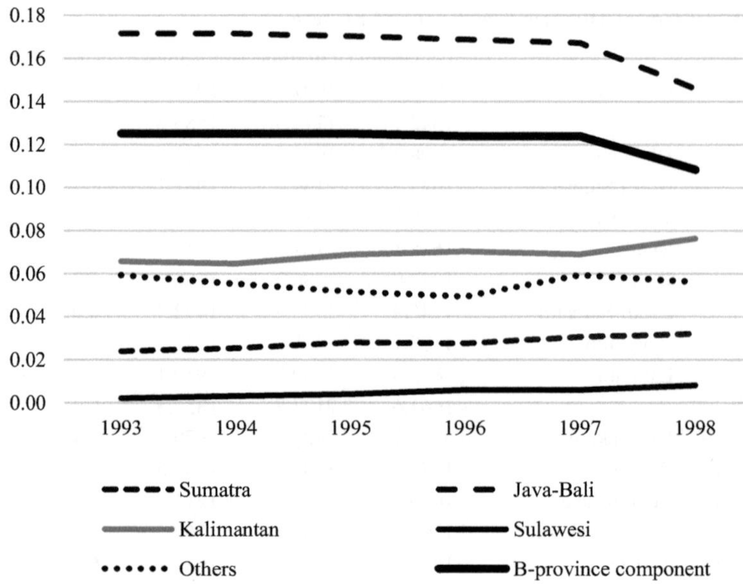

Fig. 6.2 Between Province Inequality by Region, 1993–1998. Note: B-province component is the between-province inequality component. (Sources) Central Bureau of Statistics (2000a)

3.1.2 Within-Province Inequalities

The within-province inequality component increased significantly from 0.119 to 0.143 in the precrisis period (see Table 6.1 and Fig. 6.1). As a result, its contribution to overall inequality rose from 45.5% to 49.7%. This increase was due primarily to the rises in the within-province inequalities of four provinces (Riau, Jakarta, West Java, and East Java). While their combined contribution to overall inequality was 31.8% in 1993, it had risen prominently to 36.4% in 1997. Of the 23 other provinces, 15 recorded an increase in within-province inequality. However, their contributions to the total increase in the within-province component of inequality were all negligible.

Of the 8 provinces in Sumatra, 6 recorded an increase in within-province inequality in the precrisis period. However, only Riau's increase was significant. In 1997, Riau had the highest level of within-province inequality in Sumatra, followed by West Sumatra and Lampung. Riau's level of inequality is largely due to the special position of the district of Batam, located just 20 km south of Singapore, which has received preferential treatment from the central government as an export-oriented industrial zone. Batam's per capita non-oil and gas GDP was much higher than that of Riau's other districts.

In the Java-Bali region, all but Bali experienced an increase in within-province inequality; in particular, Jakarta, West Java, and East Java recorded significant increases. In 1997, East Java had the highest level of within-province inequality, accounting for 20.9% of overall inequality. This is due to the existence of a few very rich districts (Kediri city, Surabaya city, and Gresik). With its limited population, Kediri city's per capita GDP was the highest in the entire country, well above Central Jakarta's figure. While falling far short of Kediri city, Surabaya city and Gresik had much larger per capita GDP than most other districts in East Java.

Within the Java-Bali region, Central Java had the second highest level of within-province inequality in 1997. This was driven mainly by the districts of Kudus and Semarang city, both of which had relatively high levels of per capita GDP. West Java had the third highest level of within-province inequality in 1997, but much lower than the levels recorded by Central Java and East Java. This is due to the fact that, unlike Central Java and East Java, which include the primary cities of Semarang and Surabaya, respectively, West Java does not have a dominant city and is relatively uniformly developed. In West Java, Tangerang city had the highest level of per capita GDP, followed by Bekasi, Serang, Cirebon city, and Bandung city.

In the Kalimantan region, West Kalimantan registered the highest level of within-province inequality in 1997. This was driven in part by Pontianak city, which had the highest level of per capita GDP. It is interesting to observe that while the province of East Kalimantan had a very high per capita non-oil and gas GDP, its level of within-province inequality is one of the lowest in Indonesia if the oil and gas sectors are excluded. In the Sulawesi region, three provinces experienced a slight increase in within-province inequality. South Sulawesi had the highest level in 1997, due in large part to Ujung Pandang's high per capita GDP. The Sulawesi region however had a very even distribution of GDP, not only among but also within provinces. In the Others region, the province of Irian Jaya had the highest level of within-province inequality in 1997.

3.2 The Impact of the Economic Crisis on Income Inequality

The Indonesian economy contracted significantly in 1998 as a result of the economic crisis. According to district-level GDP data, national average per capita non-oil and gas GDP fell by 11.9% in 1998 (see Table 6.2), retreating to its 1995 level. However, the impact was spatially heterogeneous; while most provinces in the Java-Bali region contracted by 10–20% in per capita GDP, the effects were much less severe in the Outer Islands.

Overall income inequality, as measured by the Theil index *T*, declined from 0.287 in 1997 to 0.266 in 1998, which is essentially the same level as in 1993–1994 (see Table 6.1 and Fig. 6.1). The two-stage nested Theil decomposition analysis reveals that about three-quarters of the decline was due to the fall in the between-province inequality component; its contribution to overall inequality declined to 40.6% from 43.1% in 1997. Consequently, the contribution of the within-province inequality component to overall inequality rose to 52.8% from 49.7%, even though the within-province inequality component, as measured by the Theil *T*, itself recorded a slight decrease. The between-region inequality component declined also, though only slightly.

3.2.1 Between-Region and Between-Province Inequalities

The economic crisis reduced Java-Bali's per capita non-oil and gas GDP by 14.8% in 1998 (Table 6.2), bringing it to the same level as in 1994–1995. In the Sumatra region, per capita non-oil and gas GDP also declined significantly, though less than in the Java-Bali region; it fell to the same level as in 1995–1996. On the other hand, the economic crisis seems to have affected Kalimantan and Sulawesi very little. As a result, between-region inequality fell from 0.021 in 1997 to 0.018 in 1998.

Java-Bali's between-province inequality played a major role in the reduction of the between-province inequality component; its contribution to overall inequality fell from 38.6% in 1997 to 35.1% in 1998 (see Table 6.1 and Fig. 6.2). Upon examining the trend in Java-Bali's between-province inequality since 1993, we find that the fall in 1998 is the continuation of a trend that began before 1997, though it is much sharper than in the precrisis period and is due to different factors.

The economic crisis affected Jakarta in a significant way. Jakarta's per capita GDP declined by 19.5% in 1998 (see Table 6.2). The resulting level is equivalent to that recorded in 1993. The economies of West and East Java also contracted substantially, though by less than that of Jakarta. The primary reason Java-Bali recorded a significant fall in between-province inequality appears to have been Jakarta's large decline in per capita GDP relative to other Java-Bali provinces. This contrasts with the precrisis period, which saw a slight decline in Java-Bali's between-province inequality, where West Java's per capita GDP grew much faster than those of the other Java-Bali provinces.

To investigate regional differences in the growth rate of GDP between 1997 and 1998, a shift and share analysis is performed using provincial GDP data from the Central Bureau of Statistics (2000b). The sector classification used in this analysis is: agriculture; non-oil and gas mining; non-oil and gas manufacturing; gas, electricity, and water; construction; trade; transport and communication; finance; and services. The result is presented in Table 6.3.

The provinces of Jakarta, West Java, and East Java contracted at much faster rates than the nation as a whole; thus, the fall in their GDP exceeded the calculated fall if these provinces had contracted at the national rate, that is, total growth minus regional share was negative for these provinces. However, there are differences in the pattern of contraction between Jakarta and the provinces of West and East Java. While the industry-mix shift component played an important role in the contraction of Jakarta, the competitive shift component played a dominant role in the contraction of West and East Java.

In Jakarta, the non-oil and gas manufacturing, finance, and construction sectors contributed significantly to a large negative industry-mix shift, reflecting the province's industrial structure, in which the combined GDP share of these three worst crisis-hit sectors was about 60%. The declines in these three sectors in the country as a whole were 18.2%, 17.3%, and 33.3%, respectively, much larger than the negative growth rate of the national economy. In Jakarta, on the other hand, these three sectors contracted by 18.0%, 9.6%, and 38.3%, respectively.

Table 6.3 Shift and share analysis for provinces, 1997–1998. Based on GDP excluding oil and gas sectors (billion rupiah)

	Province	Actual Growth (A)	Regional Share (*RS*) (B)	Total Shift (C) = (A) − (B) = (D) + (E)	Industry-Mix Shift (*IMS*) (D)	Competitive Shift (*CS*) (E)
1	Aceh	−380	−824	444	169	275
2	North Sumatra	−2733	−3139	406	368	38
3	West Sumatra	−520	−1010	490	203	287
4	Riau	−155	−1080	925	−57	982
5	Jambi	−282	−398	116	56	60
6	South Sumatra	−1082	−1551	470	127	342
7	Bengkulu	−109	−220	110	64	46
8	Lampung	−500	−909	409	91	317
9	DKI Jakarta	−12,163	−8776	−3387	−2742	−645
10	West Java	−12,744	−8583	−4161	−567	−3595
11	Central Java	−5750	−5201	−549	170	−719
12	Yogyakarta	−596	−667	71	31	40
13	East Java	−10,424	−8108	−2316	−49	−2267
14	Bali	−306	−954	648	173	475
15	West Kalimantan	−340	−911	571	94	476
16	Central Kalimantan	−297	−541	244	161	83
17	South Kalimantan	−404	−781	377	135	242
18	East Kalimantan	−317	−1440	1122	256	866
19	North Sulawesi	−89	−475	386	88	299
20	Central Sulawesi	−92	−292	201	83	118
21	South Sulawesi	−570	−1248	678	302	377
22	Southeast Sulawesi	−95	−207	112	36	77

(continued)

Table 6.3 (continued)

	Province	Actual Growth (A)	Regional Share (*RS*) (B)	Total Shift $(C) = (A) - (B) = (D) + (E)$	Industry-Mix Shift (*IMS*) (D)	Competitive Shift (*CS*) (E)
23	West Nusa Tenggara	−125	−424	300	122	178
24	East Nusa Tenggara	−77	−358	281	119	162
26	Maluku	−183	−388	205	49	156
27	Irian Jaya	931	−916	1847	518	1329
	Total	−49,402	−49,402	0	0	0

Source: Central Bureau of Statistics (2000b)

In West Java, the non-oil and gas manufacturing, finance, and construction sectors contributed to a large negative competitive shift, with their growth rates of −21.4%, −40.3%, and −46.2%, respectively. On the other hand, the non-oil and gas manufacturing and trade sectors contributed significantly to East Java's large negative competitive shift, with their growth rates of −24.3% and −17.8%, respectively. In West Java and East Java, the industry-mix shift component was also negative, owing to very large negative growth in the non-oil and gas manufacturing and construction sectors, whose combined GDP shares in West and East Java were 44% and 36%, respectively. Nonetheless, the industry-mix shift component (which is based upon the growth rates of industries in the nation) was much less significant than the competitive shift component, because of the prominence of the agricultural sector in these provinces and because the agricultural sector was much less affected by the economic crisis in the nation as a whole.

In contrast to the Java-Bali region, the Kalimantan and Sulawesi regions both recorded an increase in between-province inequality in 1998 (see Table 6.1 and Fig. 6.2). The reason seems to have been that the richest province in each region (East Kalimantan for Kalimantan and North Sulawesi for Sulawesi) performed better than the other provinces in each region, though all the provinces experienced negative growth in per capita GDP (see Table 6.2). According to the shift and share analysis, East Kalimantan and North Sulawesi had a positive total shift (= actual total regional growth minus regional share of the national growth), and more than three-quarters of the total shift was accounted for by the competitive shift component (see Table 6.3). East Kalimantan and North Sulawesi seem to have had a competitive advantage in non-oil and gas manufacturing and trade. In North Sulawesi, these two sectors achieved large positive growth, whereas in East Kalimantan they neither grew nor contracted.

Sumatra's between-province inequality was stable between 1997 and 1998 (see Table 6.1 and Fig. 6.2). In the Sumatra region, Riau performed relatively well. In 1998, Riau became the richest province in Sumatra in terms of per capita GDP (see Table 6.2). Like East Kalimantan and North Sulawesi, it appears to have had a strong competitive advantage in non-oil and gas manufacturing and trade; its competitive shift component explained most of its total shift (Table 6.3).

3.2.2 Within-Province Inequalities

In the Java-Bali region, all provinces except Jakarta experienced a fall in within-province inequality between 1997 and 1998 (Table 6.1). Jakarta's within-province inequality rose in 1998, but this was the continuation of a precrisis trend. Jakarta's rise in within-province inequality over the 1993–1998 period seems to have been due to a rising disparity between Central Jakarta, the second richest district in Indonesia next to Kediri city, and the other Jakarta districts. In 1998, Central Jakarta experienced an 8% fall in per capita GDP, while the other Jakarta districts recorded falls of 20% or more.

Together with the fact that districts in West Java adjacent to Jakarta (Tangerang, Bekasi, and Bogor) also recorded falls of 20% or more in per capita GDP, the economic crisis had very strong adverse effects on the greater Jakarta metropolitan area including Jakarta, Tangerang, Bekasi, and Bogor. The severe economic downturn in the area would have had enormous direct and indirect effects not only on the other districts of the Java-Bali region but also on the Outer Islands, because the greater Jakarta metropolitan area generated about a quarter of total Indonesian non-oil and gas GDP, and there are numerous interindustry linkages between the area and other regions, especially provinces in the Java-Bali region.

East Java experienced a slight decline in within-province inequality, but it still had the highest level of inequality in Indonesia. Like the greater Jakarta metropolitan area, East Java's major urban areas had been affected very adversely by the crisis; the relatively rich districts of Surabaya, Sidoarjo, and Gresik experienced per capita GDP growth rates of −17%, −18%, and −13%, respectively. On the other hand, Indonesia's richest district, Kediri, recorded only a minor reduction in per capita GDP (−3%). Central Java's within-province inequality declined significantly, almost retreating to its 1993 level. Again, the crisis-hit Central Java's major urban areas hardest; Semarang, Kendal, Demak, and Kudus recorded significant falls in per capita GDP (−19%, −13%, −12%, and −13%, respectively). These observations, together with the greater Jakarta metropolitan area's very severe economic conditions in 1998, confirm that Indonesia's economic crisis was a crisis afflicting urban Java (Booth, 2000). It also hit most of the other parts of the Java-Bali region, but to a lesser extent.

In the Sumatra region, all provinces except West Sumatra and Riau experienced a fall in within-province inequality in 1998 (see Table 6.1). Lampung recorded a significant decrease in its within-province inequality, due to a substantial reduction in the per capita GDP of Bandar Lampung, the richest district in the province. Among Sumatra's districts, Banda Aceh, Tebing Tinggi, Medan, Binjai, Sawah Lunto, Palembang, and Bandar Lampung registered relatively large falls in per capita GDP (around −15%). But, Batam, the richest district in Sumatra, was not significantly affected by the crisis, suffering only a 4% decline in per capita GDP. As in the Java-Bali region, the economic crisis in Sumatra seems to have hit major urban areas hardest.

In the Kalimantan region, the province of South Kalimantan recorded a significant increase in within-province inequality, because per capita GDP grew by 3% in Kota Baru, its richest district, but fell substantially in its second and third richest districts (Barito Kuala and Banjarmasin) (by 9% and 14%, respectively) (see Table 6.1). Among the municipalities in Kalimantan (Pontianak, Palangka Raya, Banjarmasin, Balikpapan, and Samarinda), only Banjarmasin had a large decline in per capita GDP, signifying that the crisis had few adverse effects on urban Kalimantan.

In the Sulawesi region, all provinces except South Sulawesi experienced a slight increase in within-province inequality in 1998, mainly because per capita GDP fell significantly in Ujung Pandang, the richest district of South Sulawesi (see Table 6.1). In North Sulawesi, four of the seven districts (Minahasa, Sangile Talaud, Gorontalo, and Bitung) recorded rises in per capita GDP, though growth rates were much lower than in the precrisis period (1–3% vs 6–12%). The crisis affected other Sulawesi districts adversely, but the effects seem to have been uniform across districts.

4 Concluding Remarks

As measured by the Theil *T* index based on district-level GDP and population data, overall inequality in per capita increased significantly over the 1993–1997 period (from 0.262 to 0.287), during which time Indonesia achieved an annual average growth rate of more than 7%. This finding does not conflict with the fact that GDP and population data from the provincial income statistics suggested quite stable inequality in per capita GDP across provinces over the same period, because, according to the two-stage nested Theil decomposition analysis, the increase is due mainly to the rise in the within- rather than between-province inequality component, especially in the provinces of Riau, Jakarta, West Java, and East Java.

The between-province inequality component increased too, but only very slightly, whereas the between-region inequality component was very stable. In the precrisis period, the within-province inequality component had played an increasingly important role in determining overall inequality, as measured using district-level data. In 1997, it accounted for about a half of overall income inequality, whereas the between-province and between-region inequality components contributed 43.1% and 7.2%, respectively. This result suggests that it would be very misleading to base a judgment about whether income inequality is increasing or decreasing solely upon provincial GDP and population data, especially when the economy is growing very rapidly and undergoing significant structural changes.

In terms of per capita GDP, the economic crisis caused the Indonesian economy to revert to its 1995 level. The impacts were very uneven across provinces and districts, however. Overall income inequality, as measured using district-level data, declined to 0.266 in 1998, which corresponded to the level prevailing in 1993–1994.

The two-stage nested Theil decomposition analysis reveals that about three-quarters of the decline was due to the fall in the between-province inequality component. The Java-Bali region played a prominent role in the fall in this component. The capital province of Jakarta was the hardest-hit province in Indonesia, owing to its heavy reliance on the non-oil and gas manufacturing, finance, and construction sectors, which were most adversely affected by the crisis; Jakarta's per capita GDP fell by almost 20%, reverting to the level recorded in 1993. The economies of other Java provinces also contracted significantly, but the impacts were less severe than in Jakarta. As a result, the per capita GDP gap between Jakarta and the other Java-Bali provinces narrowed. Among the Outer Islands, Sumatra experienced a 7% decrease in per capita GDP, but the economic crisis does not seem to have affected Kalimantan and Sulawesi very severely. As a result, the between-region inequality component fell in 1998.

The impact of the economic crisis was borne disproportionately by Java-Bali's major urban areas. In the provinces of Jakarta and West Java, the greater Jakarta metropolitan area including Jakarta, Tangerang, Bekasi, and Bogor was severely affected; with the exception of Central Jakarta, all of its districts recorded a decline of 20% or more in per capita GDP. As a result, within-province inequality fell in West Java. It also fell in Central and East Java, again because of a very large decline in per capita GDP in their major urban districts. These observations confirm that Indonesia's economic crisis was a crisis afflicting urban Java. However, with the exception of Batam, Sumatra's major urban districts also experienced a relatively large decline in per capita GDP. Thus, the crisis seems to have adversely affected Sumatra's urban areas, like those of the Java-Bali region.

References

Akita, T. (2003). Decomposing regional income inequality in China and Indonesia using two-stage nested Theil decomposition method. *The Annals of Regional Science, 37*(1), 55–77.

Akita, T., & Lukman, R. A. (1995). Interregional inequalities in Indonesia: A sectoral decomposition analysis for 1975–92. *Bulletin of Indonesian Economic Studies, 31*(2), 61–81.

Armstrong, H. W., & Taylor, J. (1985). *Regional Economics and Policy*. Blackwell.

Booth, A. (2000). The impact of the Indonesian crisis on welfare: what do we know two years on? In C. Manning & P. van Diermen (Eds.), *Indonesia in Transition: Social Aspects of Reformasi and Crisis* (pp. 145–162). Institute of Southeast Asian Studies.

Bourguignon, F. (1979). Decomposable income inequality measures. *Econometrica, 47*(4), 901–920.

Central Bureau of Statistics. (1997). *Gross Regional Domestic Product of Regencies/Municipalities in Indonesia, 1993-1995*, Jakarta.

Central Bureau of Statistics. (1998). *Gross Regional Domestic Product of Regencies/Municipalities in Indonesia, 1994-1997*, Jakarta.

Central Bureau of Statistics. (2000a). *Gross Regional Domestic Product of Regencies/Municipalities in Indonesia, 1995-1998*, Jakarta.

Central Bureau of Statistics. (2000b). *Gross Regional Domestic Product of Provinces in Indonesia by Industrial Origin, 1996-1999*, Jakarta.

Esmara, H. (1975). Regional income disparities. *Bulletin of Indonesian Economic Studies, 11*(1), 41–57.

Shorrocks, A. F. (1980). The class of additively decomposable inequality measures. *Econometrica, 48*(3), 613–625.

Uppal, J. S., & Handoko, B. S. (1986). Regional income disparities in Indonesia. *Ekonomi dan Keuangan Indonesia, 34*(3), 286–304.

Williamson, J. G. (1965). Regional inequality and the process of national development: A description of the patterns. *Economic Development and Cultural Change, 13*(4), 3–45.

Chapter 7
Inter-provincial Inequality in Labor Productivity and Efficiency in Indonesia: A Factor Decomposition Analysis

Abstract Efficiency is defined as the ratio of the actual to the optimal output. Accordingly, labor productivity (output-labor ratio) is expressed as a product of optimal labor productivity, also known as pure labor productivity, and efficiency. As a large insular and the world's fourth most populous East Asian middle-income nation, Indonesia achieved a substantial reduction in regional inequality in labor productivity during the last quarter-century. However, such large disparities persist beyond the policy goals. This study incorporates efficiency factors in the decomposition analysis that explore the sources of inter-provincial inequality in labor productivity, using balanced panel data on 26 provinces in Indonesia during 1990–2015. Our frontier analysis through conventional and bootstrap Data Envelopment Analysis computes pure labor productivity and efficiency and finds efficiency convergence. We then perform Theil's second measure-based factor decomposition analysis and find that a substantial decline in inter-provincial labor productivity gaps is attributable to efficiency convergence. Conversely, pure labor productivity increased inter-provincial inequality and became a key factor in determining inequality in labor productivity.

Keywords Regional inequality · Labor productivity · Data envelopment analysis · Factor decomposition analysis · Indonesia

1 Introduction

Regional development policies allocate available resources to enhance regional competitiveness and/or mitigate the considerable regional gap in competitiveness. Output-labor ratio, also known as labor productivity, is regarded as a proxy for regional competitiveness (Armstrong & Taylor, 2006). Efficiency is defined as the ratio of the actual to the optimal output values, where the actual output value is

This chapter is written by Mitsuhiko Kataoka based partly on Kataoka (2018).

T. Akita, M. Kataoka, *Regional Inequality and Development*, New Frontiers in Regional Science: Asian Perspectives 63,
https://doi.org/10.1007/978-981-19-2968-7_7

determined by optimal output and efficiency. Accordingly, labor productivity is expressed as a product of two variables: optimal labor productivity (hereinafter referred to as pure labor productivity) and efficiency. Despite its importance in regional development, the level and changes in the regional distribution of labor productivity and the above two proximate factors have been only infrequently examined in empirical research and policy debates.

As a large insular and the world's fourth most populous East Asian middle-income nation, having an extensive distribution of abundant natural resources, Indonesia is a regionally diverse economy with widely different socioeconomic provinces: the largest urban agglomeration capital province (Jakarta), resource-rich off-Java provinces (Ache, Riau, East and South Kalimantan, and Papua), internationally popular tourist destinations (Bali and Yogyakarta), emerging industrial clustering provinces (West and East Java), and labor-intensive agricultural provinces (all remaining provinces). The gaps in regional competitiveness are a major policy issue in Indonesia. The nation is also beset by large spatial output and factor imbalances: nearly two-thirds of its economic activities are concentrated in on-Java provinces, which account for only 6% of the land (Kataoka, 2021). The government tackled these disproportions by implementing various policies, including administrative directions in its 5-year national development plans and integrated economic development zones, interregional migration to thinly populated off-Java provinces, equity-oriented intergovernmental fiscal transfers, and decentralization reforms (Hill et al., 2008; Kataoka, 2020). However, the policy outcomes were still below the expected goals.

Figure 7.1 shows the choropleth map of the provincial distribution of labor productivity and its growth. In 1990, the relative ratio of the highest labor productivity to the lowest was over 23 (highest: East Kalimantan at 64.7 million IDR; lowest: East Nusa Tenggara at 2.8 million IDR). The provinces with higher productivity are the capital province of Jakarta and resource-rich off-Java provinces, such as Aceh, Riau, East Kalimantan, and Papua, while the lower productivity provinces are the non-resource-rich off-Java remote provinces, such as Bengkulu, Lampung, Central Sulawesi, West Nusa Tenggara, and East Nusa Tenggara. The productivity growth rate also varies by province. Resource-rich provinces show lower growth rates, while several lower productivity ones show higher growth rates. The relative ratio of the highest labor productivity to the lowest declined to nearly 15 by 2015 (Highest: Jakarta at 105.1 million IDR; lowest: East Nusa Tenggara at 7.0 million IDR). However, the labor productivity gaps across provinces remain enormous, although it has largely declined during this period.

Since Esmara's (1975) pioneering work, many studies have examined regional income and factor imbalances; however, to the best of our knowledge, few have quantified the effects of efficiency factors on regional income inequalities in Indonesia.[1] To address this gap, Kataoka (2018) used nonparametric frontier analysis

[1] See Alisjahbana and Akita (2020) and Kataoka (2021) for more details on the previous studies on regional income inequality in Indonesia.

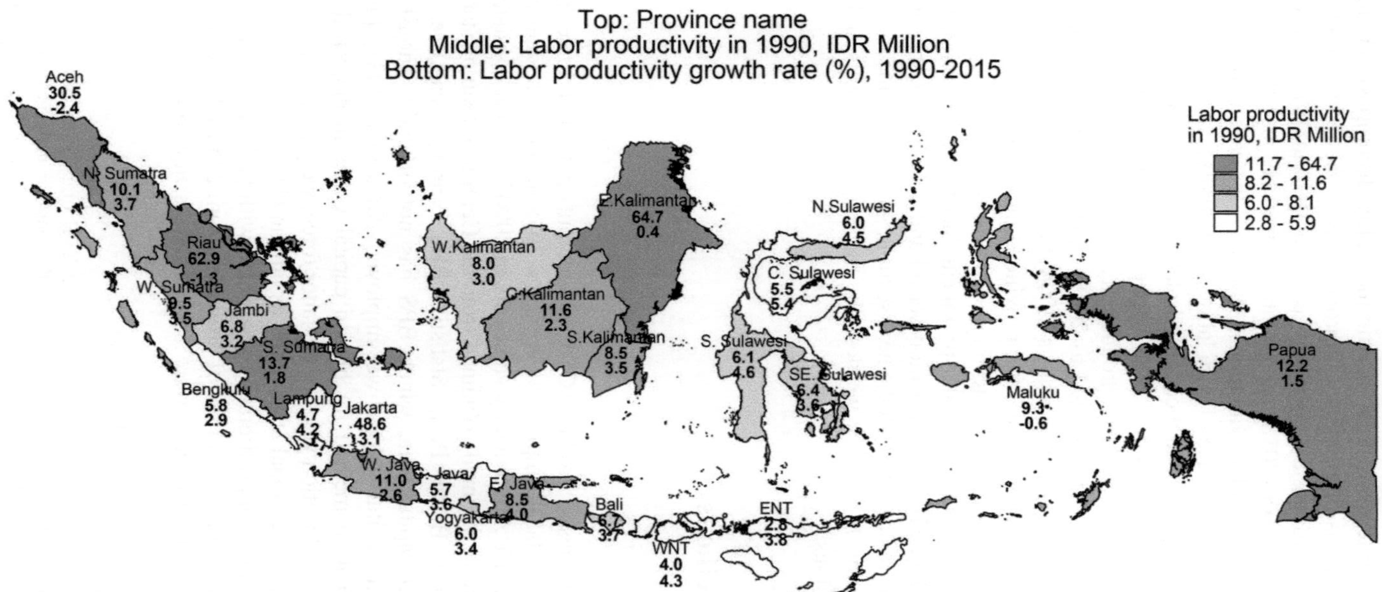

Note 1: The provincial average of the compound annual growth rate in labor productivity for 1990-2015: 2.8%.
Note 2: North, South, East, and West are abbreviated as N, S, E, and W, respectively.
Note 3: WNT and ENT are abbreviated as West Nusa Tenggara and East Nusa Tenggara, respectively.

Fig. 7.1 Provincial distribution of labor productivity in Indonesia

approaches of conventional data envelopment analysis (DEA)[2] to incorporate the efficiency factor into inter-provincial income inequality decomposition and found considerable contributions of efficiency improvements to the reduction in regional income inequality for Indonesia's 26 provinces from 1990 to 2010. However, the efficiency values in Kataoka (2018) are possibly biased because the conventional DEA method ignores any random variations. Moreover, his decomposition analysis paid little attention to the presence of pure labor productivity, which determines the long-term trend of inter-provincial inequality in labor productivity.

To rectify these shortcomings, this study applies the bootstrap DEA technique to compute the bias-corrected pure labor productivity and efficiency for each province of Indonesia's 26 provinces from 1990 to 2015, extended from the conventional DEA technique. Then, using Cheng and Li's (2006) factor decomposition technique, we explore the factors contributing to inter-provincial inequality in labor productivity. This study also applies a filtering technique to remove regional cyclical stocks and quantify the long-term trends in inter-provincial inequality for each factor. This study extends Kataoka's (2018) observation period and analyzes labor productivity and its proximate in greater detail. In the next section, we describe the methods and data used in this study. In Sect. 3, we describe the empirical results and Sect. 4 presents our conclusions.

2 Data and Methods

2.1 Data

We use the gross domestic product (GDP) for output and labor force, physical capital, and human capital for inputs, covering the 26 contiguous Indonesian provinces from 1990 to 2015. All monetary values are in 2000 base-year constant prices. All provincial data were originally obtained from the Central Bureau of Statistics of Indonesia (Indonesian: Badan Pusat Statistik, BPS, Various years), except for physical and human capital data, which BPS has not officially published. For physical and human capital values, we employed Kataoka's (2021) provincial estimates. The evaluation method for human capital varies in empirical studies. We define the average education years of the labor force, weighted by the provincial labor force's share of educational attainment, as human capital.

In Indonesia, the regional proliferation associated with political reforms after the 1997–1998 crisis increased the number of provinces from 27 in 1997 to 34 in 2015. Namely, eight additional provinces were established as new provinces, and one

[2]DEA was originally applied in frontier analysis at microlevel units, such as firms and plants; however, it subsequently became a popular tool in regional economic analysis as an alternative to growth accounting and regression analysis after Charnes et al. (1989) study evaluating the relative efficiency of 28 Chinese cities (Enflo & Hjertstrand, 2009; Schaffer et al., 2011).

province, East Timor, became an independent nation.[3] However, the data were not adjusted for these changes. To solve these inconsistent areal unit problems, we aggregated new and existing province data in the corresponding year for the solution, following several previous studies (Kataoka, 2013, 2018, 2020, 2021; Mendez, 2020; Mendez & Kataoka, 2020).

Table 7.1 presents the summary statistics for the input and output variables in 1990 and 2015.[4] Welch's mean comparison test confirms that the means of all variables, except human capital, increased between 1990 and 2015, as did their statistical significance. Additionally, the output variables increased the inequalities across provinces, as measured by the coefficient of variation, while the input variables decreased them.

2.2 Methods

This study incorporates the efficiency factor for inter-provincial inequality decomposition analysis in labor productivity through the two stages of analysis: (1) DEA-based frontier analysis and (2) Theil's second measure-based factor decomposition analysis. We define efficiency in a province as the ratio of the actual to the optimal output, where a province achieves best-practice performance. Thus, labor productivity is expressed as a product of pure labor productivity and efficiency. Let Y_i, Y_{ei}, and L_i be the actual output, optimal output, and labor in province i, respectively. Labor productivity in province i, denoted by $x_i = \frac{Y_i}{L_i}$ is expressed as follows:

$$x_i = xe_i \cdot oe_i \tag{7.1}$$

where $xe_i = \frac{Y_{ei}}{L_i}$ and $oe_i = \frac{Y_i}{Y_{ei}}$ are pure labor productivity, that is, a proxy for the optimal level of regional competitiveness and efficiency, which is equivalent to the overall technical efficiency (oe) in DEA. The former is labor productivity when the overall technical inefficiency is removed.

To generate pure labor productivity and efficiency, we applied a DEA-based frontier analysis, given actual input and output observations. After linearizing the product in Eq. (7.1) using the natural logarithm, it additively decomposes regional inequality in labor productivity into three components: regional inequality in pure labor productivity, regional inequality in efficiency, and an interpretive residual term.

[3]The eight newly established provinces are North Maluku (Maluku, 1999), West Papua (Papua, 1999), Banten (West Java, 2000), Bangka-Belitung (South Sumatra, 2000), Gorontalo (North Sulawesi, 2000), Riau Islands (Riau, 2002), West Sulawesi (South Sulawesi, 2004), and North Kalimantan (East Kalimantan, 2012). The name of the original province and the year when the new province was established are shown between parentheses (Kataoka, 2021).

[4]The output and factor input data for all 26 provinces over 1990–2015 is shared online.

Table 7.1 Descriptive statistics

Variable	GDP (Y, trillion IDR)		Labor (L, million)		Physical capital (K, trillion IDR)		Human capital (H, years)		Labor productivity (x, Million IDR)	
Year	1990	2015	1990	2015	1990	2015	1990	2015	1990	2015
Mean	34.2	112.9	3.0	4.7	59.5	244.1	5.56	8.64	14.5	23.5
Median	10.7	39.7	1.4	2.3	14.8	94.9	5.46	8.60	8.2	17.9
Minimum	3.2	9.9	0.5	1.0	3.0	11.3	4.06	6.20	2.8	7.0
Province	Bengkulu	Maluku	Southeast Sulawesi	Bengkulu	Southeast Sulawesi	Maluku	West Nusa Tenggara	Papua	East Nusa Tenggara	East Nusa Tenggara
Share (%)	0.4	0.3	0.7	0.8	0.2	0.2	–	–	–	–
Maximum	154.0	549.4	15.8	25.9	450.3	1644.3	9.00	11.18	64.7	105.1
Province	Jakarta	West Java	East Java	West Java	Jakarta	Jakarta	Jakarta	Jakarta	East Kalimantan	Jakarta
Share (%)	17.3	18.7	20.4	21.2	29.1	25.9	–	–	–	–
CV	1.332	1.408	1.429	1.344	1.747	1.496	0.179	0.110	1.196	0.891

Note: CV is the coefficient of variation

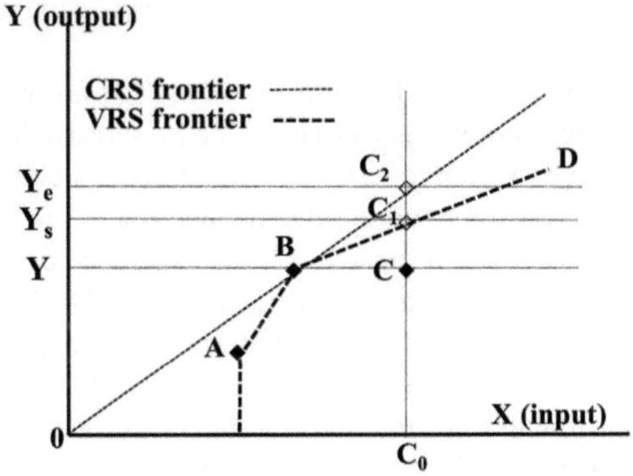

Fig. 7.2 Graphical illustration of the CRS/VRS frontiers

2.2.1 DEA-based Frontier Analysis

DEA is a linear programming method used to compute the relative input-output efficiency for each decision-making unit (DMU) that uses inputs to produce outputs.[5] DEA derives a piecewise linear surface, called a "frontier," which connects the best-performing DMUs and envelops the remainder in the observed data. The frontier differs according to the returns-to-scale (RTS) assumptions that underlie the model. Two assumptions are typically applied: constant returns-to-scale (CRS) and variable returns-to-scale (VRS).

Figure 7.2 illustrates the piecewise linear frontiers for the four observed DMUs, A–D. The diagonal passing through 0B represents the CRS frontier, whereas the concave envelope, ABD, represents the VRS frontier. All DMUs on the CRS frontier, such as DMU B, utilize resources at the maximum level and allocate resources at the optimal level, i.e., those operating at the most productive scale size. In contrast, all DMUs on the VRS frontier, such as DMUs A and D utilize resources at the maximum level. The relative distance between the actual and projected production values on the frontier indicates the efficiency score, which is assigned to each DMU and ranges from zero to unity. DMUs on the frontier are efficient, and the corresponding score values are equal to unity, whereas those that are not on the frontier are inefficient, and their scores are below unity (Cooper et al., 2006).

DEA models have two orientations: input- and output-oriented. The former (latter) minimizes (maximizes) the DMUs' level of input (output) without changing the output (input) values. DMU B on a straight line is efficient under both CRS and VRS, whereas all the observed DMUs, except for C, are efficient under VRS. Under the output-oriented orientation, C_1 and C_2 are projected DMUs under the VRS and CRS, respectively, as they maximize the DMUs' levels of output, given an unchanged input C_0. On the y-axis, Y, Y_s, and Y_e are the actual and projected output values on the VRS and CRS frontiers at C's input value C_0, respectively. Defining the overall technical efficiency score as $oe_i = Y_i/Y_{ei}$,the relationship between the oe score and the proximate variables is expressed as

[5] See Coelli et al. (2005) and Cooper et al. (2006) for a more detailed and technical discussions on DEA.

$$oe_i = pe_i \cdot se_i, \tag{7.2}$$

where pe_i ($=Y_i/Y_{si}$) and se_i ($=Y_{si}/Y_{ei}$) are pure technical efficiency and scale efficiency scores, respectively. The *pe* score helps assess the ability of a DMU to utilize a given resource, whereas the *se* score helps assess the optimality of the operation size. In other words, the former (latter) indicates the DMU's resource utilization (allocation) efficiency. The *oe* score helps assess the comprehensive ability of a DMU to utilize and allocate resources. DMUs with inefficient utilization below their maximum level are attributable to managerial underperformance, whereas those allocating at a nonoptimal level (i.e., too large or too small an operation size) are attributable to imperfect competition, government regulation, and financial access constraints. Y_e is the output value at the most productive scale size, where it removes overall technical inefficiency. When DMU C increases above the C_2 level, the frontier 0B shifts upward. Such an output increase embodies technological progress.

The study in this section treats a province as a DMU and uses output-oriented CRS and VRS models, considering limited province-specific resource endowments and the presence of economies or diseconomies of scale in Indonesia's provinces. Assume that each province i ($i = 1, \ldots, n$) uses m inputs X_{ij} ($j = 1, \ldots, m$) to produce a single output Y_i: In the output-oriented DEA model, Y_{si} and Y_{ei} are the projected outputs of province i without pure technical inefficiency and overall technical inefficiency, respectively. Our application uses three input variables of physical and human capital and labor, denoted as K, H, and L, and a single output variable proxied by GDP, denoted as Y.

We conducted the following linear programming routine to obtain the pe_{i0} score of one of the n provinces under evaluation (output-oriented VRS model), denoted province $i0$:

$$\begin{aligned} &\text{Max}_{\theta,z}\theta \\ &\text{s.t.} \quad \theta\, Y_{i0} \le \textstyle\sum_{i=1}^{n} z_i Y_i \quad (i = 1, 2, \ldots, n) \\ &\qquad \textstyle\sum_{i=1}^{n} z_i X_{ij} \le X_{i0j} \quad (j = K, H, \text{and } L) \\ &\qquad \textstyle\sum_{i=1}^{n} z_i = 1 \\ &\qquad z_i \ge 0. \end{aligned} \tag{7.3}$$

where θ and z are the decision variables, ($1/\theta$) represents the pe_{io} score, and z is an unknown optimal weight for each province that takes a nonnegative value. After removing the second-last constraint, we obtained the oe_{io} scores under CRS.

Additionally, we considered stochastic noise in terms of efficiency measurement. The efficiency scores derived from the conventional DEA estimator are "calculated" rather than statistically "estimated." The conventional frontier is defined only relative to the best-practice productions in the observed set of finite-sample data. If more efficient provinces exist outside the sample data, the "true" frontier might lie above the conventional frontier. Therefore, upward biases are theoretically evident in the conventional DEA estimator (Enflo & Hjertstrand, 2009; Toma et al., 2017). To address this drawback, we apply the bootstrapping technique developed by Simar and Wilson (1998, 1999, 2000) to estimate the bias-corrected efficiency score and obtain confidence intervals. The bootstrap procedure generates a multiple pseudo-dataset by drawing with replacement from an original sample and then produces multiple estimates that can be used for statistical inference. The true model is assumed to lie between the lower and upper intervals. In this study, 2000 bootstrap replicates were used.

2.2.2 Theil's Second Measure-based Factor Decomposition Analysis

This subsection shows Theil's second measure-based factor decomposition analysis, introduced by Cheng and Li (2006), which identifies the factors determining inter-provincial inequality in labor productivity and the *oe* score derived from Eqs. (7.1) and (7.2).[6] For inequality decompositions in labor productivity, *let* μ_x, μ_{xe}, and μ_{oe} be the simple provincial average values of x_i and their corresponding multiplicative elements, xe_i and oe_i (i.e., $\left[\mu_x = \left(\frac{1}{n}\right)\sum_{i=1}^{n} x_i\right]$). Then, the inter-provincial inequality of labor productivity was measured using Theil's second measure, also known as Theil L index (Anand, 1983; Theil, 1967), as follows:

$$L_x = \sum_{i=1}^{n} \left(\frac{1}{n}\right) \ln \left(\frac{1/n}{x_i / \sum_{i=1}^{n} x_i}\right) = \sum_{i=1}^{n} \left(\frac{1}{n}\right) \ln \left(\frac{\mu_x}{x_i}\right) \quad [L_x \geq 0], \tag{7.4}$$

Note that the inequality value in Eq. (7.4) is weighted by the total number of province units (1/*n*). Substituting Eq. (7.1) into Eq. (7.4) and multiplying the quotient inside the natural logarithm by $[(\mu_{xe} \cdot \mu_{oe})/((\mu_{xe} \cdot \mu_{oe}))]$ yields

$$\begin{aligned} L_x &= \sum_{i=1}^{n} \left(\frac{1}{n}\right) \ln \left(\frac{\mu_{xe}}{xe_i} \cdot \frac{\mu_{oe}}{oe_i} \cdot \frac{\mu_x}{\mu_{xe} \cdot \mu_{oe}}\right) \\ &= \left(\frac{1}{n}\right) \sum_{i=1}^{n} \ln \left(\frac{\mu_{xe}}{xe_i}\right) + \left(\frac{1}{n}\right) \sum_{i=1}^{n} \ln \left(\frac{\mu_{oe}}{oe_i}\right) + \ln \left(\frac{\mu_x}{\mu_{xe} \cdot \mu_{oe}}\right) \\ &= \sum_{i=1}^{n} \left(\frac{1}{n}\right) \ln \left(\frac{1/n}{xe_i / \sum_{i=1}^{n} xe_i}\right) + \sum_{i=1}^{n} \left(\frac{1}{n}\right) \ln \left(\frac{1/n}{oe_i / \sum_{i=1}^{n} oe_i}\right) \\ &\quad + \ln \left(\frac{\mu_x}{\mu_{xe} \cdot \mu_{oe}}\right) \\ &= L_{xe} + L_{oe} + + \ln \left(\frac{\mu_x}{\mu_{xe} \cdot \mu_{oe}}\right), \end{aligned} \tag{7.5}$$

where L_{xe} and L_{oe} are strict Theil L indices of pure labor productivity and overall technical efficiency, respectively. This is because the weight given before the natural logarithm is the total number of provincial units (1/*n*) and takes nonnegative values.

[6] Section 5 of Chap. 3 provides a detailed account of the method.

Conversely, the third term is not a Theil index as it takes a negative value. In addition, it does not provide any interpretation. Transforming this term to be interpretive, we express the covariance of the two element variables, denoted as ***cov((xe, oe)***, as follows:

$$\begin{aligned} cov(xe, oe) &= \left(\frac{1}{n}\right)\sum\nolimits_{i=1}^{n}(xe_i - \mu_{xe})(oe_i - \mu_{oe}) \\ &= \left(\frac{1}{n}\right)\sum\nolimits_{i=1}^{n}(xe_i \cdot oe_i) - \mu_{oe} \cdot \left(\frac{1}{n}\right)\sum\nolimits_{i=1}^{n} xe_i \\ &\quad - \mu_{xe} \cdot \left(\frac{1}{n}\right)\sum\nolimits_{i=1}^{n} oe_i + \mu_{xe} \cdot \mu_{oe} \\ &= \left(\frac{1}{n}\right)\sum\nolimits_{i=1}^{n} x_i - \mu_{xe} \cdot \mu_{oe} - \mu_{xe} \cdot \mu_{oe} + \mu_{xe} \cdot \mu_{oe} = \mu_x - \mu_{xe} \cdot \mu_{oe} \end{aligned} \tag{7.6}$$

Equation (7.6) is modified as follows:

$$\mu_x = cov(xe, oe) + \mu_{xe} \cdot \mu_{oe}. \tag{7.7}$$

Then, dividing both sides by $(\mu_{xe} \cdot \mu_{oe})$, we obtain:

$$\frac{\mu_x}{\mu_{xe} \cdot \mu_{oe}} = \frac{cov(xe, oe)}{\mu_{xe} \cdot \mu_{oe}} + 1. \tag{7.8}$$

Substituting Eq. (7.8) into Eq. (7.5), we obtain:

$$\begin{aligned} L_x &= \left(\frac{1}{n}\right)\sum\nolimits_{i=1}^{n} \ln\left(\frac{\mu_{xe}}{xe_i}\right) + \left(\frac{1}{n}\right)\sum\nolimits_{i=1}^{n} \ln\left(\frac{\mu_{oe}}{oe_i}\right) + \ln\left(\frac{cov(xe, oe)}{\mu_{xe} \cdot \mu_{oe}} + 1\right) \\ &= L_{xe} + L_{oe} + \lambda(xe, oe), \end{aligned} \tag{7.9}$$

where $\lambda(xe, oe)$ denotes the interaction term, which can be positive, negative, or zero if the two element variables are positively correlated, negatively correlated, or not correlated, respectively. On the left-hand side of Eq. (7.8), all three mean values take positive values, and then $\frac{\mu_{oe}}{(\mu_{pe} \cdot \mu_{se})} = \left(\frac{cov(pe, se)}{\mu_{pe} \cdot \mu_{se}} + 1\right) > 0$. When the two element variables are negatively correlated, Eq. (7.8) takes a nonnegative value below unity, and the interaction term in the natural logarithmic transformation in Eq. (7.9) shows negative values. Accordingly, the third term in Eq. (7.9) becomes an interpretative residual term.

Similarly, we obtain as follows from Eq. (7.2):

$$L_{oe} = L_{pe} + L_{se} + \lambda(pe, se). \tag{7.10}$$

Subsequently, using Eqs. (7.9) and (7.10), we decompose the inter-provincial inequality in labor productivity and efficiency and quantify the contribution of each factor to the overall inter-provincial inequality.

3 Results

This section presents the two empirical results of (a) the DEA-based frontier analysis and (b) Theil's second measure-based factor decomposition analysis for 1990–2015. The former measures the relative input-output efficiency for each province, whereas the latter quantifies each decomposition factor contributing to the overall inequality in labor productivity. To explore the long-term trend of inter-provincial inequalities, we applied Hodrick–Prescott filtering (1997) to remove the cyclical component from the original values and derive the long-run trend component.[7]

3.1 *Measuring Conventional and Bias-corrected Relative Efficiency by Province*

We computed the conventional and bias-corrected bootstrap DEA efficiency scores and pure labor productivity of 26 provinces for 1990–2015.[8] Table 7.2 summarizes the efficiency scores based on the trend components in the first and last observation years (see Table 7.4 for the results of the efficiency scores in each province). The following findings are noteworthy.

First, the conventional *oe* and *pe* efficiency scores in 1990 and 2015 show greater values than the corresponding bias-corrected values at the minimum, mean, and median values. The conventional *oe* and *pe* measures exhibit the presence of the best-practice provinces with conventional scores of 1, while the bias-corrected measures do not. This indicates that the conventional efficiency scores are overestimated and hold positive bias values, as the bias-corrected frontier theoretically lies above the conventional frontier. These findings were also confirmed for all provinces (see Table 7.4). Note that the bias-corrected *se* scores likely exceed one, unlike other bias-corrected scores, which range between zero and unity. The bias-

[7] Our filtering technique is applied to each of input and output variable with a smoothing parameter of 6.25. This smoothing parameter value has been employed by Ravn and Uhlig (2002) and has been applied in several studies on Indonesia (Gunawan et al., 2019; Kurniawan et al., 2019; Mendez & Kataoka, 2020).

[8] We use command *teradialbc* developed by Badunenko and Mozharovskyi (2016) in Stata for computations. We applied a homogeneous smoothed bootstrap method to estimate the bias-corrected scores.

Table 7.2 Summary of conventional and bias-corrected efficiency scores and pure labor productivity

		Conventional measures				Bias-corrected measures			
Variable	Year	*oe*	*pe*	*se*	*xe*	*oe*	*pe*	*se*	*xe*
Minimum	1990	0.175	0.225	0.175	7.14	0.139	0.188	0.192	9.59
	2015	0.435	0.556	0.435	8.10	0.393	0.525	0.449	9.29
	2015/1990	3.6	3.6	3.6	0.5	4.2	4.1	3.4	−0.1
Maximum	1990	1.000	1.000	1.000	65.85	0.776	0.800	1.067	96.59
	2015	1.000	1.000	1.000	103.84	0.947	0.941	1.030	128.35
	2015/1990	0.0	0.0	0.0	1.8	0.8	0.6	−0.1	1.1
Mean	1990	0.511	0.669	0.771	27.01	0.382	0.532	0.718	35.70
	2015	0.795	0.872	0.914	29.47	0.725	0.805	0.902	32.90
	2015/1990	1.8^{*}	1.1^{*}	0.7^{*}	0.3	2.6^{*}	1.7^{*}	0.9^{*}	−0.3
Median	1990	0.336	0.609	0.872	25.47	0.264	0.535	0.798	31.77
	2015	0.831	0.893	0.992	23.53	0.770	0.851	0.963	24.74
	2015/1990	$3.6^{\dagger}$	$1.5^{\dagger}$	$0.5^{\dagger}$	−0.3	$4.3^{\dagger}$	$1.9^{\dagger}$	$0.8^{\dagger}$	−1.0
Coefficient of variation	1990	0.653	0.461	0.344	0.551	0.604	0.411	0.334	0.612
	2015	0.232	0.155	0.171	0.708	0.215	0.133	0.165	0.786
Skewness	1990	0.612	−0.092	−0.964	1.026	0.555	−0.249	−0.748	1.374
	2015	−0.633	−0.801	−2.124	2.197	−0.892	−1.142	−2.204	2.411
# of efficient provinces	1990	7	10	7	–	0	0	0	–
	2015	6	9	8	–	0	0	0	–

Note: 2015/1990 indicates the compound annual growth rate (%)

All conventional and bias-corrected efficiency scores, except the conventional *se* score, showed statistically significant differences ($p < 0.05$) in the distribution function between 1990 and 2015, based on the Kolmogorov-Smirnov test

All conventional and bias-corrected efficiency values showed statistically significant differences ($p < 0.05$) in the distribution function between the *pe* and *se* scores in 1990 and 2015, based on the Kolmogorov-Smirnov test

* Denotes statistically significant difference ($p < 0.05$) between 1990 and 2015 based on Welch's mean equality test

† Denotes a statistically significant difference ($p < 0.05$) between 1990 and 2015 based on the nonparametric equality-of-medians test

corrected *se* scores were calculated from the bias-corrected *oe* and *pe* scores, which were in turn independently estimated based on multiple pseudo-replicates of inputs and outputs in the bootstrap CRS and VRS models (see Eq. (7.3)). The values of the pseudo-dataset between the two models are not identical; thus, the maximum values of the *se* scores are possibly over unity.

Second, regarding the changes in the conventional and bias-corrected *pe* and *se* scores for 1990–2015, the provincial mean and median values grew. Both Welch's mean equality test and the nonparametric equality-of-medians test (Wilcoxon matched-pairs signed-rank test) confirm the aforementioned results for all scores. Table 7.4 shows that most provinces experienced positive growth for both conventional scores, indicating they improved relative efficiencies both in resource utilization and allocation for the observation period. Several rich-resource provinces with higher productivity, such as Aceh and Riau provinces, failed to improve efficiency.

Third, comparing the conventional and bias-corrected values between the *pe* and *se* scores in 1990 and 2015, the *pe* score shows lower mean and median values than the *se* score. However, our statistical test results only verified the above results for bias-corrected measures. Table 7.4 shows that 15 (14) provinces show greater conventional scores in resource allocation (*se*) than those in resource utilization (*pe*) in 1990 (2015). Nearly over half of all provinces took resource utilization inefficiency more seriously than resource allocation. The Kolmogorov-Smirnov test confirmed that *pe* and *se* scores had different distribution functions in 1990 and 2015. For the distribution of resource allocation efficiency, Papua province had in 2015 was an outlier of the *se* score in the lower long tail. Policies to adjust the operation scale should be considered for outlier provinces in a negatively skewed distribution.

Fourth, for the coefficient of variation, the inter-provincial disparities for all efficiency scores declined from 1990 to 2015. This refers to σ-convergence, which simply indicates an inequality reduction among provinces over time. In 1990, *pe*'s disparity is larger than *se*'s disparity; however, the decline in *pe*'s disparity is larger than the decline in *se*'s disparity. In 2015, *pe*'s disparity became smaller than *se*'s disparity. The provincial gaps in resource utilization efficiency decreased more than those in resource allocation efficiency, although they both declined over the entire period. Figures 7.3a–c plot each of the three conventional efficiency scores in 1990 (x-axis) against the corresponding average annual growth rates for 1990–2015 (y-axis). All figures show negative and significant coefficient values with a high coefficient of determinant values, that is, the regression line has a downward slope. Our Ramsey RESET test failed to reject the null hypothesis of no omitted variables for all efficiency scores. This indicates statistically significant absolute β-convergence, meaning the lower efficiency provinces grew faster than the higher efficiency ones and all provinces converged towards the same steady state.[9] Although the figures are not shown, we verified the presence of absolute β-convergence in the bias-corrected measures.

Lastly, in pure labor productivity, Indonesia experienced stagnant growth, unlike the relative efficiencies. The inter-provincial gaps, measured by the coefficient of

[9] Section 5 of Chap. 2 provides a detailed account of the method.

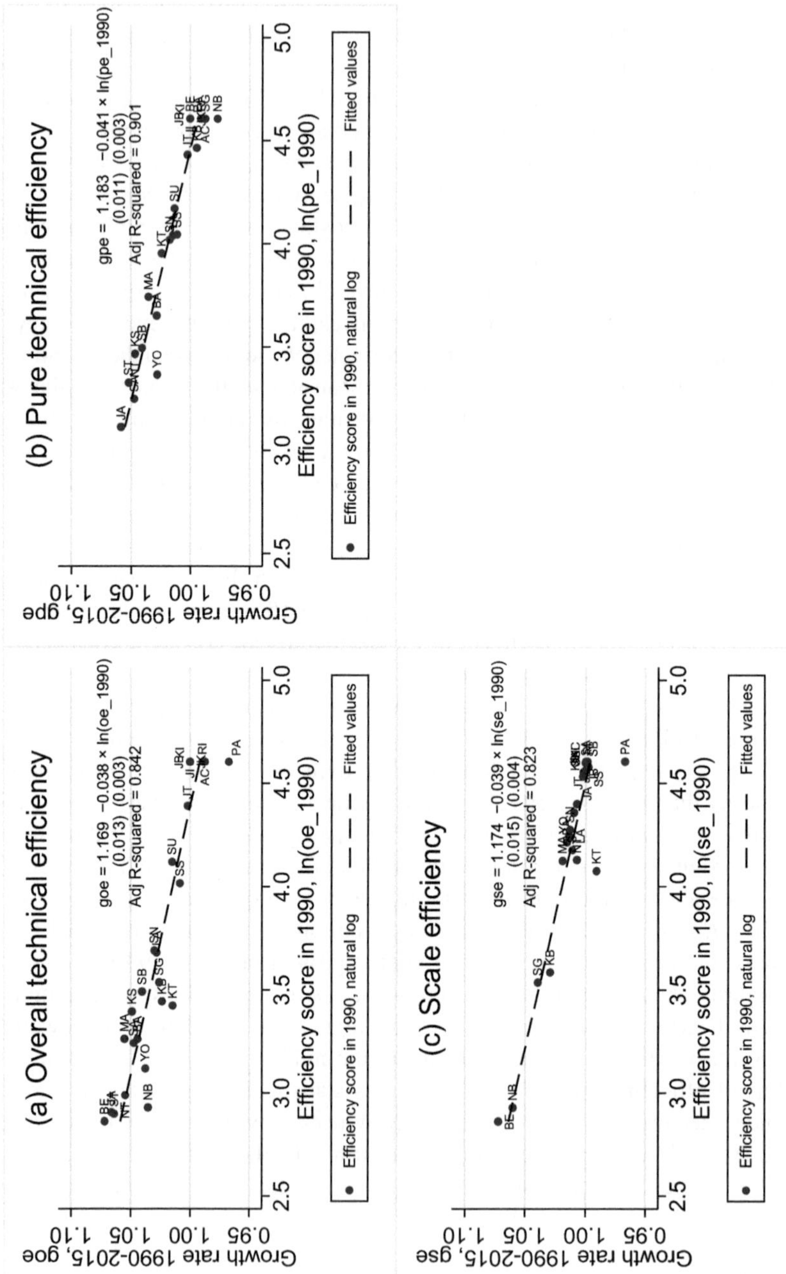

Note 1: All scores are measured based on the trend component.
Note 2: The efficiency score values are multiplied by 100.

Fig. 7.3 **(a–c)** Efficiency growth rate during 1990–2015 against the efficiency score in 1990 (Conventional measures)

variation, increased from 1990 to 2015. This finding provides insights into our key research question regarding inter-provincial gaps in pure labor productivity contributing to those in labor productivity.

3.2 *Exploring the Sources of Inter-provincial Inequality in Labor Productivity*

Next, we present the results of the inequality decomposition analysis derived from Eqs. (7.9) and (7.10). Our analysis incorporates both conventional and bias-corrected measures. Figures 7.4a, b (Fig. 7.4c, d) illustrate the inequality decomposition in labor productivity and the overall technical efficiency using conventional measures (bias-corrected measures) for 1990–2015. As a supplement, Table 7.3a, b describe those in the initial and last study periods. Several interesting findings are presented below.

From Fig. 7.4a, c, the inter-provincial inequality in labor productivity decreased from 0.405 in 1990 to 0.203 in 2015. The inequality declined by half but remained beyond the target level. This decreasing trend is consistent with previous studies, such as Kataoka (2018) and Mendez and Kataoka (2020). As we use the trend components to quantify the long-term trend of the source of productivity inequalities, there is no evidence of major regional cyclical shocks due to the Asian financial crisis of 1997/1998 and the global financial crisis of 2007/2008.

In the inequality decomposition of both the conventional and bias-corrected measures in labor productivity, the inequalities in the *oe* score monotonically and largely decreased (Fig. 7.4a, c). In the conventional measures in Table 7.3a, the *oe* score inequalities show a large decline from 0.208 to 0.030, while the contribution to inequality in labor productivity fell from 51.4% in 1990 to 14.8% in 2015. Conversely, the inequality in pure labor productivity (*xe*) declined until the mid-1990s, then increased until the mid-2000s, subsequently remaining stable (Fig. 7.4a). For 1990–2015, the inequality values increase from 0.147 to 0.170, and the contribution rose from 36.3% in 1990 to 83.7% in 2015 (Table 7.3a). Their interaction terms have minor positive values, ranging between 0.051 and 0.003. Regarding the inequality change for 1990–2015, the declining inequality in labor productivity is largely attributed to the inequality in overall technical efficiency, which accounted for 88.1% of the decreasing inequality in labor productivity. On the other hand, the increasing inequality in pure labor productivity offsets only around 10%. This trend is also consistent with Cheng and Li's (2006) observations on China for 1978–1998. The results based on the bias-corrected measures shown in Fig. 7.4c and Table 7.3b confirm the robustness of the results based on the conventional measures.

In Fig. 7.4b, the inter-provincial inequality in both the *pe* and *se* scores monotonically decreased from 1990 to 2015. In Table 7.3a, the inequalities in the conventional *pe* score and the *se* score declined from 0.125 in 1990 to 0.013 in 2015 and from 0.092 in 1990 to 0.020 in 2015, respectively. Their interaction terms had minor values ranging between −0.009 and 0.001 (Fig. 7.4b). Regarding the

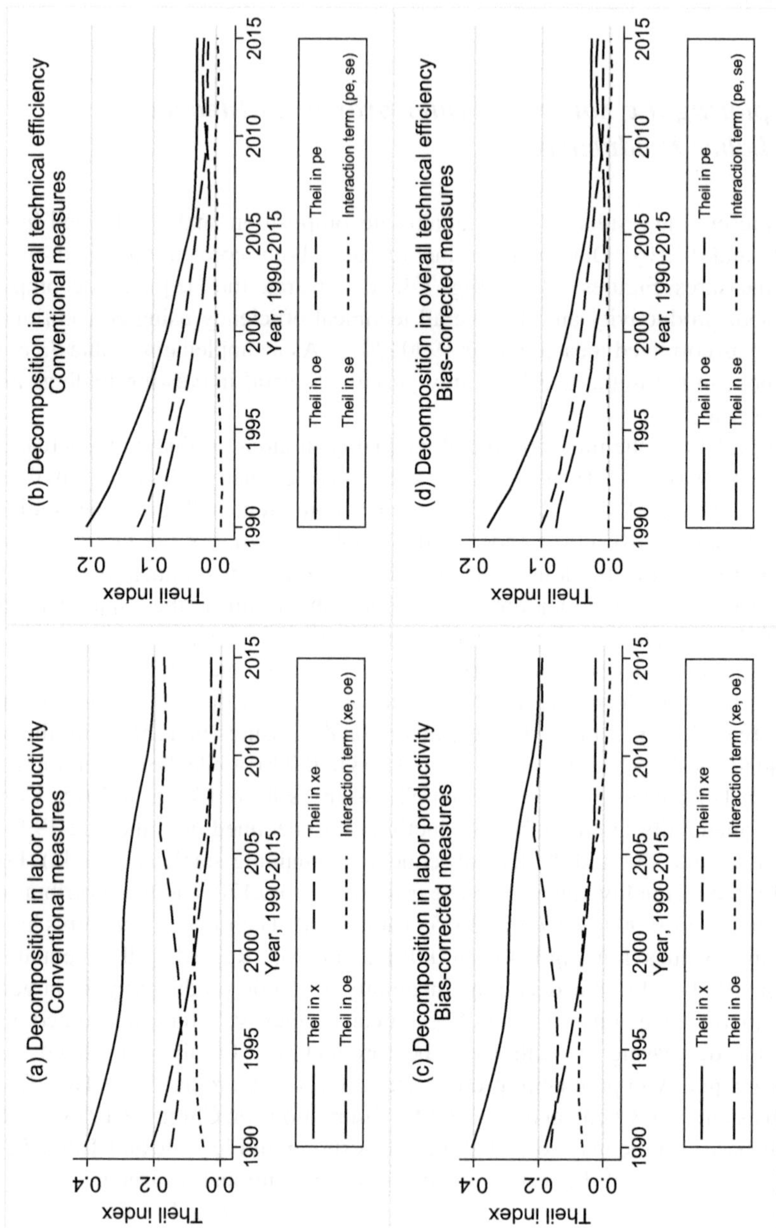

Note: x labor productivity, xe pure labor productivity, oe overall technical efficiency, pe pure technical efficiency, se scale efficiency.

Fig. 7.4 (a–d) Inequality decomposition in labor productivity and overall technical efficiency

Table 7.3 Inequality decomposition in 1990 to 2015

	1990		2015		Change during 1990–2015	
Year	Value	Contrib. (%)	Value	Contrib. (%)	Value	Contrib. (%)
(a) Conventional measures						
L_x	0.405	100.0	0.203	100.0	−0.202	100.0
L_{xe}	0.147	36.3	0.170	83.7	0.023	−11.4
L_{oe}	0.208	51.4	0.030	14.8	−0.178	88.1
λ(xe, oe)	0.051	12.6	0.003	1.3	−0.048	23.9
L_{oe}	0.208	100.0	0.030	100.0	−0.178	100.0
L_{pe}	0.125	60.1	0.013	43.3	−0.112	62.9
L_{se}	0.092	44.2	0.020	66.7	−0.072	40.4
I(pe, se)	−0.009	−4.5	−0.002	−6.8	0.007	−4.1
(b) Bias-corrected measures						
L_x	0.405	100.0	0.203	100.0	−0.202	100.0
L_{xe}	0.162	40.0	0.193	95.1	0.031	−15.3
L_{oe}	0.180	44.4	0.027	13.3	−0.153	75.7
λ(xe, oe)	0.064	15.7	−0.016	−7.9	−0.080	39.5
L_{oe}	0.180	100.0	0.027	100.0	−0.153	100.0
L_{pe}	0.101	56.1	0.010	37.0	−0.091	59.5
L_{se}	0.078	43.3	0.018	66.7	−0.060	39.2
I(pe, se)	0.000	0.2	−0.001	−4.1	−0.002	1.0

inequality changes for 1990–2015, the contributions of the decreasing inequality in pure technical efficiency and scale efficiency accounted for 62.9% and 40.4% of the decreasing inequality in overall technical efficiency, respectively. Associated with the results in Fig. 7.3a–c, this implies that the inequality convergence in resource utilization efficiencies (*pe*) had larger impacts than the inequality convergence in resource allocation efficiencies (*se*). The bias-corrected decomposition results in Fig. 7.4d and Table 7.3b confirm the robustness of the conventional results.

The decrease in inter-provincial overall technical efficiency inequality substantially contributed to a decrease in labor productivity inequality. In contrast, pure labor productivity increased inter-provincial inequality and played a significant role in inter-provincial labor productivity inequality, which remained high. To catch up with the higher labor productivity provinces, pure labor productivity growth as well as efficiency improvement are essential for lower labor productivity provinces. However, fully efficient provinces can choose only pure labor productivity growth, as efficiency improvement cannot recur once the production level becomes fully efficient. Figure 7.5 plots the *oe* scores and labor productivity by the province in 2015. Among the lower labor productivity provinces, all inefficient provinces can increase labor productivity by increasing either pure labor productivity, efficiency, or both. However, fully efficient ones such as Bengkulu (BE) and Maluku (MA) can increase labor productivity by only increasing pure labor productivity. Therefore, the government carefully considers the province-specific policy discretion.

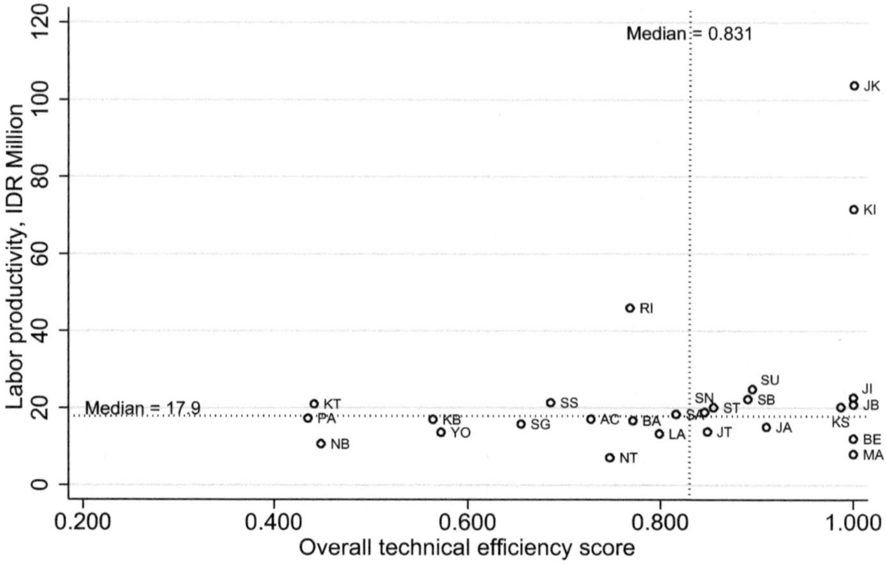

Note: See Table 7.4 for the corresponding province name of the marker label abbreviation.

Fig. 7.5 Overall technical efficiency versus labor productivity in 2015

4 Concluding Remarks

This study incorporates efficiency factors in the decomposition analysis that explore the sources of inter-provincial inequality in labor productivity. Our DEA-based frontier analysis derived the values of pure labor productivity and efficiency and found that Indonesia's provinces improved their relative efficiencies in terms of resource utilization and allocation. Specifically, they experienced β-convergence as well as σ-convergence in production efficiency. From the decomposition analysis, Indonesia substantially reduced its inter-provincial labor productivity gaps through both relative efficiency convergence effects. Pure labor productivity increased inter-provincial inequality and became a key factor in determining inter-provincial inequality in labor productivity, which remains high. Our bias-corrected analysis based on bootstrap DEA measures confirms the robustness of the aforementioned results based on the conventional DEA measures.

For a further inter-provincial inequality reduction in labor productivity, either pure labor productivity growth, efficiency improvement, or both are vital for lower labor productivity provinces; however, fully efficient provinces with lower labor productivity can no longer improve efficiency once they become fully efficient. Therefore, the government should carefully consider province-specific policy discretion. Finally, our study could not empirically detect whether the efficiencies of all provinces converged towards the same steady state. Testing single or multiple equilibria in the convergence pattern can be thus a possible extension of this study.

Appendix

Table 7.4 Conventional and bias-corrected efficiency scores for 1990 and 2015 (Trend components)

	1990							2015						
	Conventional			Bias-corrected				Conventional			Bias-corrected			
Province (Code)	oe	pe	se	oe	C.I. in oe	pe	C.I. in pe	oe	pe	se	oe	C.I. in oe	pe	C.I. in pe
	(1)	(2)	(3)	(4)	(5)	(6)	(7)	(8)	(9)	(10)	(11)	(12)	(13)	(14)
1. Aceh (AC)	1.000	1.000	1.000	0.746	[0.434, 0.928]	0.800	[0.495, 0.988]	0.728	0.729	0.998	0.700	[0.658, 0.729]	0.710	[0.674, 0.727]
2. North Sumatra (SU)	0.615	0.648	0.950	0.491	[0.323, 0.585]	0.565	[0.444, 0.639]	0.895	0.895	1.000	0.822	[0.719, 0.889]	0.845	[0.757, 0.892]
3. Riau (RI)	1.000	1.000	1.000	0.701	[0.333, 0.936]	0.780	[0.397, 0.984]	0.768	0.796	0.965	0.674	[0.521, 0.761]	0.740	[0.622, 0.793]
4. West Sumatra (SB)	0.328	0.330	0.995	0.253	[0.154, 0.317]	0.274	[0.174, 0.327]	0.891	0.891	0.999	0.854	[0.795, 0.889]	0.858	[0.808, 0.888]
5. Jambi (JA)	0.183	0.225	0.815	0.141	[0.087, 0.175]	0.188	[0.130, 0.222]	0.910	0.928	0.981	0.855	[0.792, 0.900]	0.877	[0.799, 0.925]
6. Bengkulu (BE)	0.175	1.000	0.175	0.139	[0.088, 0.166]	0.723	[0.229, 0.984]	1.000	1.000	1.000	0.868	[0.727, 0.986]	0.875	[0.561, 0.997]
7. South Sumatra (SS)	0.555	0.570	0.973	0.437	[0.286, 0.525]	0.491	[0.384, 0.561]	0.686	0.746	0.919	0.628	[0.545, 0.682]	0.707	[0.649, 0.743]
8. Lampung (LA)	0.396	0.568	0.698	0.308	[0.189, 0.385]	0.506	[0.394, 0.562]	0.799	0.812	0.984	0.755	[0.707, 0.792]	0.778	[0.73, 0.809]
9. West Java (JB)	1.000	1.000	1.000	0.694	[0.286, 0.961]	0.788	[0.370, 0.985]	1.000	1.000	1.000	0.851	[0.582, 0.987]	0.890	[0.683, 0.997]
10. Jakarta (JK)	1.000	1.000	1.000	0.675	[0.295, 0.951]	0.735	[0.327, 0.984]	1.000	1.000	1.000	0.809	[0.453, 0.988]	0.878	[0.561, 0.995]

(continued)

Table 7.4 (continued)

	1990							2015						
	Conventional			Bias-corrected				Conventional			Bias-corrected			
Province (Code)	oe	pe	se	oe	C.I. in oe	pe	C.I. in pe	oe	pe	se	oe	C.I. in oe	pe	C.I. in pe
	(1)	(2)	(3)	(4)	(5)	(6)	(7)	(8)	(9)	(10)	(11)	(12)	(13)	(14)
11. Central Java (JT)	0.807	0.840	0.960	0.601	[0.301, 0.785]	0.711	[0.355, 0.826]	0.849	0.886	0.958	0.757	[0.601, 0.845]	0.835	[0.698, 0.882]
12. Yogyakarta (YO)	0.226	0.289	0.781	0.179	[0.113, 0.220]	0.257	[0.202, 0.285]	0.572	0.574	0.997	0.550	[0.516, 0.572]	0.556	[0.527, 0.571]
13. East Java (JI)	1.000	1.000	1.000	0.701	[0.274, 0.949]	0.739	[0.300, 0.980]	1.000	1.000	1.000	0.869	[0.623, 0.992]	0.889	[0.668, 0.997]
14. Bali (BA)	0.261	0.385	0.677	0.209	[0.132, 0.255]	0.346	[0.284, 0.381]	0.771	0.772	1.000	0.741	[0.697, 0.772]	0.750	[0.716, 0.769]
15. West Kalimantan (KB)	0.313	0.869	0.360	0.252	[0.162, 0.302]	0.729	[0.528, 0.850]	0.564	0.755	0.747	0.532	[0.477, 0.562]	0.712	[0.64, 0.753]
16. Central Kalimantan (KT)	0.307	0.521	0.589	0.243	[0.148, 0.297]	0.427	[0.250, 0.511]	0.442	0.941	0.469	0.396	[0.32, 0.439]	0.875	[0.759, 0.937]
17. East Kalimantan (KI)	1.000	1.000	1.000	0.682	[0.312, 0.941]	0.735	[0.306, 0.986]	1.000	1.000	1.000	0.835	[0.617, 0.988]	0.879	[0.596, 0.996]
18. South Kalimantan (KS)	0.298	0.321	0.930	0.230	[0.141, 0.288]	0.269	[0.177, 0.317]	0.987	1.000	0.987	0.947	[0.889, 0.986]	0.919	[0.825, 0.996]
19. North Sulawesi (SA)	0.256	0.257	0.994	0.205	[0.127, 0.248]	0.217	[0.138, 0.254]	0.816	0.818	0.997	0.783	[0.736, 0.816]	0.781	[0.728, 0.816]
20. Central Sulawesi (ST)	0.181	0.278	0.652	0.143	[0.087, 0.176]	0.240	[0.182, 0.274]	0.855	0.991	0.862	0.817	[0.766, 0.852]	0.941	[0.851, 0.989]
21. South Sulawesi (SN)	0.400	0.557	0.719	0.329	[0.209, 0.395]	0.506	[0.428, 0.549]	0.846	0.849	0.996	0.796	[0.727, 0.841]	0.809	[0.752, 0.846]
22. Southeast Sulawesi (SG)	0.343	1.000	0.343	0.276	[0.175, 0.334]	0.719	[0.229, 0.977]	0.655	0.722	0.907	0.620	[0.579, 0.65]	0.670	[0.566, 0.72]

23. West Nusa Tenggara (NB)	0.187	1.000	0.187	0.151	[0.095, 0.183]	0.722	[0.231, 0.988]	0.449	0.556	0.807	0.430	[0.402, 0.448]	0.525	[0.471, 0.554]
24. East Nusa Tenggara (NT)	0.199	0.320	0.622	0.160	[0.098, 0.194]	0.275	[0.201, 0.315]	0.748	1.000	0.748	0.703	[0.647, 0.742]	0.873	[0.559, 0.997]
25. Maluku (MA)	0.261	0.422	0.619	0.208	[0.129, 0.251]	0.362	[0.245, 0.416]	1.000	1.000	1.000	0.872	[0.708, 0.993]	0.878	[0.561, 0.996]
26. Papua (PA)	1.000	1.000	1.000	0.776	[0.461, 0.931]	0.727	[0.233, 0.986]	0.435	1.000	0.435	0.393	[0.327, 0.432]	0.875	[0.558, 0.996]
Minimum	0.175	0.225	0.175	0.139		0.188		0.435	0.556	0.435	0.393		0.525	
Maximum	1.000	1.000	1.000	0.776		0.800		1.000	1.000	1.000	0.947		0.941	
Mean	0.511	0.669	0.771	0.382		0.532		0.795	0.872	0.914	0.725		0.805	
Median	0.336	0.609	0.872	0.264		0.536		0.831	0.893	0.992	0.770		0.852	
CV	0.653	0.461	0.344	0.604		0.412		0.232	0.155	0.171	0.215		0.133	
Score ≧1	7	10	7					6	9	8	0	0	0	3

Notes: CV is coefficient of variation. CI refers to 95% confidence intervals. All provinces' bias-corrected scores fell within 95% confidence intervals. Bias-corrected scale efficiency scores are omitted from the table

References

Alisjahbana, A., & Akita, T. (2020). Economic tertialization and regional income inequality in a decentralized Indonesia: a bi-dimensional inequality decomposition analysis. *Social Indicators Research, 151*, 51–80.

Anand, S. (1983). *Inequality and poverty in Malaysia: Measurement and decomposition*. Oxford University Press.

Armstrong, H., & Taylor, J. (2006). *Regional economics and policy*. Blackwell.

Badan Pusat Statistik (BPS). (Various years). *Statistical yearbook of Indonesia*. BPS.

Badunenko, O., & Mozharovskyi, P. (2016). Nonparametric frontier analysis using Stata. *The Stata Journal, 2016*(16), 550–589.

Charnes, A., Cooper, W. W., & Li, S. (1989). Using data envelopment analysis to evaluate efficiency in the economic performance of Chinese cities. *Socio-Economic Planning Sciences, 23*, 325–344.

Cheng, Y.-S., & Li, S.-K. (2006). Income inequality and efficiency: a decomposition approach and applications to China. *Economics Letters, 91*, 8–14.

Coelli, T. J., Prasada, R., & Battese, G. E. (2005). *An introduction to efficiency and productivity analysis* (2nd ed.). Kluwer Academic Publishers.

Cooper, W. W., Seiford, L. M., & Tone, T. (2006). *Data envelopment analysis: a comprehensive text with models, applications, references and DEA-solver software*. Springer.

Enflo, K., & Hjertstrand, P. (2009). Relative sources of European regional productivity convergence: a bootstrap frontier approach. *Regional Studies, 43*, 643–659.

Esmara, H. (1975). Regional income disparities. *Bulletin of Indonesian Economic Studies, 11*, 41–57.

Gunawan, A., Mendez, C., & Santos-Marquez, F. (2019. November) Regional income disparities, distributional convergence, and spatial effects: evidence from Indonesia. MPRA Working Paper No. 95972.

Hill, H., Resosudarmo, B. P., & Vidyattama, Y. (2008). Indonesia's changing economic geography. *Bulletin of Indonesian Economic Studies, 44*, 407–435.

Kataoka, M. (2013). Capital stock estimates by province and interprovincial distribution in Indonesia. *Asian Economic Journal, 27*, 409–428.

Kataoka, M. (2018). Inequality convergence in inefficiency and interprovincial income inequality in Indonesia for 1990–2010. *Asia-Pacific Journal of Regional Science, 2*, 297–313.

Kataoka, M. (2020). Total factor productivity change in Indonesia's provincial economies for 1990–2015: Malmquist productivity index approach. *Letters in Spatial and Resource Sciences, 13*, 233–243.

Kataoka, M. (2021). Perspiration versus inspiration: sources of national and provincial output growth in Indonesia [1990–2015] using province-level non-parametric frontier analysis. *Asia-Pacific Journal of Regional Science*. https://doi.org/10.1007/s41685-021-00222-7

Kurniawan, H., de Groot, H. L., & Mulder, P. (2019). Are poor provinces catching-up the rich provinces in Indonesia? *Regional Science Policy and Practice, 11*, 89–108.

Mendez, C. (2020). Regional efficiency convergence and efficiency clusters. *Asia-Pacific Journal of Regional Science, 4*, 391–411.

Mendez, C., & Kataoka, M. (2020). Disparities in regional productivity, capital accumulation, and efficiency across Indonesia: a club convergence approach. *Review of Development Economics*. https://doi.org/10.1111/rode.12726

Ravn, M. O., & Uhlig, H. (2002). On adjusting the Hodrick-Prescott filter for the frequency of observations. *The Review of Economics and Statistics, 84*, 371–376.

Schaffer, A., Simar, L., & Rauland, J. (2011). Decomposing regional efficiency. *Journal of Regional Science, 51*, 931–947.

Simar, L., & Wilson, P. W. (1998). Sensitivity analysis of efficiency scores: how to bootstrap in nonparametric frontier models. *Management Science, 44*, 49–61.

Simar, L., & Wilson, P. W. (1999). Estimating and bootstrapping Malmquist indices. *European Journal of Operational Research, 115*, 459–471.

Simar, L., & Wilson, P. W. (2000). Statistical inference in nonparametric frontier models: the state of the art. *Journal of Productivity Analysis, 13*, 49–78.

Theil, H. (1967). *Economics and information theory*. North-Holland.

Toma, P., Miglietta, P. P., Zurlini, G., Valente, D., & Petrosillo, I. (2017). A non-parametric bootstrap-data envelopment analysis approach for environmental policy planning and management of agricultural efficiency in EU countries. *Ecological Indicators, 83*, 132–143.

MIX
Papier aus verantwortungsvollen Quellen
Paper from responsible sources
FSC® C105338

If you have any concerns about our products,
you can contact us on
ProductSafety@springernature.com

In case Publisher is established outside the EU,
the EU authorized representative is:
Springer Nature Customer Service Center GmbH
Europaplatz 3, 69115 Heidelberg, Germany

Printed by Libri Plureos GmbH
in Hamburg, Germany